ISBN 978-0-331-05689-1
PIBN 10261566

1 MONTH OF
FREE
READING

at

www.ForgottenBooks.com

By purchasing this book you are
eligible for one month membership to
ForgottenBooks.com, giving you
unlimited access to our entire
collection of over 1,000,000 titles via
our web site and mobile apps.

To claim your free month visit:

www.forgottenbooks.com/free261566

English
Français
Deutsche
Italiano
Español
Português

www.forgottenbooks.com

Mythology Photography **Fiction**
Fishing Christianity **Art** Cooking
Essays Buddhism Freemasonry
Medicine **Biology** Music **Ancient
Egypt** Evolution Carpentry Physics
Dance Geology **Mathematics** Fitness
Shakespeare **Folklore** Yoga Marketing
Confidence Immortality Biographies
Poetry **Psychology** Witchcraft
Electronics Chemistry History **Law**
Accounting **Philosophy** Anthropology
Alchemy Drama Quantum Mechanics
Atheism Sexual Health **Ancient History**
Entrepreneurship Languages Sport
Paleontology Needlework Islam
Metaphysics Investment Archaeology
Parenting Statistics Criminology
Motivational

USEFUL REFERENCE SERIES. NO. 5.

ABBREVIATIONS AND TECHNICAL TERMS USED IN BOOK CATALOGS AND IN BIBLIOGRAPHIES

BREVIATIONS | TECHNICAL TERM

AND | USED IN

HNICAL TERMS | BIBLIOGRAPHIES

ED IN BOOK CATALOGS | AND BY THE BOOK
ND BIBLIOGRAPHIES | AND PRINTING TRADES

In Eight Languages | *In Eight Languages*

BY | BY

. K. WALTER | AXEL MOTH

WITH A BRIEF LIST OF ABBREVIATIONS OF
HONORARY TITLES AND PLACES OF
PUBLICATION

1917
HANDY EDITION
RE-ISSUE OF TWO BOOKS
BOUND IN ONE

BOSTON
THE BOSTON BOOK COMPANY

ABBREVIATIONS AND TECHNICAL TERMS
USED IN BOOK CATALOGS AND IN BIBLIOGRAPHIES

BY

FRANK KELLER WALTER

VICE-DIRECTOR, NEW YORK STATE LIBRARY SCHOOL

THE F. W. FAXON COMPANY

BOSTON, 1919

The Riverdale Press
BROOKLINE
MASS.

PREFACE

THIS list was begun as an expansion of Miss Mary Medlicott's *Abbreviations in Book Catalogues* which was issued in 1906 by the Boston Book Company as Bulletin of Bibliography, pamphlet No. 15. It has so far outgrown the limits of the original list as to have become a quite independent production. Special thanks, however, for the original plan and for much of the subject matter of the present list are due to Miss Medlicott's list and to a manuscript *List of bibliographical terms and abbreviations* compiled in 1906, under the direction of Mr. E. C. Williams, by Miss Eliza Townsend for the use of the Western Reserve Library School.

Originality can hardly be claimed for any work so obviously dependent on previous similar attempts nor, although longer than most previous attempts, can any claim to more than approximate completeness be made for this list. Perhaps the chief point of difference from other lists is the greater attention paid to terms and abbreviations frequently used in current catalogues of second-hand booksellers but which, as they describe peculiarities of individual copies, are seldom found in more formal bibliographies. Arbitrary symbols used only in particular works are usually explained in the works themselves and are therefore seldom included here. The inclusions are almost entirely bibliographic rather than literary, that is, confined to terms used in the description of books rather than in the titles proper. The chief exception is the inclusion of a partial list of honorary titles likely to be met in author entries. Many terms have been included which are almost certain to be superfluous for the expert bibliographer but, as the expert seldom ought to need an elementary list to aid him, the needs of beginners have been given first consideration.

It is perhaps unnecessary to state that this is a list of terms in actual use, good, bad and indifferent, and not a code of forms recommended for use in catalogues and bibliographies. Some unusual terms used in descriptions of manuscripts and incunabula have been omitted. For these, Cappelli's *Dizionario de abbreviature*, Chassant's *Dictionnaire des abréviations* and Prou's *Manuel de paléographie latine et française* (*3d ed. Par. 1910*) should be consulted. Older spellings which are not radically different from present usages are not usually indicated. They can easily be found in good dictionaries.

The lists of honorary titles and of places of publication are confessedly incomplete. For such abbreviations, titles and place names as are omitted, consult the authorities cited at the head of each of these two sections.

Special thanks are due to Mr. A. Hafner of G. E. Stechert & Co., New York, for current catalogues from which many of the entries were taken; to the Grolier Club and its librarian, Miss Ruth S. Grannis, for access to bibliographic works in the club library; to Mr. A. J. F. van Laer, Archivist, New York State Library, for corrections and additions in the Dutch, French and Italian sections; to Miss Gudrun Holth of the New York State Library School for similar help in the Swedish and Danish-Norwegian sections; to Mr. John T. Fitzpatrick of the Legislative Reference Section of the New York State Library for correcting the proof of the Spanish section; to Mr. Adam J. Strohm of the Detroit Public Library for correcting that of the Swedish section and to Miss Edna M. Sanderson of the New York State Library School for correcting proof. Whatever accuracy or usefulness the list may possess is in large part due to their assistance.

F. K. W.

NOTE TO THE REVISED EDITION

In the present revision a number of errors which crept into the final proofs, in spite of repeated readings by several competent collaborators thoroughly familiar with the languages represented, have been corrected. Several librarians and booksellers have given further aid in the revision. Among them special mention is due to Mr. Alfred Hafner and the staff of G. E. Stechert & Co., and to Mr. Moth and Miss Plummer of the New York Public Library. Although an honest attempt at accuracy has been made it is not probable that all old errors have been detected or all new ones avoided. It is hoped that such as do remain may not prove misleading, however much they may vex the soul of the fastidious bibliographer.

Several considerations, among them the expense of bibliographic publications, have prevented any considerable changes in content or scope. This is still a tentative preliminary list based, both as to inclusion and exclusion, on observation of the difficulties most frequently met in the use of ordinary trade bibliographies. It can, consequently, claim neither well-balanced proportion, entire consistency nor completeness.

A very considerable number of other abbreviations and terms, less common but in frequent use, has been collected, and librarians and booksellers are invited to contribute (with definite citations of authority or source) any unusual ones with which they may meet, for inclusion in a probable supplementary list. Even with the greatest amount of competent assistance the difficulties inherent in the compilation of a list like this are great; without such assistance any satisfactory compilation is practically out of the question.

F. K. W.

ALBANY, N. Y., May, 1912.

viii

PARTIAL LIST OF AUTHORITIES CONSULTED

(General dictionaries of the different languages, general encyclopedias and current catalogs of booksellers are not included.)

Årskatalog for svenska bokhandeln, 1910. Stockholm, 1911.

BECK, C. Jahrbuch der Bücherpreise. v. 1., 1906. Leipzig, 1907.

BLACKBURN, C. F. Hints on catalogue titles. London, 1884.

Book prices current. v. 1 — date. London, 1886 — date.

BREUL, KARL. Handy bibliographical guide to the study of the German language and literature. London, 1895.

BROWN, JAMES DUFF. Manual of practical bibliography. London, 1910.

BRUNET, J. C. Manuel du libraire et de l'amateur de livres. 6 v. Paris, 1860–65.

CAPPELLI, Ad. Dizionario di abbreviature latine ed italiane usate nelle carte e codici specialmente del medio evo. Milan, 1906.

CHASSANT, L. Dictionnaire des abréviations latines et françaises usitées dans les inscriptions lapidaires et métalliques, les manuscrits et les chartes. 3d ed. Paris, 1866.

CIM, ALBERT. Le livre. 5 v. Paris, 1908.

COLLINS, F. HOWARD. Authors' and printers' dictionary. London, 1909.

EBERT, F. A. General bibliographical dictionary. 4 v. Oxford, 1837.

GALLARDO, BARTOLOME JOSE. Ensayo de una biblioteca española de libros raros y curiosos. Madrid, 1863.

HEINSIUS, WILHELM. Allgemeines Bücher-Lexicon, 1700–1827. 7 v. Leipzig, 1812–29.

HINRICHS, J. H. Halbjahrs-katalog, 1910. Leipzig, 1910.

HINRICHS, J. H., *Pub.* Fünf-Jahrs Katalog. 8 v. Leipzig, 1851–1905.

HOEPLI, ULRICO. Catalogo completo delle edizione Hoepli, 1871–1911. Milan, 1905–11.

KAYSER, C. G. Vollständiges Bücher-Lexicon, 1907–10. Leipzig, 1911.

KLEEMEIER, F. J. Handbuch der Bibliographie. Wien, 1903.

KLEMMING, G. E. Sveriges bibliografi, 1481–1600. Upsala, 1889.

MAIRE, ALBERT. Manuel pratique du bibliothécaire. Paris, 1896.

MEDLICOTT, MARY. Abbreviations used in book catalogues. Boston, 1906.

NORDISK Boghandlertidende (Weekly) Copenhagen.

OTHMER, GUSTAV. Vademecum des Buchhändlers und Bücherfreundes. 5th ed. Leipzig, 1903.

OTTINO, GIUSEPPE. Bibliografia. Milan, 1892.

POWER, JOHN. Handy book about books. London, 1870.

PROU, MAURICE. Manuel de paléographie latine et française, 3d ed. Paris, 1910.

ROGERS, W. T. Manual of bibliography. London, 1891.

ROUVEYRE, EDOUARD. Connaissances nécessaires à un bibliophile. 5th ed. 10 v. Paris, 1899.

SALVA Y MALLEN, PEDRO. Catalogo de la bibliotheca de Salva. 2 v. Valencia, 1872.

CONTENTS

ENGLISH ABBREVIATIONS AND TERMS

A.

*A. D.   Autograph document.

A. D. S.   Autograph document signed.

A. L.   Autograph letter.

A. L. S.   Autograph letter signed.

A. N. S.   Autograph note signed.

a. v.   Authorized version.

abbr.   Abbreviation(s).

abr.   Abridged.

acct.   Account.

add.   Additional, addition(s).

adv.   Advance. (*e.g.*, adv. no.)   advance number.

adv.   Advertised, advertisement(s).

aft., aftw.   Afterwards.

anal.   Analysis, analytical.

annot.   Annotations, annotated, annotator.

anon.   Anonymous.

app.   Appendix.

apprec.   Appreciation.

apx.   Appendix.

arr.   Arranged.

asm.   Assembly. (*e.g.*, **asm. doc.**, assembly document.)

auth.   Author, authorized.

* The presence of a seal is frequently indicated by *.

B.

b. Born.

B. C. Before Christ.

b. l. Black letter.

bas. (baz.). Basil (bazil), red sheep, roan.

bd. Bound.

bdg. Binding.

bds. Boards.

bibl., bibliog. Bibliography.

bister (bistre). A dark brown color. "Sepia tone."

biog. Biography, biographic, biographical.

bk. Book.

bnd. Bound.

bxd. Boxed, *i.e.*, in a box.

C.

c. Circa, about.

c. Copyright.

c. o. s. Condemned or suppressed.

c. p. China paper. (India paper.)

ca. Circa.

cancels. Leaves replaced by corrected extra leaves.

cent. Century.

cf. Calf.

cf. Confer (compare).

cf. ext. Calf extra.

chap. Chapter(s).

Chr. Christian.

chron. Chronological.

circuit edges. Edges of cover turned over edges of book as in " Teachers' bibles."

cl., clo. Cloth.

cl. bds. Cloth boards, *i.e.*, boards covered with cloth.

col. Collector.

col., cold. Colored.

col. Column(s).

coll. Collected, collection(s).

com. Committee, commerce, commercial.

comment, commt. Commentator.

comp. Compiled, compiler(s).

comp. Complete.

conc. Concerning.

cong. Congress, congressional.

cont. Containing, contents, continued.

cont. Contemporary. (*e.g.*, **cont. cl.,** contemporary cloth.)

contin. Continuing.

cop. Copy, copyright.

cor., corr. Corrected, corrections.

cp. Compare.

Cr. Crown (English coin).

cr. 8°, cr. O., cr. 8vo. Crown octavo.

crit. Critical.

Crown octavo. About 5 by $7\frac{1}{2}$ in.; — **4to,** $7\frac{1}{2}$ by 10 in.

crwn. Crown.

cyc. Cyclopedia.

D.

d. Died.

d. e. Deckle edges.

D. Duodecimo. 12mo. ($17\frac{1}{2}$ to 20 cm.)

D. S. Document signed.

Dan. Danish.

Demy 8vo. Demy octavo, $5\frac{1}{2}$ by $8\frac{3}{4}$ in.; — **4to,** about $8\frac{3}{4}$ by 11 in.

dentelle borders. Lace-like tooling or printing on borders.

dept. Department.

diagr.(s). Diagram(s).

diss. Dissertation.
divinity calf. Plain dark brown calf binding.
doc. Document.
dom. Domestic.
doublures. Cover linings or ornamental end papers.

E.

e. d. l. Edition de luxe.
e. i. Extra-illustrated.
e. p. c. Editor's presentation copy.
ea. Each.
ed., edit. Edited, edition, editor.
edn. Edition.
el. fo. Elephant folio.   (About 14 by 23 in.)
elem. Elementary, elements.
emb. Embossed.
encyc. Encyclopedia.
eng.(s). Engraving(s).
Eng. English.
engr. Engraving(s).
enl. Enlarged.
etch. Etching(s), etcher.
ex. Executive.   (*e.g.,* **ex. doc.,** executive document.)
ex. Extra.   (*e.g.,* **mor. ex.,** morocco extra.)
expl. Explained, explanatory.

F.

f. Folio (sheet).
F. Folio.   (30 cm. and over.)
f. e. p. Fore-edges painted.
F. P. Fine paper.
fac.(s), fac.-sim.(s). facsimile(s).
fcap., fcp. foolscap.
Fe. 48mo.   (7½ to 10 cm.)

4

ff. Folios.

fict. Fiction.

fl. Flourished.

flex. Flexible.

fo., fol. Folio.

foolscap octavo. About $4\frac{1}{4}$ by $6\frac{3}{4}$ in.; — **quarto,** about $6\frac{3}{4}$ by $8\frac{1}{2}$ in.

fold. Folded, folding.

for. Forel.

forel. (forrel). Heavy rough parchment used on old books.

foxed. Pages brown spotted.

fr. From.

Fr. French.

front. Frontispiece.

G.

g. Gilt.

g. Guinea(s).

g. e. Gilt edges.

g. g. e. Gilt, with gilt edges.

g. h. Gilt head (gilt top).

g. l. Gothic (black) letter.

g. m. e. Gilt marbled edges.

g. t. Gilt top.

g. t. e. Gilt top edge.

Ger., Germ. German.

gloss. Glossary.

glt. Gilt.

gn. Guinea(s).

gr. Group(s). (Of portraits.)

Gr. Greek.

gs. Guineas.

gt. Gilt.

gt. Great. (*e.g.*, **gt. f.**, great folio.)

gu. Guinea.

H.

h. m. p., h. p. Handmade paper.

h. c. Half calf.

hdbk. Handbook.

hf. Half. (*e.g.*, **hf. cf.**, half calf; **hf. cl.**, half cloth; **hf. mor. ex.**, half morocco extra.)

hist. Historical, history.

hm. Half morocco.

I.

i. J. p. Imperial Japanese paper.

I. p. India paper.

I. p. p. India paper proofs.

il. Illustrated, illustration(s), illustrator(s).

illum. Illuminated.

illus. *See* **il.**

imp. Imperfect, imperial, imported.

imp. Imported.

imp. fol. Imperial folio.

Imperial octavo. About 11 by $7\frac{1}{2}$ in.; — **quarto,** about 15 by 11 in.

impr. Improved.

incl. Including.

incr. Increased.

int. Interleaved.

introd. Introduction, introductory.

Ital. Italian.

Ital. Italics.

J.

J. p. Japan paper.

J. p. p. Japan paper proofs.

J. v.   Japanese vellum.

J. v. p.   Japanese vellum proofs.

jt.   Joint.

juv.   Juvenile.

L.

l.   Large.

l.   Leaf.

l. g.   Gothic letter (litteræ gothicæ).

l. p.   Large paper.

l. p. p.   Large paper proofs.

l. s.   Letter signed.

l. t. p.   Large thick paper.

l. v. p.   Large vellum paper.

l. W. p.   Large Whatman paper.

lang.   Language.

Lat.   Latin.

law calf, law sheep.   Plain uncolored leather (calf or sheep).

lea.   Leather.

leather velvet.   Ooze leather.

lev.   Levant.

lex. 8vo.   Lexicon octavo.

lf.   Lettering faded.

lg.   Large.

lib.   Library.

lit.   Literary, literature.

ll.   Leaves.

M.

m. e.   Marbled edges.

m. o. p.   Manuscript on paper.

m. o. v.   Manuscript on vellum.

med.   Medical, medicine.

medium 8vo. About 9½ by 6 in.; — **4to,** about 12 by 9½ in.

mem. Memoir.

misc. Miscellaneous.

—mo. Size mark. (*e.g.,* **12mo.** (duodecimo), etc.)

mo. Month, monthly.

mor. Morocco.

mor. ext. Morocco extra.

ms.(s). Manuscript(s).

musl. Muslin.

mut. Mutilated.

N.

Net.

New.

. d. No date.

. ed. New edition.

. p. No place (of publication).

. s. New series.

n. u. Name unknown.

nar. Narrow.

nat. National.

no. Number.

O.

O. Octavo. (20 to 25 cm.)

o. p. Out of print.

o. v. On vellum.

ob., obl. Oblong. (*e.g.,* **obl. 8vo,** oblong octavo.)

orig. Original.

P.

p. Page(s).

p. Paper.

p. 8vo., p. 8°, p. O.   Post octavo.

p. l.   Preliminary leaf or leaves.

p. o. a. s.   Printed on asses' skin (shagreen).

p. o. f.   Painted on fore-edge.

p. o. r. p.   Printed on rice paper.

p. o. s.   Printed on silk or satin.

p. p.   Proof plates.

pa.   Paper.

pam.   Pamphlet.

pap.   Paper.

parch.   Parchment.

pb.   Published.

phot.   Photograph(s), photogravure(s).

pict.   Pictorial.

pl.   Plate(s).

pl. pap.   Plate paper.

plts.   Plates.

pm.   Pamphlet(s).

pol.   Polished.

pop. ed.   Popular edition.

por., port.(s).   Portrait(s).

post octavo.   About 5 by 8 in.; — **quarto,** about 8 by 10 in.

Pott (pot) 8vo.   About 4 by 6¼ in.; — 4to, about 6¼ by 8 in.

pref.   Preface, prefixed.

pp.   Pages.

pph.   Pamphlet.

prel. ll.   Preliminary leaves.

preprint.   Advance copy or print.

pres.   Presentation.

priv. pr.   Privately printed.

ps., pseud.   Pseudonym, pseudonymous.

pt.(s).   Part(s).

pub. Published, publisher.
pubd. Published.
publ. Published, publisher, publication.

Q.

Q. Quarto (25 to 30 cm.).
q. v. Quod vide (which see).

R.

r. e. Red edges.
R. e. Royal edition.
r. f. Rough finish (paper).
R. O., r. 8vo. Royal octavo.
rec. Record.
rect., r°., Recto (right-hand page). Front of printed
  leaf.
red. Reduced.
rep. Report(s), reporter(s).
rev. Revised, revision.
rn. Roan.
ro. Roan.
Rom. Roman.
Roxb. Roxburghe binding.
roy. 8vo. Royal octavo. About 6¼ by 10 in.; —
  4to, about 10 by 12½ in.
Rus., Russ. Russia.
Rxb., Rxbgh. Roxburghe binding.

S.

S. 16mo. (15 to 17½ cm.).
s. Series.
s. a. Sine anno (without date of publication).

s. a., l., et n. Sine anno, loco, et nomine (without date, place, and name of printer).

s. d. Sans date (without date).

s. e. Special edition.

s. l. Sine loco (without place of publication).

s. n. Sine nomine (without name of printer).

s. p. Small paper.

s. v. Sub voce or verbo (under the word or title).

Sc. He (or she) engraved it.

Sci. Science, scientific.

sd. Sewed.

sel. Selected, selection(s).

sen. Senate.

sep. Separate.

seq. Sequentes, sequentia. (The following; the next.)

ser. Series.

sess. Session.

Sf. 64mo. (Sexagesimo-quarto. Up to $7\frac{1}{2}$ cm.)

Sh. Sheep.

Sh. Shelfworn.

Shp. Sheep.

Sig. Signature.

sm. $4°$ or **4to** or **Q.** Small quarto.

soc. Society.

spr. Sprinkled.

sq. Square.

st. Stitched.

subs. Subscription.

sup. ex. Super-extra, " de luxe."

superroyal 8vo. About $6\frac{3}{4}$ by $10\frac{1}{4}$ in.; — **4to**, about $10\frac{1}{2}$ by $13\frac{1}{2}$ in.

swd. Sewed.

Swed. Swedish.

T.

t. Type (*i.e.*, size of printed part of page).

T. 24mo. (12 to 15 cm.)

tabby. Watered (moire) silk.

t. e.g. Top edge gilt.

t. p. Thick paper.

t. p. Title page.

t. p. m. Title page mutilated.

t. p. w. Title page wanting.

tab. Table(s).

tall copy. Copy on large paper.

temp. Temporary.

theol. Theological, theology.

thk. Thick.

tr., trans. Translated, translation(s), translator(s).

Tt. 32mo. (10 to 12½ cm.)

typog. Typographical, typography.

U.

unb., unbd. Unbound.

unc., unct. Uncut. (Pages not trimmed in rebinding.)

und. Undated.

unopened. Folds of leaves not opened.

unp. Unpaged.

V.

v. Volume(s).

v. d. Various dates.

v. y. Various years.

vel., vell. Vellum.

vers. Verso (left-hand page), back of printed page.

vig. t. Vignette title.

vign. Vignette(s).
vo. Verso.
vocab. Vocabulary.
vol.(s). Volume(s).

W.

w. Wanting.
w. Waterstained.
w. With.
w. a. f. With all faults.
W. p. Whatman paper.
wkly. Weekly.
wormed. Worm-eaten.
wraps. Wrappers.

X.

xylog. Xylographic. Engraved on wood. Relating
to " block books."

Y.

y. b., yr. bk. Year book.
yapp. Binding with flexible " circuit edges."
yrly. Yearly.

FRENCH ABBREVIATIONS
AND TERMS

A.

a. acier, année.

a. (av.) a. avec adresse.

à comp. à compartiments. In sections, paneled.

à dent. à dentelle. Tooled with lace-like designs.

à fond. Thoroughly, completely.

abîmée (reliure-). Binding damaged, in poor condition.

abrégé. Abridgment, abstract, summary.

abt. abonnement. Subscription.

acheté. Purchased.

acier (sur-). On steel, steel engraving.

acte. Formal document. **acte de notaire.** Notarial instrument.

-aîné. Senior. (*e.g.*, Dorbon-aîné (Dorbon, Sr.).)

ais de bois. Wooden covers.

allem. allemand. German.

anc. ancien. Old.

ancienne maison. Formerly (literally, " old house"). (*e.g.*, ancienne maison Martin & cie (formerly Martin & Co.).)

année. Year.

annoté. Annotated.

app., append. appendice. Appendix.

apparition (dès l'-). On (or from) date of publication.

aquarelle. Water-color.

assemblé. Gathered and folded, "in sheets."

atl., atlan. (format) atlantique. Atlas (folio).

augmenté. Enlarged.

autographe. Autograph. **-ié.** Autographed.

av. avec.

avant-propos. Preface, introduction.

avec. With.

B.

bas. basane; — **gran.**, basane granit (granulée); — **m.** (**mar.**), basane maroquin; — **rac.**, basane racinée.

basane. Sheepskin; — **granit,** Mottled sheep; — **granulée.** Granulated sheepskin. "Imitation shagreen" or morocco; — **grenée,** Grained sheep; — **maroquin,** Imitation morocco; — **racinée,** Tree sheep.

bel, belle. Fine, beautiful; — **état,** Fine condition; — **ex.,** bel exemplaire, Fine copy.

bistré. Tawny, dark brown. "Sepia."

bl. bleu, also blanc.

blanc. Blank, white.

blas. blason. Coat of arms.

bleu. Blue.

boîte (en-). Boxed.

bon état. Good condition.

bord. bordure. Border, edge.

boucles de mét. boucles de métal. Metal clasps.

bouquineur. Lover of old books.

bouquiniste. Cheap second-hand bookseller.

bouton. Knob, boss.

Br. Bradel.

br. broché. Sewed, stitched, paper covered.

Bradel. A style of French half-binding with cloth or paper back and paper sides.

broch. broché. Sewed, stitched, paper covered.
brochure. Pamphlet.
brun. Brown.
bruni. Browned, discolored, "foxed."

C.

c. centimes.
c. couronné.
c.-à-d. c'est-à-dire.
c. d. R. cuir de Russie.
c. et ferm. coins et fermoirs.
cachet. Seal. (Of letter or document. Usually represented by *.)
cadre. Frame, ornamental border.
cahier. Sheet, "signature," manuscript book, quire.
car., caract. caractères; — **élz.,** caractères élzéviriens; — **goth.,** caractères gothiques; — **rom.,** caractères romains.
caractères. Characters, letters; — **cursifs,** or **italiques,** Italics; — **élzéviriens,** Elzevir type; — **gothiques,** Black-letter, "text"; — **romains,** Roman characters.
cart. cartonnage, cartonné; — **Brad.,** Cartonnage Bradel; — **percal.,** cartonnage percaline.
carton. Correction sheet, "cancel." Cardboard box.
carton. cartonnage. **En carton.** In cardboard box; bound in boards.
cartonnage. Board binding; — **Bradel,** board binding, Bradel style; — **d'éditeur,** Publishers' board binding; — **percal.,** Cloth back with board sides.
cassé. Broken.
catal. Catalogue; — **raisonné,** Subject catalog.
cdé. cordé.
cercle. Club, society.

c'est-à-dire. That is to say (i. e.).

cf. conférer.

ch. chiffré.

chagr. chagrin, shagreen. Leather with granulated surface. Properly, asses' skin, but applied also to morocco and other grained leathers.

charte. Charter.

chif. chiffré. Numbered.

chromol. chromolithographe.

ci-dessus. Above.

ci-dessous. Below.

cité. Cited, quoted.

citr. citron, lemon colored.

cliché. Stereotyped, stereotype plate.

coin. Corner. (*e.g.*, **coins et fermoirs,** Metal corners and clasps.)

col. Colonne.

collé. Pasted, glued.

colonne. Column.

coloré. Colored.

commenté. Annotated.

commerce. Trade; **non destiné au —,** Privately printed, not for sale; **pas en (dans le) —,** Not in the trade, not usually sold.

comp. complet, complète. Complete.

conférence. Lecture.

conférer. Compare.

cons. conservé. Preserved. (*e.g.*, **bien conservé,** Well preserved, in good condition.)

cordé. With bands. (*e.g.*, **vél. cordé,** Vellum binding with bands. " In vellum, with bands.")

corrigé. Corrected.

couché. *See* **papier.**

coul. couleur. Color.

coupé. Leaves opened.

couronné. Approved, crowned by the Academy.

couv. couvert, couverture.

couvert. Covered.

couverture. Cover, wrapper; — **cons., couverture conservée,** Cover preserved, original cover; —**imp., couverture imprimée,** Printed cover or wrapper.

cplt. complet, complète.

croquis. Sketch, outline drawing.

cuir. Leather; — **de Russie,** Russia leather; — **de s., san.,** or **sang.,** cuir de sanglier, Pigskin; — **de s. g.,** cuir de sanglier gaufré, Gauffered pigskin; — **maroquin,** morocco; — **maroquiné,** Imitation morocco.

cul-de-lampe. Tailpiece.

Cursif. (ve). Cursive letters, italics.

D.

d. demi. (q. v.); **d. b. (d.-bas.),** demi-basane; **d. ch.,** demi-chagrin; **d. m. (-mar.),** demi-maroquin; **d. rel.,** demi-reliure; **d. t.,** demi-toile; **d. v.,** demi-veau; **d. vél.,** demi-vélin.

d. doré. **d. s. t.,** doré sur tranche. (*See also* **doré.**)

dans les marges. In the margins.

déboité. Loosened in the joints.

déchiré. Torn.

déchirures. Tears.

découpé. Cut out of, detached.

découpure. Piece cut out. •

défectuosité. Defect, imperfection.

défraichi. Dulled, faded, shopworn. (*e.g.,* **rel. défraichie,** Binding faded.)

dél. délié. Binding loosened.

demande. Order.

demi. Half; — **basane,** Half sheep; — **chagrin,**

Half shagreen; — **maroquin,** Half morocco; — **re-liure,** Half binding; — **toile,** Half cloth; — **veau,** Half calf; — **vélin,** Half vellum.

dent. dentelle. Lace-like tooling or ornament; — **int. (intér.),** dentelle intérieure, Lace-work tooling on inside of cover.

dérel. dérelié. Unbound, binding gone.

des. dessin. Design, drawing.

diff. différent. Different. (*e.g.*, **reliure diff.,** Binding not uniform.)

dommage. Injury, damage.

dor. doré; — **s. pl.,** doré sur plats; — **sur tr.,** doré sur tranches.

doré. Gilt; — **sur plats,** Gilding on sides; — **sur tranches,** Gilt edges.

dorure. Design in gilt.

dos. Back (of book); — **brisé,** Loose back; — **cassé,** Broken back; — **de vélin,** Vellum back; — **fac. (factice),** false back, wrapper; — **orné,** Decorated back.

douzaine. Dozen.

dzn. douzaine.

E.

e. a. entre autres.

e. b. en bois.

e. t. d. en taille-douce. Copperplate.

eau(x)-forte(s), gravure(s) à l' —. Etching(s).

éb. ébarbé. Trimmed, cut.

écaille. "Tortoise shell" binding, usually scarlet calf.

écriture. Writing.

éd. éditeur, édition.

éditeur. Publisher.

édition. Edition.

élég. élégant, élégamment. Elegant, elegantly.

empiré. Spoiled.

en. In; — **bois,** In wood (wood-cuts); — **taille-douce,** Copperplate; — **tête,** At the top, the top, head (of book), headpiece, vignette.

encadrement. Frame, border.

enchère. Auction. **aux —s, vente à l' —,** Sale by auction.

endom. (-m.). endommagé. Damaged.

enlevé. Missing.

enluminé. Illuminated.

ens. ensemble, ensuite.

ensemble. Together, as a whole, complete.

ensuite. Next, following.

entre autres. Among others.

entrelac. Interlacing, wreath.

env. environ, envoi.

environ. About.

envoi. Parcel, something sent; — **autogr.,** Autographed presentation copy; — **d'auteur,** "Authors' copy" with authors' autograph, sentiment, etc.; — **d'auteur signé,** Presentation copy signed by the author; — **d'éditeur,** Publishers' presentation copy.

époque (de l' —). Contemporary.

épuisé. Exhausted, out of print.

err. errata.

ess. essai(s). Essay(s).

est. estampe, estampé.

estampe. Print, engraving, stamp. **Magasin d' —s,** Print-shop; **Marchand d' —s,** Dealer in prints.

estampé. Stamped, embossed.

et. and; — **suiv.,** — suivant, And following.

ét. étude.

état. State, condition; — **de neuf,** — **neuf,** "As new."

étude. Study.

étui. Case, box.

exemp. exemplaire. Copy; — **à témoins,** Trimmed copy with some untouched corners or edges; — **neuf,** New copy; — **numéroté,** Numbered copy.

ex-libris. Bookplate.

expédié a l'examen. Sent on approval.

expl. exemplaire.

F.

f. (ff.). feuille(s), feuillet(s). Folio.

f. à fr. fer à froid.

f. atl. format atlantique.

f. d. filets dorés.

facs. facsimile(s).

factice. False, artificial.

f. d. s. l. p. filets d'or sur les plats.

f. ob. format oblong.

fasc. Fascicule. Number (part) of a serial or book.

fauve. Fawn-colored, tawny.

faux-titre. False or bastard title.

fc. franco.

fe. feuille, feuillet; — **n. chiff.,** feuillet non chiffré.

fer. Tool; — **à froid,** Blind tooling.

ferm. (-s). fermoir(s). Clasp(s).

feu. "The late." (*e.g.,* "Feu Auguste Renard." "The late Auguste Renard.")

feuill. feuilleton.

feuille. Leaf, sheet; — **hebdomadaire,** Weekly newspaper; — **périodique,** Periodical; — **volante,** Flyleaf, loose sheet, broadside; **en —s.,** "In sheets."

feuillet. Leaf; — **blanc,** Blank leaf, flyleaf; — **chiffré,** Numbered page; — **non chiffré,** Unnumbered leaf; — **refait,** "Cancel," corrected page for insertion in place of incorrect one.

feuilleton. Flysheet, light literature, part of newspaper devoted to light literature.

ff. feuilles, feuillets.

ffc. feuillets chiffrés.

ffnch. feuilles (feuillets) non chiffrés.

fig.(-s). Figure(s); — **col.,** figure(s) coloriée(s) (colorées); — **s. b.,** figures sur bois.

figure(-s). Figure(s), illustration(s); — **coloriée(s)** (**colorées**), Colored figures; — **sur bois,** Wood cuts.

fil. filet(-s).

filet. Fillet, ornamental line or band; —**s d'or sur les plats,** Gilt fillets on the sides; — **dorés,** Gilt fillets; — **sur les bords,** Gilt fillets on the edges.

filigrane. Water mark.

fl. d. l. fleur de lis.

fleuron. Tailpiece. Floral ornament.

fnc. feuillet non chiffré.

fol. folio.

folio. Folio; — **atlantique,** Atlas folio.

forel. Rough, heavy parchment.

form. format. Size; — **atlas,** Atlas folio; **Grand —,** Large size; — **oblong,** Oblong; **petit —,** Small size.

fr. franc(s).

franco. Prepaid.

frappé. Stamped, tooled; — **en or et à froid,** Gold and blind tooled.

frc.(-s). franc(s).

froid, à-. Blind tooling.

front., frontisp. Frontispiece.

fx. tit. faux titre.

G.

g. gaufré, gravé, grand.

g. e. t. d. gravé en taille-douce.

g. de marges. grand de marges.

g. p. grand papier; **g. p. d. H.,** grand papier de Hollande; **g. p. v.,** grand papier vélin.

gauf. gaufré. Goffered; — **à froid,** Goffered without gilt; — **d'or,** Goffered in gilt.

gf. gaufré.

glacé. Glazed, glossy.

goth. gothique.

gr. grand; — **in-8°,** Large 8vo.

gr. grand; — **marg.,** grandes marges; — **pap.,** grand papier.

gr. gravé, gravure; — **en t.-d.,** gravé (gravure) en taille-douce; — **gr. s. b.,** gravé (gravure) sur bois.

grain, à — s. Grained.

grand. Large; — **es marges,** Wide margins; — **papier,** Large paper.

grav. gravé, gravure.

gravé. Engraved; — **à l'eau-forte,** Etched; — **en taille-douce,** Engraved on copper; — **sur acier,** Engraved on steel; — **sur bois,** Engraved on wood; — **sur cuivre,** Engraved on copper.

gravure. Engraving. (For compounds *see* **gravé.**)

gris. Gray.

Grol. Grolier. Style of decorated binding.

H.

h. hauteur. Height.

héliogravé. Photo-engraved; — **gravures,** Photogravures.

héritiers. Heirs.

hommage. Compliments; — **de l'auteur,** With the compliments of the author.

hors commerce. Not in the trade. Not usually sold.

hors texte. Not in the text.

I.

impr. imprimé, imprimerie.

imprimé. Printed.

imprimerie. Printing establishment.

in. In. In composition to express book sizes. (*e.g.*, **in-f.,** in-folio (Folio); **pet. in-fol.,** petit in-folio (Small folio); **in-8,** in-octavo (Octavo); **in-8° écu** (Crown octavo); **in-seize** (16mo), etc.)

inédit. Unpublished.

init. initiale(s), Initial(s).

int. intérieur. Interior.

interfolié. Interleaved.

J.

j. jaune.

jans. janséniste.

janséniste. Jansenist. A severe unornamented French style of binding.

jaune. Yellow.

jésus. Superroyal (book or paper size). (*e.g.*, **in-8 jésus,** Superroyal octavo; **grand** —, Imperial. *e.g.*, **in-8 grand jésus,** Imperial octavo.)

journal. (**-naux**). Journal, newspaper, periodical.

L.

l. largeur.

l. lettre; — **a.,** lettre autographe; — **a. s.,** lettre autographe signée; — **s.,** lettre signée.

l. g. lettres gothiques.

largeur. Breadth, width.

lavé. Washed.

lég. léger. Slight. **légères mouillures,** Slight "fox marks."

lettre. Letter; — **autographe,** Autograph letter; — **autographe signée,** Autograph letter signed; —**s gothiques,** Gothic letters; —**s onciales,** Uncial letters; — **ornées,** Decorative letters; — **signée,** Letter signed.

lettrine. Heading, reference, small superior letter, referring to footnote.

libraire. Bookseller; **libraire-éditeur,** Bookseller and publisher.

librairie. Bookstore, bookselling; — **ancienne,** Old bookstore. (*i.e.*, Second-hand.)

ligne. Line.

ligné. Lined.

lith., litho., lithog. lithographie, lithographié.

lithographie. Lithograph.

lithographié. Lithographed; — **par** —, Lithographed by (the artist); — **de** —, Printed by (the publisher).

livr. livraison. Part or number of a book or serial.

livre. Book.

livre. Old French coin of various values.

livres d'occasion. Second-hand books.

ll. lignes.

ll. ll. longues lignes. Long lines.

lv. livres (coin).

M.

main de papier. Quire of paper.

m. maroquin; **m. ant.,** maroquin antique; **m. br.,** maroquin brun; **m. cit,** maroquin citron; **m. d. d. m.,** maroquin doublé de maroquin; **m. d. d. t.,** maro-

quin doublé de tabis; **m. d. l.,** maroquin de luxe;
m. gr., maroquin grené; **m. fil.,** maroquin à filets;
m. j., maroquin jaune; **m. jans.,** maroquin jansénist;
m. l., maroquin lilas; **m. n.,** maroquin noir; **m. o.,**
maroquin olive; **m. pl.,** maroquin plein; **m. r.,** maroquin rouge; **m. v.,** maroquin vert; **m. viol.,** maroquin violet; **d.-m.,** demi-maroquin.

manch. manchettes. Side notes.

manuscrit. Manuscript.

manque. Lacks. (*e.g.,* " Manque la couverture supérieure (inférieure)," "Lacks the front (back)
cover.")

manquent. Are lacking.

mar. maroquin. (**q. v.**)

marb., marbr. marbré. Marbled.

marge. Margin; **grandes —s.,** Wide margins.

maroquin. Morocco; — **antique,** Antique morocco;
— **bleu,** Blue morocco; — **brun,** Brown morocco;
— **citron,** Lemon-colored morocco; — **doublé de
maroquin,** Morocco binding lined with morocco;
— **doublé de tabis,** Morocco binding lined with
tabby; — **à filets,** Morocco binding with decorative lines and bands; — **grené,** Grained morocco;
— **jaune,** Yellow morocco; — **janséniste,** Morocco
binding, Jansenist style; — **lilas,** Lilac morocco; —
noir, Black morocco; — **olive,** Olive morocco; —
plein, Full morocco; — **rouge,** Red morocco; —
vert, Green morocco; — **violet,** Violet morocco;
demi-maroquin, Half-morocco.

marque d'imprimeur. Printer's mark.

majuscule. Capital letter.

marron. maroon.

mauv. mauvais. Bad.

mes. mesure. Measure, dimensions.

min. miniature.

minuscule. Lower case letter. Small capital.

mod. moderne. Modern. **à la —,** Modern style.

moins. Except. (*e.g.,* **"Comp. moins le t. 7,"** "Complete with the exception of vol. 7.")

mouil., mouill. mouillure. Water-stain, "Fox mark." **—s et piqures,** Fox marks and wormholes.

mouton. Sheepskin.

N.

n. nerf, neuf, non, numéroté, nouveau (-velle).

n. ch. (nch). non chiffré.

n. e. non ébarbé.

n. ms. notes manuscrites.

n. per. nouvelle période.

n. rel. non relié.

n. rogn. (n. r.) non rogné.

n. s. nouvelle série.

nch. non chiffré.

nerf. Raised band, tape, cord (binding). **à —s,** " Raised bands."

neuf., neuve. New.

neumes. Medieval musical notes (literally, breathings). "Plain chants."

nn. numéroté.

nombr. nombreux(se). Numerous.

non. Not; — **chiffré,** Unnumbered; — **coupé,** Unopened; — **ébarbé,** Untrimmed, rough edges; — **livré au commerce,** "Not in the trade"; — **rel.** (**relié**), Unbound; — **rogné,** Uncut.

notes manuscrites. Manuscripts.

nouv. nouveau, nouvelle.

nouvelle. New; — **période,** New series; — **série,** New series.

num. numéro, numéroté.

numéro. Number, issue (periodical).

numéroté. Numbered.

O.

obl., oblg. oblong, oblongue.

oblongue. Oblong.

œuvre. Book, work; —s complètes, complete works.

oncial. Uncial, Rounded letters used in early mss.

orn. orné. Ornament.

orné. Ornamented, decorated.

ornement. Ornament, decoration.

ouv., ouvr. ouvrage. Work. (*e.g.*, **ouv. cité,** Work cited.)

P.

p. papier; **p. de H.,** papier de Hollande; **p. ord.,** papier ordinaire; **p. v.,** papier vélin, papier vergé; **p. v. b.,** papier vélin blanc; **p. vél.,** papier vélin.

p. de tr. peau de truie.

p. f. petits fers.

p. v. t. par voie télégraphique.

page de garde. Flyleaf.

pap. papier.

papier. Paper; — **couché,** Coated paper; — **de Chine,** China paper, India paper; — **de Hollande,** Holland paper; — **glacé,** Glazed or glossy paper; — **faux vergé,** Machine laid paper; — **grand,** "large paper"; — **jaspé,** Marbled paper; — **léger,** Lightweight paper; — **ordinaire,** "Small paper," ordinary paper; — **sparte,** Esparto paper; — **ramie,** Straw paper; — **satiné,** Calendered paper; — **vélin,** Vellum or parchment paper; — **vergé,** Laid paper.

par voie télégraphique. By telegraph.

paraphe. Paraph, signature consisting of initials.

paraphé. Initialed.

parch., parchem. parchemin. Parchment.

partie. Part.

pas en commerce. " Not in the trade."

peau. Leather; — **de Rus. (Russie),** Russia leather;
— **d. tr. (de truie),** Sowskin, pigskin.

peignées, tranches. Grained edges.

per. période.

percal. percaline. Book cloth, book muslin.

pet. petit.

petit. Small; —**s fers,** Small tools or tooling; — **grattage,** Small scratch or rubbing. (The word grattage
is also used in connection with palimpsests, rubbed;
literally, scraping.)

peu. Little, few; — **commun,** Scarce; — **frais
(fraîche),** Soiled, shopworn.

photogr. photographe, photographique.

photographique. Photographic.

piq. piqué, piqûres.

piqué. Wormeaten.

piqûres. Wormholes.

pl. planche, plein.

pl. planche. Plate; — **col.,** planche coloriée (colorée),
Colored plate; — **enl.,** planche enluminée, Illuminated, hand-colored plate.

plaq. plaquette. Booklet, small thin book.

plats. Sides (of book); — **de papier,** Paper sides; —
dorés, Sides gilt; — **toile,** Cloth sides.

plch.(s). planche(s).

plein(e). Full; — **toile,** Full cloth; — **veau,** Full calf.

plié. Folded.

pointillé, gravé au —. Stippled.

pontuseau(x). Watermark(s). (*i.e.,* " cross ribs.")

port (le —). Transportation charges, postage.

portef. portefeuille. Portfolio, holder.

porto. Postage, carriage charge.

portrait. Portrait.

pour paraître prochainement. To appear shortly.

précis. Summary.

prél. préliminaire. Preliminary.

prem. premier. First.

prix. Price; — **courant,** Price current; — **coûtant,** Cost price; — **fixe,** Fixed price, no discount; — **fort,** List price; — **réduit,** Reduced price.

ptr.(s). portrait(s).

Q.

quaterne. Quire (quaternio, 4 double leaves or 16 pages).

qq. quelques. Some.

R.

r. reliure, rogné, rouge.

r. pl. reliure pleine.

rac. raccommodé. Repaired.

rame de papier. Ream of paper.

rarissime. Very rare.

réclame. Catchword at bottom of page.

recouvr. recouvrement. New cover, rebinding. (*e.g,* **vél. à recouvr.,** Rebound in vellum.)

recueil. Collection.

rédigé. Arranged, drawn up, compiled.

réduit, prix —. Reduced.

refait à la main. Reproduced in manuscript.

réglé. Ruled, lined, directed.

réglure. Ruling. (*e.g.*, **réglure à la mine de plomb,** Ruling made with lead pencil; — **au crayon,** Pencil ruling.)

rehaussé. Decorated.

réimpression. Reprint.

rel. relié, reliure.

relié. Rebound.

relieur. Book binder.

reliure. Binding; — **ang. (anglaise),** English binding; — **aux armes,** Armorial binding; — **brisée,** Binding cracked or broken; — **cassée,** Binding broken; — **d' éditeur,** Publisher's binding; — **défaite,** Binding loose; — **du temps,** Contemporary binding; — **en bois,** Bound in wood boards; — **en sus,** Binding extra (cost); — **fat. (fatiguée),** Binding worn; — **moderne,** Modern binding; — **orig. (originale),** Original (contemporary) binding; — **orig. g. ferm.** — **(originale, gaufré, fermoirs),** Contemporary binding with goffered edges and clasps; — **pleine,** Full binding; — **usagée, usée,** Binding worn.

remarque. Small marginal sketch.

remise. Discount; — **de 20%,** Discount of 20%.

réparé. Repaired, mended.

restauré. Restored.

revu. Revised; — **et corrigé,** Revised and corrected.

rog. rogné.

rogné. Cut, edges trimmed; — **en haut,** Top edges trimmed.

rom. (romain.). Caractères romains. Roman characters.

roman. Novel, romance.

rouge. Red; — **et noir,** Red and black, rubricated.

rousseur. "Fox mark," red spot.

ruban. Ribbon bookmark.

S.

s. sans.

s. c. sur cuivre.

s. d. sans date.

s. ind. typ. sans indices typographiques.

s. l. sans lieu; — — **n. d.,** sans lieu ni date.

s. libr. sans libraire.

s. typ. sans typographe.

saisi. Confiscated, suppressed.

sangl. (cuir de —). cuir de sanglier.

sans. Without; — **indices typographiques,** Without typographic marks, *i.e.*, name of place, printer or date; — **libraire,** Without name of publisher; — **lieu,** Without place of publication; — **lieu ni date,** Without place or date; — **typographe,** Without name of printer.

satiné. Calendered (paper).

sceau. Seal (letter). Usually indicated in catalogues by *.

scient. scientifique. Scientific.

sér. série. Series.

seulem. seulement. Only.

siècle. Century.

sig. signature, signé.

sigle. Initial letter used by way of abbreviation. (*e.g.*, **S.** for Saint.)

signat. signature.

signature. Signature.

signé. Signed.

soc. société. Society.

sommaire. Summary, compendium, abstract.

souffert. p. p. of souffrir. (To suffer.) Injured, damaged.

souple. Flexible.

sous presse. In press.

souscription à forfait. Subscriptions taken, at definite price, regardless of extent of work, or number of parts that will appear.

spéc. spécial. Special.

sup. (suppl.). supplément. Supplement.

sv., svv. suivant, suivants (es). Following. (*e.g.*, v. pp. 29 svv., See pages 29 and following.)

T.

t. tête; — **d.,** tête dorée.

t. titre; — **gr.,** titre gravé. Engraved title.

t. toile; — **pl.,** toile pleine.

t. tome.

tache. Spot, stain; — **d'encre,** Ink stains; —**s de rousseur,** " Fox spots."

tacheté. Spotted, stained.

taille-douce. Copperplate.

tel que paru. In the same condition as when it appeared, as it appeared, as published.

témoins. Marks, evidence.

tête. Head (of book); — **dorée,** Gilt top.

timbre. Stamp, seal; **papier timbré,** Stamped paper.

timbre-poste(s). Postage stamp(s).

tirage. Edition, impression; — **à part,** Reprint, "separate."

tiré. Printed, struck off; — **à** — **exemplaires,** Limited to — copies; — **à petit nombre,** Limited edition.

tit. titre; — **cour.,** titre courant; — **r. et. n.,** — rouge et noir.

titre. Title; — **courant,** Running title, catch title; — **gravé,** Engraved title; — **rouge et noir,** Title in red and black.

toile. Cloth; — **pleine,** Full cloth (binding). (For colors *see under* **Maroquin.**)

tom. tome. Volume.

tout ce qui a paru, tout paru. All that has (have) appeared.

tr. traduction, traduit, tranche.

traduction. Translation.

tr. tranche; — **cis.,** tranche ciselée; — **d. (dor.),** tranche dorée; — **j.,** tranche jaspée; — **m.,** tranche **marbrée;** — **s. d. (super. dor.),** tranche supérieure dorée; — **p.,** tranche peignée; — **r.,** tranche rouge.

trad. traduction. Translation.

traduit. Translated.

tranche. Edge; — **ciselée,** Ornamentation cut in edge, goffered; — **dorée,** Gilt edge; — **jaspée,** Sprinkled edge; — **marbrée,** Marbled edge; — **peignée,** Grained edge; — **rouge,** Red edge; — **supérieure dorée,** Gilt top.

typ. typographe, typographie, typographique.

typographe. Printer.

typographie. Printing office; typography.

typographique. Typographical.

U.

unciale. *See* **oncial.**

unif. uniforme.

usé. Used, worn.

V.

v. veau; **v. p.,** veau porphyre, veau plein.

v. voyez. See.

v^e. veuve.

veau. Calf. (*See under* **Maroquin** for styles); — **écaille,** Scaled or "tortoise shell" calf; — **fauve,** Plain calf, law calf; — **porphyre,** Porphyry calf.

vél.   vélin; — **bl.,** vélin blanc.

vélin.   Vellum; — **blanc,** White vellum.

vergé.   Laid (paper), literally "ribbed."

vergeure.   Rib (line in paper made by rib of wire mesh on which it was laid).   The cross wires are called **pontuseau(x).**

veuve.   Widow (of).

vient de paraître.   Just published.

vign.   vignette.

vve.   veuve.

W.

Wh.   Whatman (paper).

GERMAN ABBREVIATIONS AND TERMS

A.

ϑ. Pfennig(e).

a. aus.

a., A. Ausgabe. Ausschnitt.

à Condition. On sale account.

a. d. J. aus dem Jahre.

a. d. Lat. aus dem Lateinischen.

a. S. andere Seite. See next page.

a. u. d. T. auch unter dem Titel.

Abb., Abbild. (gn.) Abbildung(en). Illustration(s), cut(s).

Abdr. Abdruck(-drücke). Copy(-ies), impression(s); **neuer —**, Reprint; **original —**, First edition, original impression; **— vor der Schrift,** Proof.

abgeschabt. Worn, shabby.

abgk. abgekürzt. Abridged, abbreviated.

Abh. Abhandlung(-en). Transaction(s).

Abklatsch. Proof sheet or impression.

Abkrzg. Abkürzung. Abridgment, abbreviation.

Abonnement(-s). Subscription(s).

Abonnent(en). Subscriber(s).

Abschn. Abschnitt. Extract, paragraph, section.

Abt., Abth. Abt(h)eilung(en). Section(s), part(s), chapter(s), division(s), classification(s).

Abzug. Proof, first impression; **— vor der Schrift,** Proof impression, "proof before letters."

Afl. Auflage.

allg., allgem., allgm. allgemein. General, universal.

Alm. Almanach(e). Almanac, calendar.

amtl. amtlich. Official.

Andere Seite. See next page.

Anf. Anfang(-fänge). Beginning, elements (in pl.).

Anhang(-hänge). Appendix(es), supplement(s).

Anm. Anmerkung(en). Note(s), annotation(s).

Ann. (Annal.). Annalen. Annals.

Ansicht, (zur—). On approval.

Antiquar. Dealer in old books.

Antiquariat. Old bookstore.

antiquarisch. Old, second-hand.

Antiquaschrift. Roman characters.

Anzeiger. Advertiser, intelligencer.

apart. Separate(ly).

Arch. Archiv(e). Record(s), archives (pl.).

Art. Artikel. Article.

Atlant(-en). Atlas(es).

auch unter dem Titel. Also under the title.

auf Wunsch. On request.

Aufl. Auflage(-n). Edition(s). (*See also* **Ausgabe.**)

Aufs. Aufsatz(-sätze). Essay(s), treatise(s).

aus. From.

aus dem Jahre. Belonging to the year —.

aus dem Lateinischen (etc.). From the Latin, (etc.).

Aufdr. Aufdruck(-drücke). Copy(-ies), impression(s).

Ausg. Ausgabe(n). Edition(s). **autoriz(s)ierte —,** Authorized ed.; **berichtigte —,** Corrected ed.; **billige —,** Cheap ed.; **c(k)orrigierte —,** Corrected ed.; **durchgearbeitete —,** Thoroughly revised ed.; **ergänzte —,**

Enlarged ed.; **Geschenk** —, Presentation ed.; **neu-bearbeitete** —, Newly revised ed.; **neue** —, New ed.; **original** —, First edition; **revidierte** —, Revised ed.; **kritisch rev.** —, Revised edition with critical notes; **unveränderte** —, Unchanged ed.; **verbesserte** —, Improved ed.; **vergrösserte** —, Enlarged ed.; **ver-mehrte** —, Enlarged ed.; **Volks** —, Popular edition.

ausgeb. ausgebessert. Repaired, completed (of imperfect copy).

ausgew. ausgewählt. Selected.

auslaufende Zeilen. Lines entire width of page, *i.e.*, not in columns.

Auslieferung durch —. Delivery through —, to be obtained from —.

Ausschnitt(e). Extract, excerpt.

Auszug. (-züge). Abridgment(s), abstract(s).

autoris(z). autorisirt(-zirt). Authorized.

B.

b. bar.

B. Band. Buch. Beiträge.

Band (Bände). Volume(s).

Bändchen. Small volume(s), booklet(s).

bar. Cash.

Bart. *See* **mit Bart.**

Bd(e). Band (Bände).

Bdchn. Bändchen.

Bdn. Bänden (Dative plural of **Band**).

Bearb. Bearbeiter. Editor.

bearb. bearbeitet. Adapted, arranged.

Bedingung(en). Term(s). (*e.g.*, zu **guten** —, On good terms.)

Bei Erschienen bereits vergriffen. Edition exhausted before announced date of publication.

Beiblatt (-blätter). (Newspaper) supplement.

beigeb. beigebunden. Bound with.

Beiheft(e). Supplement(s).

Beil. Beilage(n).

Beilage(n). Addition(s), enclosure(s), (newspaper) supplement(s).

bein. beinahe. Almost, nearly.

Beiname. Surname.

Beitrag(-träge). Contribution(s).

bes. besonders. Especially, particularly.

beschäd. beschädigt. Damaged.

Beschlag(-schläge). Clasp(s).

beschnitten. Cut closely, cropped.

besorgt. (Orders) filled; (books) procured, edited, prepared for publication.

betr. betreffend. Relating to, concerning; *e.g.*, das — **Buch,** The book referred to.

bez. bezüglich. Referring to, respecting.

beziehungsweise. Respectively, concerning.

bezüglich. Relating (to), respecting.

bezifferte Blätter. Numbered leaves.

bezw. bzw. beziehungsweise.

Bg. Bogen.

Bh. Buchhandlung.

Bib. Bibliothek.

bibl. bibliographisch, Bibliographic.

Bibl. Bibliotheca. Library (used of series).

Bibliothek. Library; — **swesen,** Library economy; — **zeichen,** Library bookplate.

Bibliothekar. Librarian.

biegs. biegsam. Flexible.

Bild(er). Picture(s).

Bildn. Bildnis(se). Portrait(s).

Bildtafel(n). List(s) of pictures.

billig. Cheap.

Bl.(l.) Blatt (Blätter). Leaf (leaves); **Fliegende —,** Flyleaf, occasional paper, broadside.

blattgross. Full page.

Bld(r.). Bild(-er).

Blds. Bildnis.

Blindpressung. Blind stamping or tooling.

Bn. Beiname.

Bogen. Section, sheet, signature.

Bogenbezeichnung. Signature letter or number.

böhm. böhmisch. Bohemian.

Bordirung, Bordüre. Border, edge.

br. broschirt.

braunfleckig. Brown spotted, " foxed."

Breite. Breadth.

breiter Rand (breite Ränder). Wide margin(s).

breitrandig. With wide margins.

Brief(e). Letter(s).

broschirt. Sewed, stitched, paper-covered.

brsch. broschirt.

Buch (Bücher). Book(s).

Buchb. Buchbinderei. Bookbindery.

Buchd. Buchdruckerei. Printing house.

Buchdruckerstock(stöcke). Printers' device, head-piece, tailpiece.

Bücheranzeige(n). Notice(s) of books.

Bücherbesprechung(en). Book review(s); — **bestand,** Stock (of books). (*i.e.*, Number of volumes.)

Bücherei. Library.

Bücherverzeichnis. Catalogue.

Bücherzeichen. Printers' mark, bookplate, bookmark.

Buchh. Buchhandel, Buchhandlung.

Buchhandel. Bookselling, book trade.

Buchhandlung. Bookstore.

Buchschmuck. Decoration, ornament.

Buchzeichen. *See* **Bücherzeichen.**

Buckel(n). Knob(s), boss(es).

Buntdruck(e). Colored print(s) or impression(s).

Buntpapierdeckel. Colored paper covers.

Butten. *See* **Bütten.**

Bütten. holländ. —, holländisches Büttenpapier.

Büttenausg. in Ldr. Buttenausgabe in Leder. (Edition on handmade paper, with leather binding.)

Büttenpapier. Handmade paper; **holländisches —,** Handmade Holland paper.

bzw. beziehungsweise.

C.

(See also **K** for words beginning with C. The two letters are frequently interchangeable.)

Cap. Capitel.

Capitel. Chapter.

cart. cartonnirt.

Cartonnage. Boards (binding).

cartonnirt. Bound in boards.

Cattunband. Bound in cloth.

ch.-sächs (k.-sächs). churfürstlich sächsisch. (**kurfürstlich —,** Electoral Saxon.)

Char. Charakter.

Charakter. Letter, character.

cisel. ciselierte. Engraved, chased.

ciselierte Beschläge. Chased metal clasps.

Columnentitel. *See* **Kolumnentitel.**

(in) Commission. On sale [by A.].

Commissionsverlag. Selling agency.

cplt. complett. Complete.

cr. Crown(s). Austrian coin.

Ctb. Cattunband.

Custos. *See* **Kustos.**

D.

d. deutsch (adj.), Deutsch (noun).

D. Dissertation.

d. d. —. datirt den —.

d. f. der folgende.

d. h. das heisst.

d. i. das ist.

d. J. des Jahres.

d. l. der letzte.

d. M. dieses Monats.

dän. dänisch. Danish.

dargestellt. Set forth.

dar. darunter. Under that.

darst. darstellend. Producing, presenting, descriptive.

das heisst. That is.

das ist. That is.

das(s). dasselbe.

dasselbe. The same.

datirt den —. Dated the —.

dauerhaft gebunden. Strongly bound.

dav. davon. Of which.

Deckelpappe(n). Board cover(s).

demnächst-erscheint. (To be) published at once.

Denkm. Denkmal.

Denkmal(-mäler). Monument(s). (In series names.)

Denkschr. Denkschrift(en). Commemorative publications.

der folgende. The following.

der letzte. The last.

derg. dergleichen. Like, similar.

des Jahres. Of the year.

desgl. desgleichen. Likewise, also.

deutsch. German (adj.).

dieses Jahr(es). This year (of this year).

dieses Monats. This month (of this month).

Diss. Dissertation.

Dissertation. Dissertation, essay, thesis.

doppelseitig. On both sides of the leaf.

Doktor. Doctor.

Dr. Doktor.

Dr. Drama.

Dr. Druck; — u. Verl., Druck und Verlag.

Drckp. Druckpapier.

Druck(e). Print(s), printing, type(s), proof(s).

Druck und Verlag. Printed and published by —.

Druckanstalt. Printing establishment.

Druckarbeit (Druckerarbeit). Presswork.

Druckbogen. Printed sheet.

Drucker. Printer.

Druckerei. Printing house. Printing.

Druckjahr. Date of printing, title-page date.

Druckort. Place of printing, imprint.

Druckpapier. Printing paper.

Drucksachen. Printed matter.

Druckschrift(en). Type(s), publication(s).

Druckseite(n). Printed page(s).

Druckvermerk. Printers' mark.

Druckversendung. Book post.

dt., dtsch. deutsch.

dünn. Thin.

Dünndr.-Pap. Dünndruckpapier. Thin printing paper, "India paper."

durchgesehen. Revised.

durchsch. Durchschossen. Interleaved.

Duodez-Ausgabe. Duodecimo, 12mo.

E.

e. ein.

eb., ebd. ebenda, ebendaselbst, ebendort.

ebda. ebendaselbst.

ebend. ebenderselbe, ebenda, ebendaselbst.

ebenda. At the same place.

ebendas. ebendaselbst.

ebendaselbst. At the same place.

ebenderselbe. The same.

ebendort. At the same place.

Ecke.(-n). Corner(s).

ehem. ehemalig, ehemals.

ehemalig. Former.

ehemals. Formerly.

eigenhändig geschriebener und unterzeichneter Brief. Autograph letter signed.

eigenhändig unterzeichneter Brief. Letter signed.

eigenhändiger Brief. Autograph letter.

Einb. Einband.

Einband(-bände). Binding(s).

Einblatt, Einblattdruck. Broadside.

eingedr. eingedruckt.

eingedruckt. Imprinted. (Illustrations) inserted into letterpress.

eingel. eingeleitet. With introduction by —.

eingeschr. eingeschrieben. Registered (mail).

Einl., Einleitg.(n), Einltg. Einleitung(en). Introduction(s).

Einschaltbild(er). Inserted illustration(s).

einseitig bedruckt. Printed on one side.

einzeln. Single, separate, retail price, price for separate parts.

einzeln verkäuflich. Sold separately.

einzeln zu haben. To be had separately.

Einzelpr. Einzelpreis.

Einzelpreis. Price for single parts or numbers. Retail price.

Einzelverkauf. Retail selling.

elg. Elegant. Elegant(ly).

Entw. Entwurf. Outline, sketch, drawing.

erg. ergänzt. Completed, supplemented.

Ergänzungsheft(e). Supplement(s).

erh. (Pr.). erhöhter Preis. Increased price.

erkl. erklärt.

Erkl., Erklärg(n). Erklärung(en).

erklärt. Explained, illustrated.

Erklärung(en). Explanation(s), illustration(s).

erl. erläuternd.

Erl. Erläuterung.

erläuternd. Explanatory, illustrative.

Erläuterung(en). Explanatory notes or appendices.

45

erm. ermässigter Preis. Reduced price.

erschienen, (so viel —). All that has (have) been published.

erscheint. Appears, announced for publication.

erscheint nicht mehr. No longer published.

Erwachsene (für —). Edition for adults.

erweit. Aufl. erweiterte Auflage. Enlarged edition.

Erzählg. Erzählung.

Erzählung(en). Story(-ies), tale(s), report(s).

Exempl. Exemplar(plare). Copy(ies).

Expl. Exemplar.

F.

f. fehlt.

f. für.

F. f. Fortsetzung folgt. To be continued.

F. u. S. f. Fortsetzung und Schluss folgt. To be continued and concluded.

Fa. Firma.

Fachblatt. Technical or professional paper.

Faksimile(s). Facsimiles.

Falsche Schrift. Wrong font.

Falz (Fälze). Guard (binding). Fold.

farb. farbig. Colored.

Farbdr. Farbdruck.

Farbdruck(e), Farbendruck(e). Colored print.

farbig. Colored. **farbiger Druck,** Colored print.

fehlt. Lacks, wanting.

ferner. Continued. (*e.g.*, **Schiller (ferner),** *i.e.*, The list or section on Schiller, continued.)

ff., fgg., flgd. folgende.

fg. folgend (sing.).

fgg. folgende (plu.).

fingerfleckig. Fingermarked, thumbed.

Firma. Firm, company.

Fksm(s). Faksimile.

Fl. Florin (Austrian).

Fl. h. Florin Holländish. Dutch florin.

Fl. Fleck(e).

fleckenlos. Free from stains. Perfectly clean.

Fliegendes Blatt. Broadside, flyleaf, occasional paper.

Fleck(e). Spot(s), stain(s).

fleckig. Spotted, stained.

flgd. folgende.

Flugblatt. Fugitive or ephemeral production.

folg(g). folgende.

folgende. Following, subsequent.

Forrell. Rough, heavy parchment.

fortgeführt. Continued.

Fortsetzung(-en). Sequel(s), continuation(s);—**folgt,** " Continued in the next."

Fraktur. Ordinary German text or black-letter.

franco (**franko**). Prepaid.

Franzband. Calf binding.

französ. französisch.

französisch. French.

freiherrlich. Baronial.

frhr. freiherrlich.

früh. Early, former. (*e.g.*, **früherer Preis,** Former price.)

Frzbd. Franzband.

fstl. fürstlich.

Fstt. Fürstentum.

für. for.

fürstl. fürstlich. Princely.

Fürstent(h)um. Principality.

Fussn. Fussnote(n). Footnote(s).

Futteral. Case, box.

G.

G. Gesellschaft. **G. m. b. H.** Gesellschaft mit be-
schränkter Haftung. Limited co., "Incorporated."

Ganzled. Ganzleder. Full leather (binding).

gb. (geb.). gebunden.

Geb. Gebrüder. Brothers.

gebr. gebräuchlich.

Gebrauchsspuren. Marks of use; **Mit —,** worn,
injured by use.

gebräuchlich. Usual, customary.

gebräunt. Browned, brown stained.

gebunden. Bound.

Ged. Gedicht.

Gedicht(-e). Poem(s).

gedr. gedruckt. Printed.

gefalzt. Folded. **gefalzte Bogen.** Folded signatures.

Gegensatz. Opposite, contrary.

geh., gebeftet. Sewed, stitched, pamphlet form.

gek. gekürzt. Abridged.

gelehrte Bibliothek. Library for scholars.

gelitten. Damaged.

gem. gemalt. Painted, drawn.

gen. genannt.

genannt. Called, named.

Genoss(en). Colleague, fellow-member.

gepr. geprägt.

geprägt. Stamped.

Ger. Gericht.

Gericht. Court of justice.

gepresst. Crushed, pressed (binding).

geripptes Papier. Laid paper, ribbed paper.

ges. gesammelt.

Ges. Geschichte.

Ges. Gesellschaft.

Ges. Gesang.

Ges. Gesetz.

gesammelt. Collected.

Gesam(m)t Pr. Gesam(m)tpreis. Complete price.

Gesam(m)tregister. Complete index.

Gesch. Geschichte.

Geschichte(-n). History, histories.

Gesamtausgabe. Collected edition, complete edition.

geschr. geschrieben.

geschrieben. Written.

Gesellschaft. Company, society, association.

Gesetz(e). Law(s).

Geschenkausgabe. Presentation edition.

geslt. gesammelt.

gest. gestempelt. Stamped, *i.e.*, Library stamp on title page.

gestochen. Engraved.

gestrichenes Exemplar. Expurgated (or censored) copy.

gez. Bll. gezählte Blätter. Numbered leaves.

Ggs. Gegensatz.

Glanzpapier. Glazed (coated) paper.

Gldschn. Goldschnitt.

gleichm. gleichmässig. Uniform, similar.

Gloss. Glossar, Glossarium.

Glossar. Glossarium (Glossarien). Glossary(-ies).

goldgeprägt. Stamped in goldleaf.

Goldleiste(n). Gold fillet(s).

Goldpressung. Gold stamping.

Goldschnitt. Gilt edges.

Got(h)ische Schrift. Gothic (black-letter) type.

gr. gross.

Gr. Groschen.

gräfl. gräflich. Pertaining to a count.

Groschen. Old German coin worth about two cents.

gross. Large.

H.

h. halb.

H. Handschrift.

H. Heft.

h. heilig.

H. Heller.

H. Höhe.

Hadernpapier. Rag (linen) paper.

halb. Half—(Binding). (*e.g.* **Halbfranz(band),** Half calf; — **kalbleder,** Half calf; — **leinwand,** Half cloth; — **schafleder,** Half roan or sheep; — **pergament,** Half vellum.)

Halbfrzbd. Halbfranzband.

Halbjährlich. Semi-annual(ly).

Handbibliothek. Reference library, pocket library.

Handbuch. Handbook, reference book.

Handel (Nicht im —). " Not in the trade."

Handexemplar. Personal professional copy.

handgeschöpft. Handmade.

Handrubrik. Titles, headings, initials, etc., illuminated by hand.

50

handschr. handschriftlich.

Handschrift. Manuscript, autograph.

handschriftlich. Manuscript, autograph (adj.).

handschriftlich ergänzt. Restored (in manuscript).

hb. halb. (*See also* **halb** for compounds.)

Hbfzb. Halbfranzband.

Hbldr. Halbleder.

Hblnb. Halbleinenband.

Hblwd. Halbleinwand.

Hdschr. Handschrift.

Heft(e). Number(s), part(s), stitched book(s).

—heft. Number. (*e.g.,* **Märzheft,** March number.)

Heilige. Saint.

Heller. Austrian and old German coin worth about
¼ cent.

herausgegeben. Published, edited.

Herausgeber. Publisher, editor.

herz. herzoglich.

herzoglich. Ducal.

Hfrz. Halbfranz.

Hft.(e). Heft(e).

Hftn. Heften. Dative pl. of **Heft.**

Hfz. Halbfranz.

hist. historisch.

historisch. Historical.

Hl. Heilige.

Hldr. Halbleder.

Hldrb. Halblederband.

Hlwd. Halbleinwandband.

Hlzschn. Holzschnitt.

Hochdruck. Printing in relief, embossed printing.

Höhe. Height.

Holzbd. Holz(ein)band.

Holzdeckel mit Lederüberzug. Wooden boards covered with leather.

Holz(ein)band. Wooden boards (binding).

Holzschnitt(e). Woodcut(s), wood engraving(s).

Holzstich(e). Woodcut(s), wood engraving(s).

Hpgt. Halbpergament.

Hr. Heller.

hrsg. herausgegeben.

Hschn. Holzschnitten. Dat. pl. of **Holzschnitt.**

Hschr. Handschrift.

hschr. handschriftlich.

hsgb. herausgegeben.

Hsgbr. Herausgeber.

Hwb. Handwörterbuch. Handy dictionary.

Hz. Halbfranzband.

I.

i. in. In.

i. A. im Auftrage. By order of, under the direction of, by authority of.

ill. (illustr.). illustriert.

illustriert. Illustrated.

im Einzelnen. Separately, at retail.

in Komm. in Kommission.

in Kommission. *See* **Commission.**

in leer. In blank.

in Quart. (in 4°), etc. Quarto, etc.

Inhalt. Contents.

Inhaltsverzeichnis. Table of contents, index.

Inschft. Inschrift.

Inschrift(en). Inscription(s).

J.

J. Jahr.
Jahrh. (rarely **Jahr.**). Jahrhundert.
Jahr(e). Year(s).
Jahrb. Jahrbuch.
Jahrbuch(-bücher). Year-book(s), almanac(s), annual(s).
Jahresbericht(e). Annual report(s).
Japanbütten. Japan handmade paper.
Jahrg. Jahrgang.
Jahrgang(-gänge). Annual set(s), series, or volume(s).
Jahrhundert. Century, centuries.
jährlich. Annual.
Jb. Jahrbuch or Jahresbericht.
Jchbt., Jchtn., Jchtnb. Juchtenband.
Jh., Jhr., Jahrh. Jahrhundert.
Jhrg. Jahrgang.
Jl. Journal.
Journal. Journal, magazine.
Juchtenband. Russia binding.

K.

(*See also* C for words beginning with K. The two letters are often interchangeable.)

K. Karte.
k. königlich.
K. Krone.
K. Kupfer.

K. K. (**K. u. K.**). Kaiserlich-königlich.

kais. kaiserlich. Imperial.

kaiserlich-königlich. Royal imperial.

Katal. Katalog.

Katalog. Catalogue.

kart. kartoniert. Bound in boards.

Karte(-n). Map(s), chart(s).

Kattunband. Bound in muslin.

Kehrseite. Verso.

kgl. Königlich.

Kk. Kupfer (plu.).

kl. klein.

klein. Small (in composition); **klein 8°,** Small octavo, etc.

Kleinoktav. Small octavo.

knapp beschnitten. Closely cut or trimmed.

Kollege(n). Colleague, fellow-member.

Kolumne(n). Column(s); — **titel,** Running title.

komplett. Complete.

Kopfverg. Kopfvergoldung. Gilt top.

kostenlos. "Gratis."

Kpf., Kpfr. Kupfer.

Kpfrt. Kupfertafel.

Kpfst. Kupferstich.

kplt. komplett.

Kr. Kreuzer. Small German and Austrian coin.

Krone. Crown (coin) of various values.

Ktnb., Ktnbd. Kattunband.

Kupfer. *See* Kupferstich.

Kupferätzung(en). Aquatint(s).

Kupferblatt(-blätter). Copperplate(s).

Kupferdruckpapier. Plate paper.

Kupferstich(e). Copperplate(s).
Kupfertafel(n). Copperplate(s).
Kunstdr.-Ausg. Kunstdruck-Ausgabe.
Kunstdruck-Ausgabe. "Art edition."
Kursivschrift. Italics.
Kustos (Kustoden). Catchword(s). Curator(s).

L.

l. letzte.
l. lies.
L. G. Leinwandband mit Goldschnitt.
l. J. laufenden Jahres.
l. M. laufenden Monats.
L. S. Leinwandband mit Silberschnitt.
läd. lädirt.
Ladenpreis. List price.
Ladenpreis aufgehoben. List price suspended.
lädirt. Damaged.
Lage. Signature, quire.
Landesbibliothek. National library.
Landkarte(n). Map(s), chart(s).
landschftl. landschaftlich. Provincial.
laufenden Jahres. Of the current year; — **Monats,**
Of the current month.
landw. landwirthschaftlich. Agricultural.
Ldnpr. Ladenpreis.
Ldr. Leder.
Ldrb(d.). Lederband.
Led. Leder.
Leder. Leather (binding).
Lederband. Leather binding.
Lederhlzbd. Lederholzband.

Lederholzband. Bound in wooden boards covered with leather.

Lederschliesse(n). Leather clasp(s).

leer. Blank.

leere Seite(n). Blank page(s); **leeres Blatt. (Blätter),** Blank leaf (leaves) or sheet(s).

Leinband (Leinenband). Cloth binding.

Leinwand. Cloth (binding); — **mit Goldschnitt,** Cloth binding with gilt edges; — **mit Silberschnitt,** Cloth binding with silvered edges.

Leinwandband. Cloth binding.

Leitf. Leitfaden.

Leitfaden(-fäden). Guide(s), textbook(s), manual(s).

Lesespur(en). Worn by use.

Lex. Lexikon. Lexicon.

Lfg(n)., Lfrg(n). Lieferung(-en).

Lieferung(-en). Number (issue) of a periodical or serial.

(in) Lieferungen erscheint. Appears in parts.

Lichtdruck(e). Photograph(s), heliotype(s).

Lh. (Lhz.). Lederholzband.

Lhbd. Liebhaberband.

Liebhaberausg. Liebhaberausgabe.

Liebhaberausgabe. " Favorite " edition, " gift-book " edition.

Liebhaberband. Fancy binding, " gift-book " format, usually extra leather binding.

Liebhaberband mit Lederecken. Three-quarters leather (leather corners).

Liebhaberbd. Liebhaberband.

lies. Read.

Linie(n). Line(s).

Lithogr(n). Lithographie(n). Lithograph(s).

Ln. Linien.

Lnb. Leinenband, Leinwandband.

Lsp. Lustspiel.

Lustspiel. Comedy.

Luxusausgabe. Edition de luxe.

Lwb(d.), Lwd. Leinwandband.

M.

M. Mappe.

M. Mark(en).

M. Märchen.

m. mit.

M. A. Miniaturausgabe.

m. e. mit ein.

m. G. mit Goldschnitt.

m. s. man sehe.

Mag. Magazin(e). Magazine(s). Storeroom.

maler. malerisch. Pictorial, picturesque.

man sehe. See.

Manuskript(e). Manuscript(s).

Mappe(n). Portfolio(s).

Mar., Maroq. Maroquin.

Märchen. Story(-ies), fiction.

Mark. Mark(s). German coin worth about 24 cents.

Marmorschnitt(e). Marbled edge(s).

Maroqbd. Maroquinband.

Maroquin. Morocco; — **band,** Morocco binding.

Massstab. Scale (of map).

med. medizinisch. Medical.

57

Mem. Memoir(-en). Memoir(s).

Mh. Monatsheft.

Mindestrabatt. Minimum discount.

Miniaturausgabe. Miniature edition (24mo).

mit. With; — **Bart,** Rough edges; — **Goldschnitt,** Gilt edges; — **Marmorschnitt,** Marbled edges; — **Silberschnitt,** Silvered edges; — **Schreibpapier durchschossen,** Interleaved with writing paper.

Mitglied(er). Member of society, firm, etc.

Mitt(h)eilg.(-n). Mitt(h)eilung(-en). Communication(s), contribution(s).

Mk. Mark.

mod. modern.

moderfleckig. Stained by mold.

modern. Modern.

Monatsheft. Monthly number.

Monatschrift(-en). Monthly publication(s).

Mschr. Monatschrift.

Muster. Style, sample, specimen; — **band,** Sample binding, high-grade binding; — **bogen,** Sample sheet; — **buch,** Book of specimens, "sample book"; — **schrift,** "Classic," standard work.

N.

n. nach.

n. neu.

n. (netto). Indicates limited discount, usually less than 25%.

n. F. neue Folge.

n. num. nicht nummerirt.

n. pag. nicht paginiert.

n. Tit. neuer Titel.

Nach. According to. After. (*e.g.*, **Federzeichen nach Phiz,** Pendrawings after Phiz.)

Nachdruck(e). Unauthorized or pirated edition or publication.

Nachdruck verboten. All rights reserved.

Nachf. Nachfolger.

Nachfolger. Successor to —.

Nachgelassene Schrift(en). Posthumous work(s).

Nachlass. (Literary) remains.

Nachnahme. Cash on delivery. Prepayment.

Nachschlagbuch. Reference book.

Nachschlagwerk. Reference work.

Nachtrag(-träge). Supplement(s), addition, addenda (pl.).

Namen-und-Sachregister. Name (author) and subject index.

naturw. naturwissenschaftlich.

naturwissenschaftlich. Relating to natural science.

ndr. nieder.

netto. net.

Nettopreis. Net price.

neu. new.

neue Folge. New series.

neuer Titel. New title.

Neugroschen. Old German coin, usually worth about 2 cents.

Neuigkeiten. New publications.

Ngr. Neugroschen.

Nicht im Handel. Not in the trade.

Nicht numeriert. Not numbered.

nicht paginiert. Unpaged.

nieder. Lower.

nn. (netto netto). Indicates price subject to increase (Kayser) or extra charge for commission, service, transportation, etc. (Hinrichs).

nnn. Strictly net. No discount to the trade. *See also* **nn.**

Notenblatt(-blätter). Sheet(s) of music.

Notenbuch(-bücher). Music book(s), singing book(s).

Notendruck(e). Printed music.

Notiz(en). Note(s), notice(s), memorandum(-da).

Novelle(n). Novel(s), tale(s).

Nr(n). Nummer(n).

Nummer(n). Number(s), serial part.

numeriert. Numbered.

O.

o. oben. original.

ô. Bookseller's sign, = " not " or " without."

o. Cart. original Cartonnage.

o. Dr. ohne Druckernamen.

o. J. ohne Jahr.

o. O. ohne Ort.

o. O. u. J. ohne Ort und Jahr.

ö. W. österreichische Währung. Austrian currency.

oben. Above.

Octav. *See* Oktav.

œsterr. oesterreichische.

öffentl. öffentlich. Public.

ohne Druckernamen. Without name of printer.

ohne Jahr. Without year of publication.

ohne Ort. Without place of publication.

Old. Original Leinwandband.

ölfleckig. Oil or grease spotted.

Oktav. Octavo.

Oktav-Ausgabe. Octavo edition, 8vo.

Orig. Original.

orig. Bd. (Origbd.). original Band. (Original band.)

Orig. Cart. Original Cartonnage.

Original. Original; — **Cartonnage,** Original boards; — **Band,** Original binding; — **Leinwandband,** Original cloth.

Origlwd. Originalleinwandband.

P.

P. Programm.

Pag. Pagina.

pag. paginiert.

pag. S. paginierte Seiten.

paginiert. Paged (numbered).

paginierte Seite(n). Numbered page(s).

Pagina(s). Page(s).

Papier. Paper.

Papierzeichen. Watermark.

Pappband. (Pappenband). " Boards."

Pappdeckel. Board covers.

Partiepreis(e). Price(s) per lot including free copy.

Perg. Pergament.

Pergament(-band). Vellum (binding).

Perkal. Percaline.

Pfg. Pfennig(e).

Pfennig(e). Pfennig. The hundredth part of a mark. About ¼ cent.

Pgms. Pergamentmanuskriptband. Manuscript volume on vellum.

Pgmt. (Pgt.). Pergament.

Port.(r), Porträt.

Porto (*pl. Portos* or *Porti*). Postage.

Portofrei. Postpaid, prepaid.

Porträt (Portraits). Portrait(s).

Pp., Ppbd., Pppbd. Pappband, Pappenband.

Pr. Preis.

pr. (preuss.). preussisch.

Pr. A. Prachtausgabe.

Prachtausgabe. Edition de luxe. Handsome edition, " library " edition.

Prachtband. Handsome binding.

Prachtlederband. Handsome leather binding.

prächt. prächtig.

prächtig. Splendid(ly), handsome(ly).

Preis(e). Price(s).

Preis einzeln. Price per separate part or volume.

Preis ð. Ladenpreis aufgehoben. List price suspended. No " fixed price " (Hinrichs).

Preisänderung(en). Change(s) of price.

preuss. preussisch.

preussisch. Prussian.

Prgt. Pergament.

Privatbibliothek. Private library.

Probeseite(n). Specimen page(s).

Probeexemplar. Sample copy.

Probenummer. Specimen number.

Progr. Programm.

Programm. Program, report, conspectus, school catalogue.

Ps. Pseudonym.

Q.

Qu. quadrat, quer.

Qu.-fol., etc. Querfolio, etc.

Quadrat. Square; — **folio,** Square folio; — **8°,** Square octavo.

Quartausgabe. Quarto, 4to.

Quartband(-buch). Quarto, 4°.

Quartant(en). Quarto(s).

Quer —. Oblong; — **folio,** Oblong folio (etc.).

R.

Rabatt. Discount, deduction.

Rahmen. Border(s), frame(s).

Rand. (Ränder). Margin(s).

randfl. randfleckig. Stained in the margins.

Randnote(n). Marginal note(s).

Randverzierung(en). Decorated margin(s).

Ratsbibliothek. Law library for legislative use.

Rd. Rand.

Rechtsurkunde(-n). Legal document(s).

Red. Redacteur, Redaction.

red. redigirt.

Redacteur, Redakteur. Editor (of a periodical).

Redaction, Redaktion. Editorial management (of a periodical).

redigirt. Edited.

Referat(e). Short review(s).

Referenz(en). Reference(s).

Register. Index, table of contents, list.

Registerband(-bände). Index volume(s).

Reichsbibliothek. Imperial library.

Reichsthaler. Old German coin worth three marks (Rix-dollar).

Reihe. Complete set or "run" of a serial.

rep. reparirt.

reparirt. Repaired.

roh. In loose sheets.

Roman. Romance, work of fiction.

rote Schnitte. Red edges.

Rthlr. Reichsthaler.

rubr. rubriziert. Rubricated.

Rücken. Back; — **erneuert,** Rebacked; — **titel,** Binders' title.

Rückenvergoldung. Back gilt.

Rückseite. Verso.

Rundschau. Review (in periodical titles).

russ. russisch.

Russfarbe. Bister (bistre). Tawny, "sepia."

russisch. Russian.

S.

s. sächsisch.

S. Seite.

s. siehe.

S. A. Sonderabdruck, Seperatabdruck.

s. d. siehe dieses or siehe dort, siehe dasselbe (**daselbst**).

S. f. Schluss folgt. To be concluded.

s. g. so genannt.

s. o. siehe oben.

s. u. siehe unten.

s. v. a. so viel als.

Sa. *See* **S. A.**

Sachregister. Subject index.

sächs. sächsisch. Saxon.

Saffian. Morocco, Spanish leather.

Saffianband. Morocco binding, roan (imitation morocco).

Saffianpapier. Morocco paper.

Sammelwerk(e). Compilation(s).

Sammler. Collector(s), compiler(s).

Sammlg. Sammlung.

Sammlung(en). Collection(s), compilation(s).

säm(m.) säm(m)t. säm(m)tlich.

säm(m)tlich. Collected, complete.

sämmtliche Werke. Collected (complete) works.

Samt. (Sammet). Velvet (binding).

Samtband (Sammetband). Velvet binding.

Sam(m)tbd. Sam(me)tband.

sämtl. sämtlich.

Sarsb. Sarsenetband. Bound in sarsenet.

Sars. Sarsanet. Sarsenet (Sarcenet).

Sauber. Clean.

Sch. Schauspiel, Schule. Schulband.

sch. schön.

schadh. schadhaft. Damaged.

Schauspiel(-e). Drama(s).

Schl. Schliessen.

schles. schlesisch.

schlesisch. Silesian.

Schliessen. Clasps.

Schluss. End; — **folgt,** To be concluded.

Schlussschrift. Colophon.

schmal. Narrow.

(In-) **Schmal folio.** Narrow folio.

Schmutztitel. Half title, false title, bastard title.

Schnitt(e). Edge(s) of a book.

schön. Beautiful, handsome.

Schreibpapier. Writing paper.

Schrift(en). Writing, characters, type(s), publication(s).

Schriftchen. Pamphlet(s), booklet(s).

Schriften. Writings. **nachgelassene** —, Posthumous works; **periodische** —, Periodical articles; **vermischte** —, Miscellaneous writings; **vollständige** —, Complete writings.

Schriftsteller. Author(s).

Schulb. Schulband.

Schulband. School book, textbook, half-leather binding.

schw. schwäbisch.

Schw. Schwank.

schwäbisch. Swabian.

Schwank (Schwänke). Farce(s).

Schwartenleder. Hogskin.

Schwarzkupfer. Mezzotint.

schwarzer Druck. Black letter.

Schweinsleder. Hogskin, pigskin.

Schwldr. Schweinsleder, Schwartenleder.

Schwsldr. Schweinsleder.

Seide(n). Silk(s).

Seidendruck. Printing on silk.

Seideneinband. Bound in silk.

Seidenpapier. Tissue paper, silver paper.

Seite(n). Page(s).

Seitenz. Seitenzahl.

Seitenzahl. Page number.

Selbstverlag. Published by the author.

selten. Rare.

Separatabdruck. Reprint, " separate."

Sf., Sfn. Saffian.

Sfnb(d). Saffianband.

siehe. See.

siehe auch. See also; — **dasselbe,** See the same (q. v.); — **dieses,** See this; — **dort,** See in that place; — **oben,** See above; — **unten,** See below.

Sign. Signature.

Silberschnitt. Silvered edges.

Skizze(n). Sketch(es).

Skyt. bd. Skytogenband. Bound in "Skytogen," a special waterproof cloth.

Sler. Sammler.

Slw. Sammelwerk.

Smtbd. Samtband.

so viel als. As much as.

sog. sogenannt. So-called.

Sonderabdruck. Separate (special) edition.

Sonderheft. Special number, part, or volume.

Sortimenter. (Retail) bookseller.

Sortimentsbuchhandel. Retail book trade.

sow. soweit. As far as, all. (*e.g.,* Sow. erschienen, All that has appeared.)

sp. spät or später.

sp lat. spätlateinisch.

spät(er). late(r).

spätlateinisch. Late Latin.

Ss. Seiten.

St. Staat, Stadt.

st. statt.

St. Stück.
Stadt. City.
Staatsbibliothek. State library.
Stadtbibliothek. City library.
Stahlst. Stahlstich.
Stahlstich(e). Steel engraving(s).
stat. statistisch. Statistical.
statt. Instead of. (*e.g.*, "Statt mk. 3, mk. 2," "2 marks instead of 3.")
Ste(n). Seite(-n).
steif geheftet. Sewed, stiff paper covers or boards.
Steindruck(e). Lithograph(s).
Steintafel(n). Lithograph(s).
Stirnseite. Recto of leaf.
stl. sämtlich.
Stnt. Steintafel.
stockfl. stockfleckig. Mildewed, fox marked.
Stück(e). Piece(s), extract(s), part(s).

T.

T. Titel.
T. A. Taschen-Ausgabe.
tadellos Exemplar. Perfect copy.
Taf. Tafel.
Tafel(n). Plate(s), index(es), register(s).
Tageblatt. Daily newspaper.
Taschen-Ausgabe. Pocket edition (16mo).
techn. technisch. Technical.
Teil(e), Theil(e). Part(s), section(s), volume(s).
teilw. teilweise. Partly; — **gebunden,** Part (of series or set) bound.

Textausgabe. Text edition.

Textfig. Textfigur.

Textfigur(en). Figures (or illustrations) in the text.

Tfl(n). Tafel(-n).

Th., Thal. Thaler.

Thaler. German coin worth three marks.

Theil. *See* **Teil.**

theol. theologisch.

theologisch. Theological.

Thl(e). Theil(-e).

Thlr. Thaler.

tintenfleckig. Ink-stained.

Titel. Title(s).

Titelausgabe. Edition with changed title or date.

Titelbild. Frontispiece.

Titelbildchen. Headpiece, vignette on title page.

Titelbl. Titelblatt.

Titelblatt. Title page.

Titeldruck. Binders' title.

Titelgolddruck. Title stamped in gold.

Titelkupfer(n). Engraved frontispiece.

Tl.(e). Teil(e).

U.

u. und. And.

u. a. und andere.

u. a. a. O. und an andern Orte.

u. ä. und ähnliche.

u. a. m. und anderes mehr. And so forth.

u. d. T. unter dem Titel.

u. f. (u. ff.). und folgende.

u. s. f. und so fort.

u. s. w.   und so weiter.

u. v. a.   und viele andere.

übers.   übersetzt.

übersetzt.   Translated.

Übersetzung(en).   Translation(s).

übertragen.   Translated.

übrs.   übersetzt.

Übrs.   Übersetzung.

ugbdn.   ungebunden.

umgearbeitete.   Revised.

Umschl.   Umschlag

Umschlag(-schläge).   Wrapper(s), cover(s).

unaufgeschn.   unaufgeschnitten.

unaufgeschnitten.   Unopened.

unbeschn.   unbeschnitten.

unbeschnitten.   Uncut.

und ähnliche.   And the like, and similar (ones).

und an andern Orten.   And elsewhere.

und andres mehr.   And so forth.

und folgende.   And the following.

und so fort.   And so forth, et cetera.

und so weiter.   And so forth, et cetera.

und viele andere.   And many others.

unentgeltlich.   " Gratis."

unfl.   unflektirt.   Unstained.

ungebunden.   Unbound.

und so weiter.   And so forth, et cetera.

und zwar.   And also, namely, as follows.

ung., ungar.   ungarisch.   Hungarian.

ungez. Bll.   ungezifferte Blätter.

ungezifferte Blätter.   Unnumbered leaves.

unnum.   unnumeriert.

unnumeriert. Not numbered.

unp. unpaginiert.

unpaginiert. Unpaged.

unsauber. Soiled, dirty.

unter dem Titel. Under the title.

unter der Presse. In press.

Unterhaltungsblatt. Literary periodical.

Unterhaltungslektüre(-n). Light reading, fiction.

unterstrichen. Underlined, underscored.

Untertitel. Subtitle.

unveränderte. Unchanged.

Urkunde(-n). Document(s), record(s).

urspr. ursprünglich.

ursprünglich. Original, first.

Urt. Urtext.

Urtext. Original text.

usf. und so fort.

usw. und so weiter.

V.

V. A. Volksausgabe.

v. J. vorigen Jahres. Of the preceding year.

v. o. vergleiche oben.

v. u. vergleiche unten.

Vakat. Blank page.

vb. verbessert.

Velin. Parchment; — **papier,** Wove paper.

Velp. Velinpapier.

veränd. verändert.

verändert. Altered, revised.

verb. verbessert.

Verband. Association, society, club.

verbessert. Improved.

Verbindung(-en). Association(s), society(-ies), club(s).

Verein(-e). Association(s), society(-ies), club(s).

Vereinigte Staaten. United States of America.

vereinz. vereinzelt.

vereinzelt. Separate, scattered (numbers or volumes); occasionally (adv.).

Verf. Verfasser. Author(s).

Verfügung (zur —). Subject to order.

vergleiche. Compare; — **oben,** See above; — **unten,** See below.

verglichen. Compared.

vergr. vergriffen. Out of print.

Verlag. Publishing house.

(im) Verlage von —. Published by —.

Verlagsänderung(-en). Change(s) of publisher.

Verlags(buch)handel. Publishing business.

Verlags(buch)händler. Publisher.

Verlagskatalog(-e). Publishers' catalogue(s).

Verlagsrecht(-e). Copyright.

verm. vermehrt.

vermehrte (Ausgabe). Enlarged (edition).

vermischte (Schriften). Miscellaneous (writings).

veröffentlicht. Published, issued.

Veröffentlichung(-en). Publication(s), public announcement(s).

Versammlung(-en). Assembly(-ies), convention(s), meeting(s).

Verslg. Versammlung.

Verzeichnis(se). List(s), index(es), catalogue(s).

vgl. vergleiche.

vglchn. verglichen.

vielfach vermehrte Ausgabe. Greatly enlarged edition.

Vokabularium. (*plu.* **ien**). Vocabulary.

Volksausgabe. Popular edition.

Volksbibliothek. Public circulating library.

Vollbild(-er). Plate(s), full-page illustrations.

vollst. vollständig. Entirely, completely.

Voranzeige(-n). Preliminary notice(s), announcement(s).

(in) Vorbereitung. In preparation.

Vorblatt. Foreleaf.

vorigen Jahres. Of the preceding year.

Vorlesung(-en). Lecture(s), reading(s).

vorrät(h)ig. In stock.

Vorsatzpapier. End paper.

Vortrag(-träge). Lecture(s), discourse(s).

Vorwort. Foreword, preface, introduction.

vorzügl. vorzüglich.

vorzüglich. Choice, excellent.

Vorzugsausgabe. Choice edition, special edition.

W.

W. Werk(-e).

W. Wissenschaft.

w. würtembergisch.

w. s. welches siehe.

w. v. welches vergleiche.

wasserfleckig. Water-stained.

Wasserzeichen. " Watermark."

Wb. Wörterbuch.

Wegekarte(-n). Road map(s).

weiss. White, blank.

welches siehe. Which see.

welches vergleiche. Which compare.

Werk(-e). Work(s).

wie neu. As new.

Wiegendruck(e). Incunabulum(-a).

Wiss. Wissenschaft.

wiss. wissenschaftlich.

Wissenschaft. Science.

wissenschaftlich. Scientific.

Witwe. Widow.

Wochenschrift. Weekly publication.

wohlfeil. Cheap.

Wörterbuch(-bücher). Dictionary(-ies).

Wurmst. Wurmstichig.

Wurmstich(-e). Wormhole(s).

wurmstichig. Wormeaten.

würt. würtembergisch.

würt(t)embergisch. Wirtembergian.

Wwe. Witwe.

Z.

Z. Zeile.

z. B. zum Beispiel.

z. E. zum Exempel.

z. T. zum Teil.

zahlr. zahlreich.

zahlreich. Numerous.

Zeichnung(-en). Drawing(s).

Zeile(-n). Line(s).

(der) Zeit. Contemporary. (Literally "Of the period ".)

Zeitschrift(-en). Periodical(s).

Zeitung(-en). Newspaper(s).

Zettel. Label(s), slip(s), card(s).

Zettelkatalog. Card catalogue.

Zg. Zeitung.

Zinkätzung(-en). Zinc etching(s).

Zoll (Zölle). Customs charge(s).

zsgstzt. zusammengesetzt.

zsgz.(-n). zusammengezogen.

Zsstzg.(-n). Zusammensetzung(-en).

Zt. (Ztg.(-n)). Zeitung(-en).

Ztschr. Zeitschrift.

Zugangsverzeichnis. Bulletin or list of additions.

zum Beispiel. For example.

zum Exempel. For example.

zum Teil. Partially, in part.

zus. zusammen.

zusammen. Together, jointly.

zusammengesetzt. Collected, compiled.

zusammengezogen. Contracted, condensed, abridged, summarized, collected.

Zusammensetzung(-en). Collection(s), compilation(s).

Zuschlag(-schläge). Additional charge(s).

Zuschlagsgebühr. Additional charge.

Zuschlagsporto. Postage extra.

DANISH–NORWEGIAN ABBREVIATIONS AND TERMS

The Norwegian often uses *t*, *p*, and *k* and *v*, where the Danish uses *d*, *b*, and *g* and *f* respectively.

A.

aarh. aarhundrede(r). Century(-ies).

aarskatalog(er). Annual catalogue(s).

ae. For words written with **ae** (*e.g.*, **bemaerkning**) see also **e** (**bemerkning**).

aendret. Changed, revised. (*e.g.*, **6te noget aendrede og forögede utgave.** 6th somewhat revised and enlarged edition.)

af. (av.). By.

afd. afdeling(er). Part(s).

alm. almindelig. Common(ly).

anden (andet). Second.

ang. angaaende. Concerning.

anh. anhang. Appendix(-dices).

anm. anmeldelse(r), anmerkning(er).

anmeldelse(r). Review(s).

anmerkning(er). Note(s).

antikvar(er). Secondhand bookseller(s).

antikvarboghandel (**-handler**). Secondhand bookstore(s).

antikvarisk. Secondhand.

arbeid(er). Work(s).

auka(d). Enlarge(d).

aut. (auth). aut(h)oriseret. Authorized.

76

avd. avdeling(er). Part(s), volume(s).
avtrk. Reprint(s).

B.

b. bind.
balk(ar). Chapter(s).
bd. bind, bundet.
bearb. bearbeidet. Revised, adapted.
bem(a)erkning(er). Remark(s), observation(s).
bemerkn. bemerkning(er). .
bibl. bibliot(h)ek(er). Library(-ies). (*e.g.*, **bibl. f. d. tusen hjem,** bibliothek for de tusen hjem. Library for the thousand homes (a well-known trade series).)
bibl's. bibliot(h)eket's. The library's. (Poss. of bibliothek.)
bidrag. Appendix(-dices), contributions.
bilag. Appendix(-dices), contributions.
billed(er). Picture(s), illustration(s).
billedbilag. Appendix of illustrations or plates.
billed bog (böger). Picture book(s).
billed bok (böker). Picture book(s).
bind. Volume(s). (*e.g.*, **Bind IV.** 3 **die hefte.** Vol. IV, pt. 3.)
bl. blad. Leaf of book; newspaper, periodical.
bl. blandt. Among. (*e.g.*, **bl. a.,** blandt andet. Among others.)
bladnotits(er). Brief article, newspaper item.
bog (böger). Book(s).
bogbind. Book cover(s).
böger under trykning. Books in press.
bogforening(er). Private circulating library(-ies).
bogfortegnelse(r). Book catalogue(s).

bogh. boghandel.

boghandel(-handler). Book-shop(s).

boghandler(e). Bookseller(s).

boghöker(e). Cheap (small), second-hand bookseller or dealer in cheap, inferior books.

boglade(r). Book-shop(s).

bogladepris(er). Publisher's price(s), retail price(s). (*e.g.*, **bogladepris 3 kr.,** Published at 3 kroner.)

bogliden. Booklet.

bogperm(er). Book cover(s).

bograbat. Trade discount.

bogstav(er). Letter(s), character(s).

bogstempel(-stempler). Library stamp(s).

bogstok. Books in stock.

bogtrykkeri(er). Printing house(s).

bok (böker). Book(s). For compounds of **bok** (the Norwegian form) *see under* **bog** (the Danish form).

bundet. Bound.

C.

chagrin. shagreen.

com. comedie(r). Comedy(-ies).

conf. confer. Confer, compare.

D.

d. del.

d. den (det, de). The.

d. död.

d. s. det samme. The same.

d. s. s. det samme som. The same as.

del(er). Part(s), volume(s).

den. (det, de). The.

död. Died.

E.

e., el. eller.

eft. efter. After.

eft., efterl. efterladte. Posthumous.

eks., eksempl.; **ekspl.,** eksemplar(er). Copy(-ies), example(s).

el. eller.

eleg. elegant. Elegant(ly).

eller. Or.

ensidig. Printed on one side.

eod. eodem. The same.

expl. exemplar(er). *See* eksemplar.

F.

f. födt.

f. följende (*sing.*), **ff.** (*plural*).

f. for. For. (*e.g.* "**f. 1 st. m. pfte.**" "For en stemme med pianoforte." For one voice with pianoforte accompaniment.)

f. eks. (f. ex.). for eksempel. For example (*e.g.*).

f. ö. for övrigt. Besides, (as) for the rest, further.

facsimile udgave(r) (faks-). Facsimile edition(s).

faksimilebidrag. Supplement of (with) facsimiles.

farvelagt. In colors, colored.

farvetavle(r). Colored plate(s).

farvetr. farvetryk. Colored print(s) or plate(s).

ff. följende. The following (*plural*).

figur(er). Figure(s), diagram(s).

fl. flere. More, others. (*e.g.*, **o. fl.,** and others.)

flg. följende. The following.

födt. Born. (*e.g.*, **f. d. 27 Juni,** Born June 27.)

följende. Following.

folkeutgave. Popular edition.

for. For.; — **hver.,** For each. *See also under f.*

forb. forbedret. Revised, improved.

foreg. foregaaende. Preceding.

forening(er). Society(-ies), club(s), union(s).

forfatter(e). Author(s).

forfatterinde(r). Author(s) (*fem.*).

forf's. forfatterens. The author's. (*e.g.,* **På forfat-terens forlag,** Printed or published for the author.)

forhandlerpris. Sale price.

fork. forkorte(t). Abbreviate(d).

forkl. forklarende. Explanatory.

forl. forlag. Publishing house(s); — **boghandel** (**-handler**), Publishing house(s); — **boghandler(e),** Publisher(s); — **ret,** Copyright. **overtaget fra andet forlag,** Taken over from another publisher; changed publisher.

foröget (foröket). Enlarged.

fortaelling(er). Story(ies), tale(s).

fr. fransk. French.

fuldstaendig. Complete.

G.

gennem. *See also* **gjennem.**

gennemsete. Revised; — **oplag** or **udgave,** Revised edition.

gjennemgaa(et). Revise(d).

gjennomsedd. Revised.

gl. gammel. Old.

graf. tab. grafisk(e) tabell(er). Graphical table(s).

guldkant(er). Gilt edge(s).

guldblad. Gold leaf.

H.

haandbog (böger), haandbok (böker). Manual(s), handbook(s), reference book(s).

haefte(r). *See* **hefte.**

haeftet. Stitched, sewed.

halvbind. Half-volume, Half of " 1 vol. in 2," etc.

halvaarlig. Semi-annual(ly).

handl. handling(er). Part(s), acts (dramatic).

hefte(r). Part(s), number(s), stitched or sewed pamphlet(s).

heftet. *See* **haeftet.**

hist. historie(r). Story(-ies), history(-ies).

hft. heftet, haeftet.

hos. By, at.

hvid. (hvit). White, blank. (*e.g.,* **indbunden med hvide (hvite) blade,** Interleaved.)

I.

i. in.

i alt. As a whole, complete, entire.

i. 8. in 8vo, etc. In octavo, etc.

ib. indbunden. Bound.

ibl. iblandt. Among.

ikke i boghandelen. Not for sale, not in the trade.

illus., illustr. illustreret. Illustrated, illustration(s).

imp. imperial. Imperial (paper and book size).

indb. indbunden(-bundet).

indbunden (-bundet). Bound. (*e.g.,* **indbunden i biblioteks bind,** Library binding; — **i shirting,** Cloth binding; — **med skindryg,** Half leather (literally, " bound with leather back "); — **i kompon-**

eret pragt bind, Bound in specially designed binding de luxe.)

indeh. indeholde(r). Contain(s).

indsl. indeslutte. Included. (*e.g.*, **indsl. i. saml. av. originale skuespil,** Included in a collection of original plays.)

indh. indhold. Contents.

isl. islandsk. Icelandic.

J.

jaevnf. jaevnför. Compare.

jfr. jaevnför, jevnför.

jevnfor (jaevnför). Compare.

jvf. jevnför.

jubil(a)eumsutgave(r). Jubilee edition.

K.

kart(er). Map(s), chart(s).

kart., karton. kartonert. ˙Bound in boards.

kartbilag. Supplement consisting of map or chart.

kgl. kongelig. Royal.

kgr. kongerike(r), kongerige(r). Kingdom(s).

kobberstik. Copperplate(s).

koll. kollört. Colored.

kolorert. Colored.

kom. komedie(r). Comedy(-ies).

komplet. Complete.

kongerike(r), (kongerige(r)). Kingdom(s).

kongl. kongelig. Royal.

kort. Brief, short.

kort. Map(s), chart(s).

kplt. komplet.

kr. krone(r). Scandinavian coin worth about 28 cents.

kulört. Colored.

kunstbilag. Art supplement.

kvartal. Quarter.

kvartalskrift(er). Quarterly periodical(s).

L.

l. eller. Or.

landkart(er). landkort. Map(s), chart(s).

levering(er). Part(s), issue(s), fascicle(s).

liden. Small; — **bok (bog),** Booklet.

lit.(h.) lit(h)ografi(er). lit(h)ograferet. Lithograph(s), lithographed.

lit.(t.) lit(t)eratur. Literature.

liten. *See* **liden.**

M.

m. med; **m. fl.,** med flere.

maalest. maalestok. Scale (of map).

maanedsskrift(er). Monthly publication(s).

maleblade. Leaves with outline illustrations for coloring.

mappe. Pocket, case. (*e.g.*, **i. mappe,** In pocket or portfolio.)

marokko. Morocco; — **lärred,** Morocco cloth.

med. With; — **flere,** And others; — **guld,** Gilt; — (meget) **mere,** Et cetera; — **forfatterens tillatelse (tilladelse) oversat,** Authorized translation (literally, " Translated with the author's permission").

meddelelse(r). Communication(s), contribution(s).

meddelt. Contributed.

medl. medlem(mer). Member(s) of a society.

medutgiver(e). Joint editor(s).

mindeudgave(r), (mindeutgave(r)). Memorial edition(s).

mus. musik. Music.

musikalier. Pieces of music, music books.

N.

n. norsk. Norwegian.

neds. pris. nedsat pris. Reduced price.

netto. Net; — **kontant,** Net cash; — **pris,** Net price.

no. nummer.

nord. nordisk. Scandinavian.

norsk. Norwegian.

nr. nummer.

nummer(e). Number(s).

ny. New.

O.

o. a. og andre (andet).

o. fl. og flere.

o. s. v. og saa videre.

oeget (oeket). *See* **öget.**

og. And; — **andre (andet),** And others, et cetera; — **flere,** And others; — **lignende,** And the like; — **saa,** Also; — **saa videre,** Et cetera.

öget (öket). Enlarged.

ogs. ogsaa. Also.

öket. *See* **öget.**

omarb. omarbeide(t). Revise(d).

omkr. omkring. Circa.

omslag. Cover, wrapper; — **(s)billede(r),** Cover illustration(s); — **stegning(er),** Cover illustrations; — **stitel,** Cover title, binder's title.

opkl. opklæbet. Mounted; — **med stokke,** Mounted on rollers.

oplag. Edition(s).

oplyst. Explained, annotated. (*e.g.*, **oplyst utg.,** Annotated edition; **oplysende bemerkninger ved** —, Explanatory notes by —.)

optr. optryk. Reprint(s).

optrykt. Reprinted.

ord. Word(s).

ordbog(-böger), (ordbok(-böker)). Dictionary(-ies).

orig. original. Original.

öre. Scandinavian coin worth about $\frac{1}{4}$ cent ($\frac{1}{100}$ krone).

overgaaet fra andet forlag. Changed publisher.

oversaettelse(r). Translation(s).

overs. oversat. Translated.

P.

p. paa; **p. gr. av (af.).** paa grund av.

paa. On, in; — **grund af (av),** Because, on account of; **overs. paa tysk,** Translated into German.

papbind. Board covers.

papir. Paper.

partipris. Wholesale price(s).

pergamentpapir. Parchment paper, vellum paper.

pergamentsbind. Vellum binding(s).

perm(er). Cover.

pfte. piano forte.

pl. planche(r). Plate(s).

plan(er). Plan(s), illustration(s).

plade(r), plate(r). Plate(s). (Metal) " Electros."

plschr. planscher. Plates.

por., port. portraet(er). Portrait(s).

ppbd. papbind.

pr. For, Per. (*e.g.*, 1 kr. pr. heft, " I krone per part.")

prgtb., prgtbd. pragtbind. Binding de luxe. (*Also* pergamentsbind, *q.v.*)

protokolpapir. Record paper, ledger paper.

R.

rabat. Discount.

raekke(r). Series.

redaktör(er). Editor(s).

red., redig. redigeret. Edited.

register. Index.

rev. revideret. Revised.

rigsdaler. Old Scandinavian coin (Rixdollar).

roman(-er). Novel(s), romance(s).

ryg(ge). Back(s).

S.

s. side(r).

saersk. saerskildt. Separate. (*e.g.*, **saerskilt avtryk,** Reprint, "separate.")

saertryk. " Separate," reprinted excerpt.

samf. Society, association. (*e.g.*, **Samf. til. udg. av. gl. nord. litt.,** Society for editing old Scandinavian literature.)

saml. samling, samlet.

samling(er). Collection(s).

samlet. Collected, compiled; **Samlede vaerker,** Complete works.

samt. samtidig. Contemporary.

se. See.

se. side(r).

separataftryk. " Separate."

separat prent. "Separate."

shirting. Cloth.

side(r). Page(s).

Skand. Skandinavien. Scandinavia.

Skand. Skandinavisk. Scandinavian.

skildr. skildring(er). Sketch(es).

Skilling. Old Scandinavian coin ($\frac{1}{4}$–$\frac{1}{2}\emptyset$).

skindryg. Leather back, half-leather binding.

skr. skrift(er). Writing(s).

skuesp. skuespil. Play(s).

sluttet. Finished, completed, stopped.

smaaskrifter. Minor writings.

sortiments boghandler(e). General retail bookseller(s).

sp. spalte(r). Column(s).

st. stemme. Voice (in vocal scores).

statist. statistik, statistisk. Statistics; statistical.

stift haeftet (stivt heftet). Stitched pamphlet with stout covers.

stk. stykke(r). Piece(s).

stor. Large.

suppl., supplem. supplement(er). Supplement(s).

T.

t. til.

t. (tit.). titel(er).

tabel(ler). Table(s).

talr. talrige (talrike). Numerous.

tavle(r). Plate(s).

tegn. tegning(er). Picture(s), illustration(s).

tekst(er), (text(er)). Text(s).

tidsskr. tidsskrift(er). Periodical(s).

tilbagekaldelse(r). Withdrawal(s).

tildels. Partly.

tillegg. (tillaeg.). Appendix(-dices).

titelblad. Title page.

tit. titel(er). Title(s).

topogr. topografisk. Topographic.

tosp. tospaltet. Double column(s).

traesn. traesnit. Woodcut(s).

tysk. German.

U.

u. uden, uten.

ud-. *See also* words beginning with **ut-** (Norwegian).

uden (uten). Without; — **titelblad,** Without title page.

udg. udgave(r); udgivet.

udgave(r). Edition(s).

udgiver(e). Editor(s).

udgivet (udgivelse). Edited, issued, published (editing, etc.).

udk. udkommer. Published.

uforandret. Unchanged.

umsett. Translated.

umskrift. Translation.

undt. undtagen. Except.

upag. upagineret. Unpaged.

upplag. Edition(s).

ut-. For words beginning with **ut-** *see also* **ud-** (Danish).

ut. uten. Without.

utarbeidet. Prepared, composed.

utdrag. Extract(s).

utg. utgave, utgiver(e), utgjevet.

utgaave. *See* **utgave.**

utgave(r). Edition(s).

utgiver(e). Editor(s).

utgjevet. Edited, issued, published.

utsolgt. Out of print.

utk., utko. utkommer. Published. (*e.g.*, **utkommer i 2 hefter,** Published in 2 parts (vols.).)

uttog. Extract(s).

utv. utvalg, utvalgt.

utvalg. Selection.

utvalgt. Selected. (*e.g.*, **utvalgte skrifter,** Selected writings.)

utvidet. Enlarged.

V.

vaaben. Coat-of-arms.

vaelskbind. Half-calf binding.

vaerk(er). Work(s).

ved. By.

vedr. vedrörende. Concerning.

velskb. velskbind. *See* **vaelskbind.**

vending(er). Act(s).

vignet(ter). Vignette(s).

DUTCH ABBREVIATIONS AND TERMS

A.

aank. aankondiging. Announcement.

aanst. aanstaande. Coming; — **uitgaven,** Coming publications.

aant. aanteekening. Annotation.

aant. aantal. Number.

afb. afbeelding(-en). Picture(s).

afbeeldsel. Portrait.

afdeel. afdeeling. Part.

afdruk(-ken). Copy(-ies), edition(s).

afdruksel. Copy, impression, print.

afgebroken. Broken off.

afgedrukt. Printed.

afgesneden. Cut, trimmed.

aflev. aflevering. Part.

afkorting. Abbreviation, discount.

afzonderlijk. Separate, separately.

alles. All; — **wat verscheen,** All that has (have) appeared.

ambtelijk. Official.

B.

b. v. bijvoorbeeld. For example.

baar. Cash.

Bataafsch. Dutch.

benevens. Besides.

Bericht(-en). Communication(s), notes, news.

beschadigd. Damaged.

beslag. Mountings. (*e.g.*, **met koper beslag,** With brass bosses, or brass mountings.)

bestelkaart. Order card.

bestellen. To order.

bijblad(-en). Supplement(s).

bijdrage(-n). Contribution.

bijgevoegd. Added.

bijgewerkte druk. Revised edition, edition brought up to date.

bijlage(-n). Appendix(-ces), illustrative documents, facsimiles.

bijzonder. Special, separate.

binnenkort. Shortly.

blad(-en). Leaf (leaves).

bladwijzer. Index, table of contents.

bladzijde(-n). Page(s).

blz. bladzijde.

boek(-en). Book(s).

boekbespreking(en). Book review(s).

boekdeel. Volume.

boekdrukker. Printer.

boekenkramer. Secondhand bookseller.

boekenlijst. Catalogue.

boekerij. Library.

boekhandelaar. Book dealer.

boekverkooper. Bookseller.

boekverkooping. Auction.

bovengenoemde. Above-named, aforesaid.

bronnen. Sources.
bundel. Collection, group, part.

C.

Chineesch papier. China (India) paper.
compleet. Complete, completely.

D.

d. a. v. daaraanvolgende. Following. (*e.g.*, 2 **Juli en**
   d. a. v. dagen, 2 July and following days.)
d. w. z. dat wil zeggen. That is to say.
deel(-en). Part(s), volume(s).
derzelfde. Of the same.
dezelfde. The same.
Duitsch. German.
dl. (dln.). deel(-en).
door. By, through.
druk. Print, copy, edition.
drukkersmerk. Printer's mark.

E.

e. k. eerstkomende. Next ensuing.
e. v. eerstvolgende. Next following.
erven. Heirs. (*e.g.*, **Erven B. van der Kamp,** Heirs
   of B. van der Kamp.)
eeuw. Century, age.
elk. Each.
en. And, and so forth.
enz. en zoo voort. Etc.
ets(-en). Etching(s).
etsgravure(-s). Etching(s).
exemplaar(-aren). Copy(-ies).

F.

f., fl. florijn (same as **gulden**). Florin, guilder = 40 cents.

familiewapen. Family coat of arms.

fonkelnieuw. Brand-new.

fraai. Handsome.

francijn. Parchment.

franco. Free; — per post, Postpaid.

G.

geb. gebonden. Bound.

gecart. gecartonneerd. Bound in boards.

geconserveerd. Preserved; **goed** —, In good condition.

gedeelte. Part of a volume.

geëtst. Etched.

geheel. All, entirely; — **en al.,** Altogether, entirely; — **verschillend,** Entirely different.

geillustr. geillustreerd. Illustrated.

gekart. gekartonneerd. Bound in boards.

gekl. gekleurd. Colored; — **platen,** Colored plates; — **kaart,** Colored map or chart.

geneesk. geneeskunde, geneeskundig. Medical science, medical.

geschept papier. Handmade paper.

getal. Number (of periodical or serial).

getijdenboek. Book of hours.

getranslateert. Translated.

gevouwen. Folded.

gewoon, gewone. Usual, ordinary.

Gl., Gld. gulden. Guilder = 40 cents.

goed geconserveerd. In good condition.

goedk. goedkoop. Cheap. ·

graveur. Engraver.

groot. Former Dutch coin worth about 2½ cents.

groot. Large; — **papier,** Large paper; —**e letter,** Capital letter, large print.

gulden. Guilder. Dutch coin worth 40 cents.

H.

h. half; — **led.,** half leder; —**.mar.,** half marokijn.

half. Half; — **leder,** Half leather; — **linnen,** Half linen, half cloth; — **marokijn,** Half morocco.

halfled. halfleder. *See* **half leder.**

halflederen band. Half leather binding.

halflinnen. *See* **half linnen.**

handel. Trade. (*e.g.,* "Niet in den handel," "Not in the trade.")

herdruk. Reprint.

herz. herziende, herziening.

herziene. Revised; **herziene uitgave,** Revised edition.

herziening. Revision.

Herv. Hervormd. Reformed.

hetzelfde. The same.

Hd., Hgd. Hoogduitsch. German.

Hollandsch. Dutch; — **papier,** Holland paper.

Hoogeschool. University.

Hoogleeraar. Professor (in university).

houtsn. houtsnee, houtsnede(-n). Wood cut(s).

Hs. handschrift. Manuscript.

I.

in bewerking. In preparation.
ingen. ingenaaid. Sewed.
inh. inhoud. Contents.
inleiding. Introduction.
inteekenaar(-naren). Subscriber(s); **bij. inteekening,**
By subscription.
inz. inzonderheid. Especially.

J.

jaar. jaargang.
jaargang. Annual (volume).
jaarlijks. Annually.
jaarlijksche aflevering. Annual volume.
jaartal. Date.
Japansch papier. Japan paper.
jg., jrg. jaargang.
Jhr. Jonkheer. Sir (title of nobility).
jl. jongstleden. Last past.

K.

Kaart(-en), kaarte(-n) (Kaerte or caerte is old spelling
for kaart). Chart, map.
kalfsleder. Calf.
Karton. Cardboard.
keerzijde. Back of leaf, verso.
klein. Small.
kl. 8vo. klein 8vo. Small 8°; — **papier,** Small paper.
kleurendruk. Colored print.
kloosterband. Monastic binding.
klrndr. kleurendruk.
kol. kolom(-men). Column(s).

kopergravure(-s). Copper engraving(s).

kop verguld. Gilt top.

kopversiering. Headpiece.

kosteloos(-ze). Without cost, free, gratis; **Catalogus op aanvraag kosteloos verkrijgbaar,** Catalogue to be had free on application.

kplt. kompleet. Complete.

kunstdrukpapier. " Art " paper.

L.

landkaart. Map.

langw. langwerpig. Oblong; — **folio,** Oblong folio.

Latijnsch karakter. Latin character, roman.

ll. laatstleden. Last past.

lett. Letter.

levensgroot. Life-size.

lichtdruk(-ken). Photo-engraving(s), heliotype(s).

lijst. List, frame.

linn. linnen. Book cloth.

linnen band (linnenband). Cloth binding.

los. Separate; — **se banden zijn verkrijgbaar,** Volumes sold (may be obtained) separately.

M.

marokijnleder. Morocco.

Mej. Mejuffrouw. Miss.

met. With.

Mevr. Mevrouw. Mrs.

middelb. middelbaar. Medium; **middelbaar onderwijs,** Secondary education.

mogelijk geb. Furnished also bound, may be obtained bound.

Mr. Meester. Doctor of laws.

mv. meervoud. Plural.

N.

naamcijfer. Monogram.

niet. Not; — **in den handel,** Not in the trade; — **afzonderlijk,** Not obtainable separately, sold only complete.

nl. namelijk. Namely.

nr. nrs. nommer(s). Number(s); **losse —,** separate nos.

numero. Number.

O.

o. a. onder anderen. Among others.

omgewerkt. Revised, rewritten.

omlijsting. Border, frame.

omslag. Cover, wrapper, case.

ongeb. ongebonden. Unbound.

ontbreekt. Wanting, lacking.

onuitgeg. onuitgegeven. Unpublished.

oorspronkelijk. Original; **in de oorspronkelijke banden,** In original binding.

op. On, upon.

oplaag. Edition. (*e.g.,* **kleine oplaag,** Small edition.)

opschrift. Inscription, superscription.

overdruk. Reprint.

P.

Pamflet(-ten). Pamphlet(s).

paskaart. Sea chart.

perkament. Parchment.

perse (ter —). In press; **gaat ter perse,** Goes to press.
personenregister. Index of names, index to persons.
plaat (platen). Plate(s), engraving(s), illustration(s).
plaatsregister. Index of place names.
platenregister. Index to plates or illustrations.
pltn. platen.
porte. portefeuille. Portfolio.
prachtband. Ornamental binding.
portret(-ten). Portrait(s).
prent. Print.
prijs. Price; — **thans,** Present price; — **vroeger,** Former price.
prijsverhooging. Advance in price; **prijsverlaging,** Reduction in price.

R.

rand. Margin, border.
redactie. Editorship; **onder redactie van,** Edited by, under the editorship of.
reeks. Series.
regel. Rule, line.
register. Index, register.
rug. Back.

S.

's. des. Of the, in the. (*e.g.*, **'s avonds,** In the evening; **'s Gravenhage,** The Hague (literally, the hague, or hedge, of the count [of Holland])).
schrijver. Author.
schutblad. Flyleaf.
serie. Series.
sierlijk. Neat, elegant.

slecht. Bad.

slechts. Only; — **150 exemplaren gedrukt,** Only 150 copies printed.

slot(-en). Clasp(s).

snede. Edge; **verguld op snede,** With gilt edges.

soepel. Flexible.

st. stuiver(s). Stiver = 2 cents.

staalgravure(-s). Steel engraving(s).

stevig. Strong, heavy, firm; **stevig papier,** Strong, durable paper.

stkn. stukken. Pieces, parts, volumes.

stuk. Piece, part, volume.

stukjes. Small, or thin, pieces; pamphlets.

T.

't. het. The.

taal. Language.

talrijke. Numerous.

tekst. Text, passage.

tijdelijk. Temporarily.

tijdschrift. Periodical.

titel. Title.

titelblad. Title page.

titelplaat. Frontispiece.

toegelicht. Explained.

translaat. Translation.

translateur. Translator.

U.

uitg. uitgaaf, uitgegeven.

uitgaaf. Edition, publication; **prijs bij uitgaaf,** Price at time of publication, publication price.

uitgave. [**uitgever.** Publisher.] — **is gestaakt,** Publication stopped, no longer published.

uitgeg. uitgegeven. Published, issued.

uitslaande plattegrond. Folding plan; — **platen,** Folding plates, illustrations.

uitverkocht. Sold out, not in stock, out of print.

V.

v. van. Of, from.

v. h. van het. Of the.

van voren. In front; — **gezien,** Seen from the front.

veiling. Auction.

vel. Sheet; **in afleveringen van 4 vel druks.,** In parts of 4 signatures or 64 pages.

velijn. Vellum.

verbinding. Joint, connection.

verguld. Gilt.

verhaal (verhalen). Story, account. (*e.g.*, **reisverhaal,** Account of a journey or voyage; travels.)

verkleind. Reduced (copy).

verkort. Abridged; —**e uitgave,** Abridged edition.

verlucht. Illuminated.

verm. vermeerderd. Enlarged; —**e druk,** Enlarged edition.

versiering. Decoration.

verslag(-en). Report(s).

verspreide geschriften. Miscellaneous writings, collected writings.

vert. vertaler, vertaling. Translator, translation.

vervaardigd. Made, prepared.

vervolgwerk(-en). Continuation(s).

verzamelaar. Collector.

verzameld. Compiled, collected.

verzameling. Collection.

vierkant. Square.

vochtvlek. Fox mark.

volkomen. Complete, perfect.

volledig. Complete.

voorrede. Preface.

voortgezet. Continued.

vooruitbetaling. Prepayment.

voorwoord. Foreword, preface.

voren. *See* **van voren.**

vrachtvrij. Freight prepaid.

vv. volgende. Following.

W.

wapen. (wapenschild). Coat of arms.

ware groote. Full size.

water. watervlak, watervlek. Stained or injured by water or dampness. (*e.g.*, **een weinig met watervlekken voorzien, een weinig door water beschadigd, door watervlekken ontsierd,** Slightly water-stained.)

wdb. woordenboek. Dictionary.

wed. weduwe. Widow.

weinig. (A) little.

wiegedrukken. Incunabula, cradle-books.

wijlen. The late (Mr. Jones).

wit. White, blank.

Z.

z. zonder; — **n. v. g.,** zonder naam van graveur. (graveerder).

z. n. en w. v. dr. en jaart. zonder naam en woonplaats van drukker en jaartal. Without name and place of printer and date.

zaakregister. Subject index.

Zakformaat. Pocket size, pocket edition.

zal. zaliger. Deceased.

zamen (te—). Together. (*e.g.*, **2 dln. tezamen,** "2 vols. in 1.")

zeer. Very. (*e.g.*, — **zeldzaam,** "Very scarce.")

zegel. Seal.

zeldzaam. Scarce, rare.

z. g. zaliger gedachtenis. Of blessed memory; zoogenaamd, So-called.

zie. See; — **ook,** See also.

zijde. Silk; side. (**Blazijde,** Page.)

zinnebeeld(-en). Symbol, emblem, emblemata.

zinspreuk. Motto.

z., zn. zoon, zonen. Son, sons. (*e.g.*, **S. Muller Fz.,** S. Muller, son of Frederik Muller, to distinguish him from his uncle or cousin S. Muller, son of — Muller; **G. B. van Goor Zonen,** Sons of G. B. van Goor.) (Used in corporate names.)

zonder. Without; — **naam van graveur (graveerder),** Without name of engraver.

zwaar. Strong, heavy.

zwart. Black.

ITALIAN ABBREVIATIONS AND TERMS

A.

abbon. abbonamento. Subscription.

abbreviatura(-e). Abbreviation(s).

accresciuto. Enlarged.

aggiunto. Added, continued, enlarged.

albo. White.

altro. Other; **fra le altre cose,** Among other things.

ampliato. Enlarged.

antiporta. Page preceding frontispiece. Sometimes applied to " false title " page.

atlante(-i). Atlas(es).

aumentato. Increased, enlarged.

autografo(-i). Autograph(s).

autotipiche(-i). Autotype(s).

B.

b. es. bell' esemplare.

bazzana. Sheep.

bianco. White, blank.

bibliot. biblioteca. Library.

bistre. Dark brown ("sepia"), colored with bistre.

busta. Box, case; — **in tela,** Cloth case.

C.

ca. carta; — **azz.,** carta azzura; — **dist.,** carta distinta; — **gr.,** carta grande; — **vel.,** carta velina.

carat. caratteri; — **got.,** caratteri gotici; — **ton.,** caratteri tondi.

caratteri. Characters; — **corsivi,** Italics; — **gotici,** Gothic characters (text or black letter); — **romani,** Roman characters; — **tondi,** Rounded letters.

carta. Paper, map; .— **azzura,** Blue paper; — **distinta,** Special paper; — **grande,** Large paper; — **pecora,** Sheepskin or parchment; — **pecorina,** Thin parchment (literally, lambskin); — **velina,** Vellum or parchment paper.

cartabello. Pamphlet, rare book, manuscript.

cartella. Label.

carticino. Errata sheet.

cartone. Boards (binding).

casa editrice. Publishing house.

chiuso. Unopened.

collez. collezione, collezioncina.

collezione(-i). Collection(s).

collezioncina(-e). Small collection(s).

colonna(-e). Column(s).

colorato. Colored.

compendio. Compendium.

compilato. Compiled; — **sopra fonti ufficiali,** Based on official sources.

compilatore. *fem.* (-trice). Compiler.

complessive. — **pag.,** Continuous paging.

con. With.

cons. conservazione. Preservation. (*e.g.,* **buona conservazione,** Good condition.)

contin., continua. continuato, continuazione.

continuato. Continued.

continuaz. continuazione. Continuation.
copertina(-e). Cover(s), wrapper(s).
cordoni. "Bands" (binding).
coros. corostoso. Grained.
corretto. Corrected.
corso. in process of; — **di stampa,** In press.
cromolitografia. Chromolithography.

D.

danese. Danish.
dedicatoria. Dedication.
diagramma(-i). Diagram(s).
dig. digerito. Digested, condensed, arranged.
dichiarato. Described, explained.
disegn. disegni.
disegno(-i). Design(s), drawing(s); — **e penna,** Pen
  drawings.
disp. disparto, disparte. Separate, separately.
documento(-i). Document(s).
dorato. Gilt.

E.

ecc., eccez. eccezione. Exception; **ad —,** With th
  exception of; **senz' —,** Without exception.
ed. edito. Edited; — **a cura di,** Edited under th
  direction of.
ed. edizione.
editore(-i). *fem.* (-**trice**). Publisher(s).
ediz. edizione; — **stim.,** edizione stimata; — **tasc.**
  edizione tascabile; — **uffic.,** edizione ufficiale;
  ult., edizione ultima.

edizione. Edition; — **di gran lusso,** Edition de grand luxe; — **di lusso,** Edition de luxe; — **interamente rinnovata,** Completely revised; — **popolare,** Popular edition; — **stimata,** Good (approved) edition; — **tascabile,** Pocket edition; — **ufficiale,** Official edition; — **ultima,** Last (latest) edition.

eleg. elegantemente.

eliotipie. Heliotype.

erede. Heir.

es. esemplare; — **abbrun.,** esemplare abbrunato; — **dist.,** esemplare, distinto.

esaur. esaurito. Out of print.

esemp. esemplare.

esemplare(-i). Copy(-ies); — **abbrunato,** Memorial copy (*i.e.*, pages with black borders); — **distinto,** Extra fine copy; — **popolare,** Popular edition.

esplicativo. Explanatory.

esterno. Foreign.

F.

fasc. fascicolo(-i). Part(s), fascicule(s).

fig. figura(-e). Figure(s), illustration(s).

filigrana(-e). Water mark(s).

flessibile. Flexible, limp.

foderato. Lined.

fogli chiusi. Leaves unopened.

foglietto. Small leaf.

foglio. Leaf, folio.

fogliolina. Leaf of a small book.

fol. foglio. Folio.

folio. (in —), Folio size.

folleto. Pamphlet, small book.

fotogr. fotografia. Photograph.
franco. Free.
fregi. Decorations, ornaments.
fotoincisione(-i). Photo-engraving(s).
fresco (fresche). Fresh, clean.
fu (il —). The late.

G.

giur. giuridico. Juridical.
greve. Seriously; — **cylindrata,** Badly wormed.
grandezza. Size; in — **naturale,** Full size.

I.

illustr., illustraz. illustrazione.
illustrazione(-i). Illustration(s). — **in nero,** Illustrations in black; — **in nero e bistre,** Illustrations in black and dark brown (sepia).
immagine(-i). Picture(s).
impronta. Impression.
improntato (imprentato). Printed, engraved.
in-. In composition with book sizes. (*e.g.,* **in-4 oblungo,** Oblong quarto; **in-4 piccolo,** Small quarto.)
inc. incisione(-i). Engraving(s); — **intercalate nel testo,** Illustrations in the text.
inciso. Engraved; — **in rame,** Engraved in copper, copper engravings.
indice. Index, table of contents.
ined. inedito. Unpublished.
inglese. English.
insepar. inseparabili. Complete, together. (*e.g.,* **2 vol —,** 2 volumes in 1.)

int. intonso.

intagliato. Engraved.

intaglio. Engraving; **intaglio in legno,** woodcut.

interamente. Entirely, completely, throughout.

int(i)ero. Complete, perfect.

intonso. Uncut, untrimmed.

intorno. About, nearly.

introd. introduzione. Introduction.

L.

l. Lira, lire. Coin worth about twenty cents.

lavoro (in —). In preparation.

leg. legato, legatura; — **all. bod.,** legato alla bodoniano; — **ant.,** legatura antica; — **in cart.,** legato in cartone; — **in pel.,** legato in pelle; — **ol.,** legatura olandese.

legato. Bound; — **alla bodoniano,** Bound " Bodoni style"; — **in cartone,** Bound in boards; — **in mezza pelle,** Bound in half leather; — **in pelle,** Bound in full leather; — **in pecora,** Bound in sheep; — **in tabi,** Bound in tabby; — **in tela,** Bound in cloth; — **in tutta seta artificiale,** Bound in full imitation silk.

legatura. Binding; — **antica.,** Old (antique) binding; — **olandese,** Dutch (style) binding.

libraio. Bookseller.

libreria. Library, bookstore; — **antiquaria,** Old bookstore.

libro(-i). Book(s), volume(s).

libretto. Small book, booklet.

librone(-i). Large book(s).

M.

macchiato. Spotted, stained.
manoscritto(-i). Manuscript(s).
marco (marchio)-che. Mark, water mark.
mezzo. Half; **mezza pelle,** Half leather; — **pergamena,** Half vellum.
migliorato. Improved.
ms. (mss.). Manoscritto(-i).

N.

nero. Black.
non è ancora pubblicato. Not yet published.
num. numero, numerato.
numero(-i). Number(s).
numerato. Numbered.
nuovo. New; **nuova edizione,** New edition.

O.

obl. oblungo. Oblong.
ott. ottimo. Best, very good; **ottima conservazione,** Excellent state of preservation, perfect condition.

P.

pag. pagina(-e). Page(s).
paginatura. Paging.
particol. particolareggiato. Detailed.
pecora. Sheep; **carta —,** Parchment, sheepskin.
pelle. Leather,
perg. pergamena. Vellum.
pianta(-e). Plan(s).
picc. piccolo. Small.

popolare. Popular; — **edizione,** Popular edition.

por cada tomo. Per volume.

porto. Postage.

prefaz. prefazione. Preface.

preparazione. Preparation; **in —,** In preparation.

prezzo complessivo. Complete price.

pub(b)licazione(-i). Publication(s).

Q.

quasi esaurito. Nearly out of print.

R.

rac. raccolta, raccolto.

raccolta. Compilation, collection.

raccolto. Compiled, collected.

reale. Royal; **folio —,** Imperial folio.

relazione. Account, statement, report.

richiamo(-i). Catchword(s) (at bottom of page).

ricorretto. Revised.

rifatto. Restored, repaired.

rilegato. Rebound.

rilegatura. Rebinding, binding material.

riprodutto. Reproduced.

riproduzione(-i). Reproduction(s).

riscontrato. Compared with, verified.

risma. Ream of paper.

ristampa. New edition, reprint; **in —,** In process of reprinting; **non —,** Not reprinted.

ristretto(-i). Abstract, compendium.

ritr. ritratto(-i). Portrait(s).

ritrattino(-i). Miniature(s).

riveduta. Revision.

riveduto. Revised; **rivedut(o) dall' autore,** Revised by the author.

S.

s. senza. Without; **s. a.,** senz'anno; **s. d.,** senza data; **s. l.,** senza luogo; **s. tip.,** senza tipografo.

sc. scudo(-i). Old Italian coin of varying values.

scinp. Scinpato. Torn, injured.

scritto. Written.

sec. secolo(-i). Age(s), century(-ies).

segno(-i). Mark, watermark.

senza. Without; **senz'anno,** Without year of publication; — **data,** Without date; — **luogo,** Without place of publication; — **tipografo,** Without name of printer.

seta artificiale. Imitation silk.

sigla(e). Single letter, initial.

silografiã. Block book printing.

sogetto(-i). Subject(s).

spagn(u)olo. Spanish.

spiegati. Explained.

spiegativo. Explanatory.

stampa(-e). Copy(-ies), impression(s).

stamperia. Printing office.

stesso. Same.

stup. Stupendo; — **es.** Stupendo esemplare.

stupendo. Excellent, very fine; — **esemplare,** Very fine copy.

sunto. Summary, extract.

T.

tabella(-e). Table(s), compendium(s).

tagl. taglio.

taglio(-i). Edge(s); — **dorato,** Gilt edge; — **rosso,** red edge.

tarlato. Wormeaten.

tarlatura. Wormholes.

tasc. tascabile. Pocket (edition).

tav. tavola(-e). Table(s), index(es), plate(s), table(s) of contents; —**e a colori,** Colored plates; — **colorata,** Colored plate; —**e doppie colorate,** Duplicate set of colored plates; — **fuori testo,** Picture (plate) not in the text; — **miniati,** Illustrations in miniature.

tedesco(-chi). German.

tela. Cloth; —**e oro,** Bound in cloth ornamented in gold; **mezza —,** Half cloth; **tutta —,** Full cloth.

testo. Text; **nel —,** In the text.

tipografia. Printing house.

tit. titolo; — **inc.,** titolo inciso.

titolo. Title, title page; — **inciso,** Engraved title page.

tr. tradotto. Translated.

traduz. traduzione. Translation.

trattato(-i). Treatise(s).

tutta. Full (all); — **pelle,** Full leather; — **tela,** Full cloth.

U.

uffic. ufficiale. Official.

ufficialmente. Officially.

V.

volume(-i). Volume(s).

LATIN ABBREVIATIONS AND TERMS

A.

a. C. ante Christum. Before Christ.

a capite ad calcem. Completely.

a. h. l. ad hunc locum. " On this passage (consult)."

a. n. absque nota. No particulars of publication.

acc. accedit, accessit.

accedit. There follows. Literally, there is added.

accessit. There has been added. There follows.

ad calcem. At bottom of page, at the end.

ad lib. (libit.) ad libitum. At pleasure.

ad usum. For the use of.

ad vivum. From life.

æ., æt. ætatis. Aged.

agenda. Rituals, liturgies, lists of memoranda.

al. alii, alia. Others.

al. alia lecta. Other readings.

appar. apparuit. (It) has appeared.

apud. From the publishing house of —.

B.

beatissimus. Most reverend.

beatus. Blessed, of blessed memory.

C.

c. f. cum figuris. With illustrations.

ca. circa.

cætera desunt. The rest lacking, or missing.

cap. caput. Chapter, chapter head, head.

cf. confer. Compare, consult.

ch. m. charta magna. Large paper.

clavis. Key.

corrigendum(-a). Correction(s).

cum. With; — **barbis,** Rough (deckle) edges; — iconibus, with figures; — **notis variorum,** With variorum notes.

D.

del. (deli., delin.). delineavit. He (she) drew it.

dir. direxit. (He) arranged, edited.

donum. Gift.

E.

e. g. exempli gratia.

ead. pag. eadem pagina.

eadem. The same; — **editio,** The same edition; — pagina, The same page.

ed. editio.

editio. Edition; — **princeps,** First edition.

editus. Published, edited.

ejusdem. Of the same —.

eod. loc. eodem loco. In the same place.

err. errata. Errors.

et. And; — **al.,** — **alia** or **alii,** And others; — **seq.,** et sequentes, And the following.

etiam. The same as, also.

ex. From; — **ædibus,** From the (publishing) house of; **ex. gr.,** exempli gratia; — **libris,** Bookplate; — **officina,** From the bookshop of; — **typ.** (ex typographia), From the printing house of.

exempli gratia. For example.

exc., excud. excudebat. (He) printed. (*e.g.*, **in ære excusum,** Printed on copper; *i.e.*, copperplate; **G. Virtue exc.,** G. Virtue printed it.)

excerptum. Selected from, selection, excerpt.

Explicit. The end. Used also in descriptive notes to indicate the colophon.

extremo. At the end.

F.

f., fe., fec., ft. fecit. (He) made it. (Usually of illustrations.) (*e.g.*, **X fecit aqua forti,** X etched it.)

finis. End; **in fine, ad finem,** At the end.

folio. Folio (book size); — **maximus,** Large folio.

folium. Leaf; **folio recto,** On the front of the leaf, right-hand page; **verso,** On the back of the leaf, left-hand page.

H.

h. e. hic est.

h. q. hic quære.

h. t. hoc titulo.

hic. This; — **est,** This is; — **quære,** Look for this.

hoc titulo. In, or under, this title.

I.

i. q. idem quod.

ib. (ibid.). ibidem. In the same place.

icones. Figures, diagrams.

id. idem. The same; **idem quod,** The same as.

ign. ignotus. Unknown.

impensis. At the cost of, published by (or for).

impr. impressus, imprimatur, imprimitur.

impressus. Printed. Used also to indicate the colophon.

imprimatur. Let it be printed. Official sign of approval.

imprimitur. It is printed.

in. In; — **albis,** " In sheets." — **extenso,** Entire, as a whole; — **fidem copiae,** a true copy; — **globo,** as a whole, complete; — **loc.,** in loco. In its place; — **pr.,** in principio, At the top, at the beginning.

in., (**init.,** or **ad init.**). initio, initium. At the beginning, the beginning.

inedita. Unpublished works.

inf. infra. Below, see below.

interp. interpres, interpretatus.

interpres. Translator.

interpretatus. Translated.

inv. invenit. (He) designed it.

ipse. Himself. (*e.g.*, **Se ipse del.,** Drawn by himself.)

J.

juxta. After, according to.

L.

l. lege, liber.

l. c. loco citato.

l. g. lit(t)eræ gothicæ.

l. i. c. Loco infra citato.

l. r. lit(t)eræ romanæ.
l. s. c. loco supra citato.
lege. Read, see.
lib. (libb.) liber(-bri). Book(s).
limine (in —). At the beginning or end.
literatim. Letter for letter.
lit(t)erae. Letters, characters; — **gothicae,** Gothic (black letter) characters; — **romanae,** Roman characters; — **unciales,** Uncial (round) letters.
loc. locus. **loc. cit.,** loco citato; **loc. inf. cit.,** loco infra citato; — **laud.,** loco laudato; — **s. cit.,** loco supra citato.
locus. Place; **loco citato,** In the place cited or quoted; **loco infra citato,** In the place cited below; **loco laudato,** In the place cited; **loco supra citato,** In the place cited above.

N.

n. natus.
n. b. nota bene.
n. v. ne varietur. Definitive; **editio ne varietur,** Definitive edition.
Nota(-æ). Note(s); **nota bene,** Take notice.

O.

ob. obiit. He (she) died.
op. opus; — **cit.,** opere citato.
opus (opera). Work(s); **opere citato,** In the work cited.

P.

p., (pin). pingebat, pinxit.
passim. Here and there, at random.

pingebat. He (she) painted it.

pinx. pinxit. *See* **pingebat.**

pnxt. pinxit.

princeps. First, original; **editio —,** First edition.

privilegium. Privilege, authorization; **Cum** privilegio, With privilege, by authority.

prostat. (He) sells, offers for sale.

pxt. pinxit.

Q.

q. quod; — **e.,** quod est; — **v. (qq. v.),** quod vide
(quæ vide).

quod. Which; — **est,** Which is; — **vide,** Which see
(pl. **quæ vide).**

R.

recto. Right-hand page of book, usually with odd
numbers; face or front of printed leaf.

rec., recens. recensvit. (He) revised, edited.

S.

s. seu, sive.

s. **sine;** — **a.,** sine anno; — **a. l. et n.,** sine anno,
loco et nomine; — **d.,** sine dato; — **l.,** sine loco; —
l. a. n., sine loco, anno, vel nomine; **s. l. a. et typ.**
(n.) sine loco, anno et typographi (nomine); — **n.,**
sine nomine; — **typ.(n.)** sine typographi (nomine).

s. socius.

s. sub. — **h. v.,** sub hoc verbo; — **v.,** sub voce.

sæcul. sæculum(-a). Age(s), century(-ies).

sc. (sculp., sculps.). Sculpebat, sculpsit.

sc. (scil.). scilicet. That is to say.

scripta. Writings.

sculpebat, sculpsit. (He) engraved it.

seq.(-q). Sequens(-ntes), sequentia. The following. (*e.g.,* **v.** 1636 **seqq.,** See page 1636 and following pages.)

seriatim. In succession, serially.

seu. Or.

sine. Without; — **anno,** Without year of publication; — **anno, loco et nomine,** Without year or place of publication or name of printer; — **dato,** Without date of publication; — **impressore,** Without name of printer; — **loco,** Without place of publication; — **loco, anno, vel nomine**; Without place, year, or name of printer; — **nomine,** Without name of printer; — **typographi (nomine),** Without name of printer.

singillatim. Separately, one by one.

sive. Or.

soc. Societas, socius.

societas. Society, association.

socius. Fellow, partner, associate.

sq. (sqq.) *See* **seq.**

ss. scilicet.

ss. superscriptus, suprascriptus.

sub. Under; — **hoc verbo,** Under this word; — **voce,** Under the word (or title).

sumpt. sumptibus. At the cost of, published by (or for).

sup. superexlibris.

sup. supplementum.

superscriptus. Written over or upon.

superexlibris. Mark of ownership on front cover.

supplementum. Supplement.

suprascriptus. Written at the top. *See also* **super-scriptus.**

T.

t. tomus.

tab. tabula(-æ). Plate(s).

text. rec. textus receptus. Received text. (*i.e.,* Text ordinarily used or cited.)

textus. Text.

titulus. Title; — **secundarius,** Half title, bastard title.

tomus(-i). Volume(s).

traductum. Translated.

typographia. Printing house.

typographus. Printer.

U.

u. ut; — **inf.,** ut infra; **u. s.,** ut supra.

ult. ultimo. At the end.

ut. dict. ut dictum. As has been said; — **infra,** As below; — **supra,** As above.

V.

v. vide.

v., vº. Verso.

v. g. verbi gratia.

v. lect. (vv. ll.), var. lect. vario lectio (variones lectiones).

vacat. (It is) blank.

vacant. Plural of **vacat.**

vario lectio (variæ lectiones). Different reading(s).

variorum. Of many writers. (*e.g.*, **editio variorum,** Edition including versions, notes, etc., of different people.)

verbi gratia. For example.

verso. Back of a leaf. (In a book, the left-hand (even-numbered) page.)

vide. See; — **etiam,** See also; — **retro,** See above.

videlicet. Namely.

viz. videlicet.

vo. Verso.

vol. volumen.

volumen(-ines). Volume(s).

vv. ll. Variæ lectiones. *See* **vario lectio.**

SPANISH ABBREVIATIONS AND TERMS

A.

acero, (en —). Steel (engraving).

acotado. Limited.

adición. Addition.

agotado. Out of print.

agotadísimo. Very scarce, entirely out of print.

agujero. Wormhole.

alemán. German.

algo. Somewhat. (*e.g.*, **algo deteriorado,** Somewhat damaged.)

ampliado. Enlarged.

anotación. Note, annotation.

anotado. Annotated.

anteportada. Page of half title; — **grabada,** Engraved half title.

antiguo. Old.

anual. Annual.

anual. anualmente. Annually.

anuario. Year book, annual.

anunciado. Announced.

apaisado. Oblong (particularly of illustrations or engravings).

apéndice. Appendix, supplement.

apolillado. Wormeaten.

aumentado. Enlarged.
autógrafo. Autograph.
autografiado. Autographed.
autor. Author.
azul. Blue.
azulado. Bluish.

B.

badana. Sheep.
bastante. Considerably; — **deteriorado,** Considerably damaged.
becerrillo. Calf.
bibliografía. Bibliography.
bibliográfico. Bibliographical.
biblioteca. Library, catalogue.
blanco. White, blank.
boletín. Bulletin.
bolsillo. Pocket; **ed. de —,** Pocket edition.
bonito. Attractive; **bonita edición,** Attractive edition; — **ejemplar,** Good (attractive) copy.
buen(a). Good; — **ejemplar,** Good copy; — **estado (de conservación),** Good condition; **buena letra,** Good print (type).

C.

c. con. With.
cabeza. Top; — **dorada,** Gilt top.
cabezal. Title page.
cada tomo. Per volume, each volume.
cantos dorados. Gilt edges.
caracteres. Letters; — **cursivos,** Italics; — **góticos,** Gothic (text or black-letter) characters.

carpeta. Portfolio, wrapper.

cartoné. Bound in boards.

cartulina. Cardboard, bristol board.

céntimo(-s). Centime(s).

cerca de. About.

chagrín. Shagreen, grained leather; **tela —,** Cloth grained to imitate shagreen, "morocco cloth"; **— flexible,** Flexible shagreen; **— mullido,** Padded morocco.

colección. Collection.

colofón. Colophon.

columna. (coluna.) Column.

con. With; **— grabados,** With engravings.

corrección. Correction.

corregido. Corrected.

cortado por el margen. Margin trimmed.

corte. Edge; **—s dorados,** Gilt edge(s); **—s de distinto color,** Edges of different colors; **—s rojos,** Red edges.

corto numero, (en —). Small number available, scarce.

cta. Account.

cuaderno. Stitched pamphlet, signature " in fours."

cuadro. Picture.

cubierta. Cover.

cuidadosamente corregido. Carefully corrected.

D.

ded. dedicatoria. Dedication.

deteriorado. Damaged.

dibujo. Drawing.

docum. documento. Document.

dorado. Gilt.

dos col. á. Double column.

E.

e. escudo; — **de a.,** escudo de armas; — **de a. i.,** escudo de armas imperiales; — **de a. r.,** escudo de armas reales.

ed. edición.

edición. Edition; — **autografiada,** Autographed edition; — **de corto numero de ejemplares,** Limited edition; — **de gran lujo,** Extra de luxe edition; — **de lujo,** Edition de luxe; — **en letra gruesa,** Large type edition.

ejemplar. Copy; **bonito** —, Attractive (pretty) copy; **bueno** —, Good copy; — **inmejorable,** Perfect copy; — **numerado,** Numbered copy.

en. In; — **cartoné,** Bound in boards.

enc. encuadernado.

encarnado. Flesh-colored.

encartonado. Bound in boards.

encuadernación. Binding.

encuadernado. Bound.

epoca, (de la —). Contemporary. (*e.g.*, **pasta de la epoca.**)

escaso. Defective, lacking.

escudo. shield; — **de armas,** Coat of arms; — **de armas imperiales,** Imperial coat of arms; — **de armas reales,** Royal coat of arms.

esmeradamente arreglado. Carefully arranged.

estropeado. Mutilated.

estuche. Case.
excelentemente. Excellently.
extranjero. Foreign.

F.

facsímil. facsimile.
faltan. Lacking, wanting.
falto. Wanting, lacking.
fecha. Date.
fha. Fecha.
fho. Fecho. Dated.
filete dorado. Gold fillet.
fol. foliación. folio.
foliación. Pagination.
foliado. Paged.
folio mayor. Large folio.
folio menor. Small folio.
folleto. Pamphlet.
forrado de tela. Lined with cloth.
fotograbado. Photogravure.
francés. French.
franqueo. Postage free.
frente. Front (cover).
frontis. frontispicio. Frontispiece.

G.

gastos de envío. Costs of transportation.
grab. grabado(s); — **en mad.**, grabado en madera.
grabado. Engraving; — **en acero**, Steel engraving;
— **en madera**, Wood engraving; — **relieve**, Engraving in relief.

gran. Large, great; — **folio,** Large folio; — **papel,** Large paper.

grueso. Thick, bulky; — **volumen,** Large, bulky volume.

guía. Guide.

H.

h. hoja.

hecho al cromo. Done in color.

hermoso. Handsome.

hoja. Leaf; — **volante,** Broadside, newspaper " extra " or supplement.

hol. holandés. Dutch.

I.

iluminado. Illuminated.

ilustración. Illustration.

ilustrado. Illustrated.

imprenta. Printing office.

impresión. Impression, edition.

impreso. Printed.

impreso. Small book, short treatise.

índice. Index.

infinidad. A great number; — **de láminas,** Numerous plates.

inglés. English.

iniciales. Initials.

inmejorable. Very remarkable; **ejemplar —,** Perfect copy.

intercalado en el texto. Intercalated in the text.

intonso. Uncut.

J.

jaspeado. Marbled.

L.

l. libro.

lam. lámina. Plate, engraving; — **doblada,** Folded plate, double-page plate; — **al agua fuerte,** etching; — **suelta,** Loose plate.

let. letra; — **curs.,** letra cursiva; — **got.,** letra gótica; — **rom.,** letra romana.

letra(s). Letter; —**s cursivas,** Italics; —**s capitales,** Capital letters; —**s góticas,** Gothic (text or black-letter) letters; — **gruesa,** Large type; — **muy gruesa,** Very large type; — **romana,** Roman letter; — **pegueña,** small type.

librería. Library, bookshop.

librero. Bookseller.

línea. Line.

litografía. Lithograph.

lomera. Back; — **jaspeada,** Marbled back; — **y puntas chagrín,** Three-quarters (back and corners) shagreen.

lomo. Back; — **cuajado de oro,** Back profusely ornamented with gold; — **tela,** Cloth back; — **jaspeado,** Marbled back.

lujoso. Ornate, elaborate.

M.

MS. (MSS.). Manuscrito(-s).

magnífico. Splendid; — **ejemplar,** Splendid copy.

mal. Bad, poor; — **ejemplar,** Poor copy.

mancha. Spot, stain. *See* **manchado.**

manchado. Spotted, stained; — **de agua,** Water-stained; — **de humidad,** " Foxed," mildewed; — **de tinta,** Ink stained.

manuscrito. Manuscript.

mapa. Map.

marcado. Marked.

margen. Margin; — **inferior,** Lower margin; — **superior,** Upper margin.

materia. Subject; **tabla de —s,** Subject index.

may. mayor.

mayor. Large (lit. "larger"); 4° —, Large quarto.

medio. Half; **media pasta,** Half leather binding.

menor. Small (lit. " smaller "); **folio —,** Small quarto.

mismo, el —. The same.

moderno. Modern.

mr.(s). maravedi(s). Old Spanish coin worth about one-sixth of a cent.

multidad. Large number; — **de grabados,** Many engravings.

muy. Very; — **escaso,** Very scarce; — **raro,** Very rare.

N.

n. número.

neto. Net.

nuevo. New; **neuva edición,** New edition.

nota. Note; **—s marginales,** Marginal notes.

num.(-s). número(-s). Number(s).

O.

obra. Work; **—s de ocasión,** Secondhand works; **—s de lance,** Secondhand books; — **rarísima,** Very rare work.

opúsculo. Short summary or treatise.

orden(es). Arrangement(s), class(es).

ordenado. Arranged.

ordenadamente. Systematically.

orl. orla. Margin, border.

orla. orlado; — **en las tapas,** Edges of covers decorated; — **orladas las páginas,** Decorative margins, ornamental borders.

P.

p. por, peseta, página.

p. a. por autorización.

p. p. porte pagado.

p. en b. página en blanco.

pag.(s). página(s).

página. Page; **—s doblas,** Folded pages; — **en blanco,** Blank page; **—s orladas,** Pages with decorated borders.

papel. Paper; — **gran,** large paper; — **acanillado,** Laid paper; — **avitelado,** Vellum paper; — **azul,** Blue paper; — **corriente,** Common (ordinary) paper; — **couché,** Coated paper; — **de arroz,** Rice paper; — **de China,** India paper; — **de hilo,** Rag paper; — **hilo,** Rag paper; — **Japón,** Japan paper; — **jaspeado,** Marbled paper; — **satinado,** Calendered paper, glazed paper; — **volante,** Small pamphlet, leaflet.

papel. Treatise, article, paper.

pasta. Leather binding (leather covered boards), roan leather; — **con adornos,** Ornamental leather binding; — **fina,** Fine leather binding; — **española,** Spanish leather binding; — **valenciana,** Valentian leather binding.

perfecto. Perfect.

pergamino. Parchment.

peseta. Spanish coin worth about 19 cents.

peso. Spanish dollar (South American coin worth about 75 cents); **peso duro (fuerte),** Old Spanish " hard dollar " or " piece of eight."

pf(s). peso(s) fuerte(s).

picadura de polilla. Wormhole.

piel. Leather; — **tabla,** Diced leather; — **valenciana,** Valentian leather.

plancha. Plate.

plano. Plan.

plegado. Folded.

pliego. Sheet of paper.

por. By.

port. portada.

portada. Frontispiece, title page; — **orlada,** Decorated title page. (*i.e.*, With decorative border.)

porte pagado. Prepaid.

precio. Price.

prel. preliminar. Preliminary.

prensa, (en —). In press.

primero. First; **primera edición,** First edition.

priv. privilegio. Privilege, copyright.

proemio. Preface, introduction.

prol. prólogo. Preface, introduction.

ps. páginas; — **ds.,** páginas doblas.
ps. pesos.
pta. (ptas.). peseta(s).
pts. pesetas.
publicación. Publication.
punta. Corner; — **redonda,** round corner; — **rebarbeado,** rough (deckle) edge.

Q.

Que se hallan de venta. Which are for sale.

R.

r. (rs.). Real(es).
rarísima. Very rare.
raro. Rare.
real(es). Old Spanish coin worth 10 to 12½ cents.
real. Royal.
rebaja. Reduction, rebate, discount.
rebarbeado. Rough.
recopilado. Compiled.
recopilador. Compiler.
recortado. Cut, trimmed.
reducido. Reduced.
reforzado. Strengthened, reënforced.
rehecho. Repaired, restored.
reimpresión. Reprint, new edition.
remendado. Mended.
remiendo. Short work, issued in limited edition,
patch.
reproducción. Reproduction.
retrato. Portrait.

revisado. Revised.

roto. Broken, damaged.

rótulo. Binder's title; — **dorado,** Back title in gilt.

rústica (á la —, en —). Unbound, paper covers.

S.

s. sin; — **a.,** sin año; — **f.,** sin fecha; — **l.,** sin lugar; — **l. n. a.,** sin lugar ni año; — **l. ni a. ni numeración.**

ser. serie(s). Series.

siglo. Century.

sign. signatura. "Signature," section, sheet.

siguiente. Following, sequent.

sin. Without; — **año.,** Without year of publication; — **fecha,** Without date; — **foliación,** Without numbered folios (leaves); — **foliar,** Unpaged; — **lugar,** Without place; — **lugar ni año ni numeración**; Without place, year, or numbered pages; — **numeración,** — **numerar,** Unnumbered; — **signaturas,** Without signature marks.

sobrepuestas. Mounted plates, etc.

sociedad. Society.

suelto. Loose.

T.

tabla. Table of contents.

tafilete. Morocco.

tamaño. Size, shape.

tapa. Cover.

tela. Cloth; — **con dorados,** Cloth binding ornamented in gilt; — **encarnada,** Flesh-colored cloth binding.

tirado. Printed; — **de ejemplares en corto numero,** Only a few copies printed; **tirada especiale,** Special edition.

tít. título. Title.

todas sus margenes, (con—). Margins entire, uncut.

tomito. Small volume.

tomo. Volume.

traducción. Translation.

traducido. Translated.

U.

último. Last, latest; **ultima edición,** Latest edition.

ultramar. Foreign.

unico publicado (Tomo i —). Only — vol. published.

V.

v. vease. See.

vendido. Out of print.

viñeta. Vignette; — **en madera,** Vignette woodcuts.

volumen. Volume.

SWEDISH ABBREVIATIONS AND TERMS*

Umlauted vowels are arranged in order with unumlauted, not by themselves as in Swedish dictionaries

A.

a. andra. Second.

adl. afdelning(ar). Section(s), part(s).

af. By.

afhandl. afhandling(ar). Papers.

aftryck. Copy(-ies), print(s), impression(s).

allm. allmän(t). General(ly), common(ly).

anledn. anledning. Occasion(s).

årg. årgång(-ar). Annual volume(s), yearbook(s).

årh. århundrade(r). Century(-ies).

årlig. Annual(ly).

ark. Signature(s).

arr. arrangerad. Arranged.

årsberättelse(r). Annual report(s).

årskatalog(er). Annual catalogue.

årsskrift(er). Annual publication(s).

aukt. (auktor.) öfvers. auktoriserat öfversättning. Authorized translation.

B.

bd. band. Volume(s), binding(s).

bearb. bearbetad. Revised.

* No claim to completeness or proportion is made for this section. It is included in default of a fuller available list elsewhere.

135

bemynd. bemyndigad. Authorized. **—öfvers.** (— öfversättning). Authorized translation.

bibl. bibliotek. Library(-ies). *Also* biblisk. Biblical.

bidrag. Contribution(s).

bifogad. Added.

bihang. Appendix(es), supplement(s).

bil. bilaga(-or). Supplement(s).

biogr. biografisk, biografi(er).

biografi(er). Biography(-ies).

biografisk. Biographical.

bl. blad. Leaf(-ves).

bl. a. bland annat. **bland annat.** Among others (*inter alia*).

bok (böcker). Book(s), part(s).

bokb. bokbinderi(-er). Bindery(-ies).

bokförl. bokförlag. Publishing house.

bokförläggare. Publisher(s).

bokförteckning(ar). Catalogue(s).

bokh. bokhandel. Bookstore(s).

boklåda. Book store.

boktr. boktryckeri(er). Printing house(s). — **bolag.** boktryckeribolag. Printing firm.

C.

chagrb. chagrinband. Shagreen binding.

D.

def. defekt. Defective, imperfect, incomplete.

del(-ar). Part(s).

distr. distribuerad. Distributed, " sold by."

distr. Distribution, distributing center, agency.

dlr. delar. Part(s).

dyl. dylik(a). The same, similar.

E.

eg. egentlig(en). Real(ly), proper(ly).

ej i bokhandeln. Not for sale.

el. eller. Or.

eleg. elegant. Elegant.

ensidigt blad. Broadside, leaf printed on one side.

ensk. enskild. Private(ly), special(ly).

ett ex. ett exemplar. One copy, single (or unique) copy.

ex., expl. exemplar. Copy(-ies).

exp. exporterad. Exported.

F.

f. för. For.

f. ö. för öfrigt. Besides, further.

f. följande. Following (*sing.*).

färglitografi. Lithographed in colors.

färgtr. färgtryck. Color print.

ff. följande. Following (*plu.*).

fig. figur(er). Illustration(s).

fl. fler(a). More, many.

följ. följande. Following, next.

följd. Series.

förbättrad upplaga. Revised (improved) edition.

föregående. Preceding.

förening(en). Association(s), society(-ies).

förf. författar. Author.

förl. förläggare. Publisher.

förord. Preface(s), introduction(s).

förteckn. förteckning(ar). List(s), index(es), catalogue(s).

fr. från. From.

franskt band. Calf binding, leather binding.

G.

genom. By, through.
genomsedd. Revised.
gldsn. guldsnitt.
gm., gnm. genom.
gotisk stil. Gothic type, " black letter."
grav. graverad. Engraved.
grav. gravyr. Engraving(s).
gsn., (guldsn.). guldsnitt. Gilt edges, gilding.

H.

h. (hfn.). häfte(n). Number(s), part(s).
häftad. Stitched.
handskr. handskrift(er). Manuscript(s).
hfn. häften. Numbers, parts.
heliogravyr(er). Heliogravure(s).
helsidespl. helsides plansch(er). Full-page plate(s).
hlfr. bd. (hlfr.). halffranskt band (halffransk). Half-calf binding.
hvarje. Each.
hvit. White, blank. — **sida,** Blank page.

I.

i allm. i allmänhet. Mostly, generally, commonly.
i st. f. i stället för. Instead of.
ibl. ibland. Among.
illustr. illustrerat. Illustration.
illustration(er). Illustration(s).
illustrerat. Illustrated.
inb. inbunden. Bound.
innehåll. Contents.
inledning(ar). Introduction(s), preface(s).

inneh. innehåller. Contains.
interfol. interfolierad. Interleaved.
intet titelblad. No title page.

J.

jämte. Besides, with.
jfr. jemför. Compare.

K.

kalfband. Calf binding.
kartonerad. Bound in boards.
kart. karta(-or).
kart. kartong.
karta(-or). Map(s), chart(s).
kartbok(-böcker). Atlas(es).
kartong. " Boards," board binding.
klb. kalfband. Calf binding.
klotb. klotband. Cloth binding.
kolor. kolorerad. Colored.
kompl. komplet. Complete(ly).
kongl. konglig. Royal.
koppartryck. Copperplate.
kplt. komplet.
kungl. kunglig. Royal.
kr. kron(ar). Scandinavian coin worth 25–26 cents.

L.

lägg. Signature(s).
ldrbd. läderband. Leather binding.
liten qvart. Small 4to (etc.).
litograf tryck. Lithograph(s).
litogr. litograferad. Lithographed.

litograferad plansch. Lithograph.
lyxband. Binding de luxe.

M.

m. med. With, and.
m. fl. med flera. And others.
m. m. med mera. Et cetera.
medd. meddelande(n). Communication(s), con-
tribution(s).
minnes bl. minnes blad. Memorial pamphlet(s).
mus. musik. Music.
musik förteckning(ar). Music catalog(s).

N.

närv (närvarande) tid. The present time.
notis(er). Note(s), notice(s).
numr. nummer, numrerad.
nummer. Number(s).
numrerad. Numbered.
ny. New; **ny upplaga (nya upplagor),** New edi-
tion(s).

O.

o. och. And.
ö. öfver. Over.
o. d. och dylika. And similar (ones).
o. s. v. och så vidare. Et cetera.
öfvers. öfversätt. Translated.
öfversedd. Revised.
oillustr. oillustrerad. Without illustrations.
omarb. omarbetad. Revised. — **uppl.,** omarbetad upplaga. Revised edition.
omkr. omkring. About (circa).

onumrerad. Unnumbered.

oöfver. *See* **öfver.**

opag. opaginerad. Unpaged.

öre. Scandinavian coin worth about $\frac{1}{4}$ cent.

orig. Original. ·

osignerat. Without signature marks.

oskuret. Uncut, unopened.

P.

pagina. Page(s).

paginering. Pagination.

papper. Paper.

perm(ar). Board covers, covers. (*e.g.* **med skindrygg o. clotpermar,** With leather back and cloth sides.)

pl. plansch(er). Plate(s).

plschr. planscher.

porto. Postage; — **fri,** Postpaid.

portr. porträtt(er). Portrait(s).

ppbd. papband. Board binding.

pris(er). Price(s).

prgtbd. pragtband. Binding de luxe.

Q.

Qvart. Quarto.

R.

redaktör(er). Editor(s).

redig. redigerat. Edited.

rör. rörande. Concerning.

S.

s. sida.

ss. såsom. For example (e.g.).

saml. samlade, samling.

samlade. Collected. (*e.g.* **samlade skrifter,** Complete works.)

samling(ar). Collection. (*e.g.* **samling dikter,** Collection of poems.)

samma. (The) same.

samt. samtidig. Contemporary.

särsk. särskild. Separate, individual.

särtr. särtryck. Abstract, separate.

se. See.

sid. sida.

sida (sidor). Page(s).

sign. signatur, signerat.

signatur(er). Signature(s).

signerat. Signed, marked.

skildr. skildring(ar). Description(s).

skr. skrift(er). Work(s), writing(s).

sp. spalt(er). Column(s).

ss. sidor. Pages.

stor. Large. (*e.g.* **stor folio,** Large folio.)

suppl., supplem. supplement(er). Supplement(s).

sv. svensk. Swedish.

svart. Black; — **och rödt tryck,** Printed in black and red.

T.

t. till. **t. ex.** till exempel. For example.

t. o. m. till och med. Till, inclusive.

tafla (taflor). Plate(s), illustration(s).

talr. talrik. Numerous.

teckn. teckning(ar). Drawing(s).

tidskr. tidskrift(er). Periodical(s).

till. To; **till exempel,** For example; **till och med,** Till, up to, inclusive.

tillägg. Appendix(-dices).

tillök. tillökad. tillökning.

tillökad. Enlarged.

tillökning(ar). Addition(s), enlargement(s).

titelblad. Title-page.

tr. tryck, tryckt.

träsnitt. Woodcut(s), wood engraving(s).

träsnitt gravyr. Woodcut.

träsnitts-tafla (taflor). Woodcut(s).

tryck. Print(s).

tryckt. Printed.

tryckort. Place of printing (or publishing).

tvåspaltad. Double column.

tvåspaltig. In two columns, double column.

tvär. Square. (*e.g.* **tvärfol,** Square folio.)

U.

ungef. ungefär. About (circa).

uppgift-(er). Notice(s), report(s), list(s).

uppl. upplaga(or). Edition(s).

utan. Without; — **år,** Without year; — **ort,** Without place of publication; — **sign,** utan signatur, Without signature mark(s); — **titelblad,** Without title page.

utarb. utarbetad. Compiled.

utdg., utdr. utdrag. Abstract(s), extract(s).

utg. utgifva, utgifven.

utgangen ur bokhandeln. Out of print.

utgifva. Edition.

utgifven. Edited.

utgifvare. Editor(s).

utk. utkomma. Appeared, issued.
utm. utmärkt. Choice, excellent.
utsåld. Out of print.

V.

volym(er). Volume(s), book(s), part(s).

BRIEF LIST OF HONORARY TITLES

Only such titles as are frequently used in connection with authors' names are included. For others, especially those indicating ecclesiastical or military rank, appellations of royalty or nobility, designation of particular official positions, or membership in societies, see prefaces to biographical dictionaries like *Who's Who, Who's Who in America, Wer Ist's*, etc., also the lists of abbreviations in *Webster's International Dictionary* and the *Standard Dictionary:* for forenames consult Cutter, C. A., *Rules for a Dictionary Catalogue, 1904,* p. 157–61.

(D.) = Dutch; (F.) = French; (G.) = German; (I.) = Italian; (L.) = Latin; (S.) = Spanish.

A.

A. Alteza (S). Altezza (I).

AA. Altezas. Highnesses. (S).

A.D. Archduke.

A.N.A. Associate of the National Academy. (U. S.)

A.R.A. Associate of the Royal Academy. (Eng.)

Adm. Admiral.

Alteza. Highness. (S.)

Altezza. (I.) Highness.

apa. (ap^a.), **apo., aplica., aplico.,** apostolica(-o). Apostolic.

arz., arzbpo. arzbispo. Archbishop. (S.)

Att., Atty. Attorney; **Att.-Gen.,** Attorney general.

B.

B. beato. Blessed, holy, (St.). (S.)

bach. bachelier, — es lettres, etc., Bachelor of letters, etc. (F.)

bart. Baronet.

B^{on}. Baron. (F.)

bp. Bishop.

br. bachiller. Bachelor (of Arts, etc.). (S.)

bt. Baronet.

C.

C.B. Companion of the Bath.

C.D.S.O. Companion of the Distinguished Service Order.

C. de J. Compañia de Jesus (S. J.). (S.)

C.G. Consul general.

C.J. Chief justice.

C.P.S. Custos Privati Sigilli. Keeper of the Privy Seal. (L.)

C.R. Custos Rotulorum. Keeper of the Rolls. (L.)

C.S. Custos Sigilli. Keeper of the seal. (L.)

cap., capn. capitan. Captain. (S.)

capl., capln. capellan. Chaplain. (S.)

Card., Cardl. Cardenal. Cardinal. (S.)

Card. Cardinal.

Ch. chancelier. Chancellor. (F.)

Ch^{er}. Chevalier. (F.)

Col. Colonel.

Comdt. Commandant. Commander. (G.)

conte. Count. (I.)

contessa. Countess. (I.)

Ct. Count.

Ct⁰. comte. Count. (F.)

Ct^esse. comtesse. Countess. (F.)

D.

D., D^a., Da. Doña. (S.)

D., D^n., Dn. Don. (S.)

D.C.L. Doctor of Civil (Common) Law.

D.S.O. Distinguished Service Order.

Dir. Directeur (F.), Direktor (G.). Director.

Doc. Docent.

Doct. Doctor.

Doz. Dozent. (G.)

Dr. D^r. Doctor.

Duc. Duke. (F.)

Duca. Duke. (I.)

E.

Ehzg. Erzherzog(-in). Archduke (-duchess). (G.)

Em., Ema., Em^a. Eminencia. Eminence. (S.)

Em., Emm. Eminentisimo. Very eminent. (S.)

Em. Eminenza. Eminence. (I.)

Emn. Eminenz. Eminence. (G.)

Episc. Episcopus. Bishop. (L.)

ER., ERr. Ehrenritter. (G.)

Erzb. Erzbischof. Archbishop. (G.)

Erzhzg. Erzherzog. Archduke. (G.)

Exc., Exc^a. Excelencia. Excellency. (S.)

Excma., Excmo. Excelentisima(-mo). Most excellent. (S.)

F.

F.M. Field marshal.

F.-M.-Lt. Feldmarschall-Leutnant. Lieutenant field marshal. (G.)

147

F.R.A. Fellow of the Royal Academy.

F.R.C.P. Fellow of the Royal College of Physicians.

F.R.C.S. Fellow of the Royal College of Surgeons.

F.R.G.S. Fellow of the Royal Geographical Society.

F.R.H.S. Fellow of the Royal Historical Society.

F.R.S. Fellow of the Royal Society.

F.S.A. Fellow of the Society of Antiquaries.

Frhr. Freiherr. Baron, baronet. (G.)

Frhrin. Freiherrin. Baroness. (G.)

Fst. Fürst(-in). Prince(-ess). (G.)

fstl. fürstlich. Princely. (G.)

G.

G.-F.-M. Generalfeldmarschall. General field marshal. Generalissimo. (G.)

G^{al}. General. (F.)

Gen., Genl. General.

Gen.-Lt. Generalleutnant. Lieutenant general. (G.)

Gen.-Maj. Generalmajor. Major general. (G.)

Gf. Graf. Count. (G.)

Gfn., Gfin. Gräfin. Countess. (G.)

Gfst. Grossfürst. Grand-duke. (G.)

Ghz. Grossherzog. Archduke. (G.)

Gob., Gobr., Gob^{r}. Gobernador. Governor. (S.)

gouv. gouverneur. Governor. (F.)

Gov. Governor.

Gov. Gen. Governor general.

Graaf. Count. (D.)

Gravin. Countess. (D.)

Grossh., Grossherz. Grossherzog. Archduke. (G.)

grossh., grossherz. grossherzoglich. Archducal. (G.)

H.

H.B.M.   His (Her) Britannic Majesty.
H.C.M.   His (Her) Catholic Majesty.
H.E.   His Eminence.
H.E.   His Excellency.
H.H.   His (Her) Highness, His Holiness.
H.I.H.   His (Her) Imperial Highness.
H.M.   His (Her) Majesty.
Hon., Honble.   Honorable.
H.R.H.   His (Her) Royal Highness.
Hauptmann.   Captain.   (G.)
Herren.   Gentlemen, Messieurs.   (G.)
H.H.   Herren.   (G.)
hl., hlg.   heilig.   Holy, " Saint."   (G.)
Hofmarschall.   Knight marshal, " seneschal."   (G.)
Hzg.   Herzog.   Duke.   (G.)
Hzgin.   Herzogin.   Duchess.   (G.)

I.

I.C.   Iurisconsult.   Counsellor-at-law.   (L.)
Il^{ma}, Ilma., Ilmo., Illma., Illmo.   Illustrisima(-o).
Most illustrious.   (S.)

J.

J.   Judge, justice.
J.C.   Jurisconsult.   Counsellor-at-law.   (L.)
J.C.D.   Juris Civilis Doctor.   Doctor of Civil Law.
(L.)
J.D.   Jurum Doctor.   Doctor of Laws.   (L.)
J.U.D.   Juris Utruisque Doctor.   Doctor of both
laws (*i.e.*, civil and canon).   (L.)

Jhr. Jonkheer. Sir. (D.)
Jkvr. Jonkvrouw. Lady. (D.)

K.

k. kaiserlich, königlich. Imperial, royal. (G.)
K. King, knight.
K. König. King. (G.)
K.B. Knight of the Bath.
K.C. King's Counsel.
K.C.B. Knight Commander of the Bath.
K.G. Knight of the Garter.
k.k. königlich kaiserlich, kaiserlich königlich. Royal imperial. (G.)
k.u.k. kaiserlich und königlich. Royal and imperial. (G.)
kais. kaiserlich. Imperial.
Kap. Kapitän. Captain. (G.)
Kg. König.
kgl. Königlich.
Khr. Kammerherr. Chamberlain. (G.)
Komdt. Kommandant. Commandant. (G.)
Kt. Knight
Kurfst. Kurfürst. Elector (electoral prince). (G.)
kurfstl. kurfürstlich. Relating to an electoral prince. (G.)

L.

L. Lady.
L. licenciado. Licentiate. (S.)
L.C. Lord Chamberlain, Lord Chancellor.
L.C.B. Lord Chief Baron.
L.C.J. Lord Chief Justice.

L.H.A. Lord High Admiral.

L.H.C. Lord High Chancellor.

L.H.D. Litterarum Humanarum Doctor. Doctor of Humanities. (L.)

L.J. Lord Justice.

L.P. Lord Provost.

Ldo. Licenciado. (S.)

Ldgf. Landgraf. Landgrave. (G.)

Lieut., Lt. Lieutenant; — **Col.,** Lieutenant colonel; — **Gov.,** Lieutenant governor.

M.

M. Madre. Mother, the Virgin. (S.)

M. Maestro. Professor, Master (of Arts, etc). (S.)

M. Majestad.

M. Marquis.

M. Monsieur.

M. Member. (*See* F. (Fellow)).

M. Mitglied. Member; **M.d.H.H.,** Mitglied des Herrenhauses, Member of the House of Lords; **M.d.L.,** Mitglied des Landtags, Member of the House of Commons (or Lower House); **M.d.R.,** Mitglied des Reichstags, Member of the Reichstag; **M.d.R.-R.,** Mitglied des Reichsrats, Member of the Imperial Council. (G.)

M.C. Member of Congress.

M.G. Major general.

M.P. Member of Parliament.

Maj. Major; **Maj. Gen.,** Major general.

March. Marchioness.

Marchese. Marquis. (I.)

Marchesa. Marchioness. (I.)

Maréchal. Marshal. (F.)

Marq. Marquis.

Marsch. Marschall. Marshal. (G.)

Mdlle. Mademoiselle.

Me., Me. Madre. The Virgin, mother (religious).

Mej. Mejuffrouw. Miss. (D.)

Mevr. Mevrouw. Mrs. (D.)

Mgr. Monsignor, Monsignore. (I.)

Min. Plen. Minister Plenipotentiary.

Mis. Marquis. (F.)

Mise. Marquise, Marchioness. (F.)

Mitgl. Mitglied. (*See* under **M.**)

Mlle. Mademoiselle.

MM. Their majesties.

MM. Messieurs.

Mme. Madame.

Mons. Monsieur (used in older English but considered highly incorrect by the French).

Mr. Meester. Doctor of Laws. (D.)

Most Rev. Most Reverend (Archbishop).

Mr., Mro., Mro. Maestro. (*See* **M.**)

Mrs. Missis, mistress.

N.

N.A. National Academician (Art).

O.

O.F.M. Ordinis Fratrum Minorum. Of the order of Friars Minors (Franciscan). (L.)

O.P. Ordinis Prædicatorum. Of the Dominican order. (L.)

O.S.A. Ordinis St. Angustini. **Of the order of St. Augustine.**

O.S.B. Ordinis St. Benedicti. **Of the order of St. Benedict.**

P.

P. Papa, padre. The Pope, father (priest). (S.)

P.C. Privy councillor.

P.D. Ph.D. Doctor of philosophy.

P^{ce}. Prince. (F.)

Pe. Padre.

père. Father (priest). (F.)

Präs. Präsident. President. (G.)

principe. Prince. (I.)

Prins. Prince. (D.)

Prov. Provost.

Prz. Prinz. Prince. (G.)

Przssin. Prinzessin. Princess.

Q.

Q.C. Queen's Counsel.

R.

R. Reverendo. Reverend. (S.)

R. Reverencia. Reverence.

R. Rex, regina. King, Queen. (L.)

R. Real. Royal.

R.A. Rear Admiral, Royal Academician (Art).

R.E. Right Excellent, Royal Engineers.

R.S.S. Regiæ Societatis Socius. Fellow of the Royal Society. (L.)

R.W. Right Worthy, Right Worshipful.

Rect. Rector.

Reg. Prof. Regius Professor.
Ridder. Knight. (D.)
Rt. Ritter. Knight, " Sir." (G.)
Rt. Hon. Right Honorable.
Rt. Rev. Right Reverend (Bishop).
Rt. Wpful. Right Worshipful.

S.

S., San. Santo, Santa. Saint. (S.)
S., Sant'. Santo, Sante. Saint. (I.)
S. Señor. " Mr." (S.)
S. Socius. Fellow, Associate, or Member of —. (L.)
S.A. Son (sa) altesse. His (Her) Highness. (F.)
S.A. Su (sua) Alteza. His (Her) Highness. (S.)
S.A.I. Su (Sua) Alteza imperiale. His (Her) Imperial Highness. (S.)
S.A.R. Son (sa) altesse royale. His (Her) Royal Highness. (F.)
S.A.R. Su Alteza real. His Royal Highness. (S.)
S.A.R. Suo (Sua) Altezza reale. His (Her) Royal Highness. (I.)
S.C.M. Sacra Cæsarea (or Catholica) Majestas. His Imperial (or Catholic) Majesty. (L.)
S.J. Society of Jesus (Jesuits).
S.M. Su Majestad. His Majesty; **S.M.A.,** Su Majestad Apostolica, His Apostolic Majesty. (S.)
S.R.M. Su Real Majestad. His Royal Majesty. (S.)
S.R.S. Societatis Regiæ Socius Fellow of the Royal Society. (F.)
S.T.D. Sacræ Theologiæ Doctor. Doctor of Divinity. (L.)

S^a. Señora. (S.)

Sa. Señora. " Mrs." (S.)

Sen. Senator.

Serg., Serj. Sergeant, Serjeant.

Sig. Signor. " Mr." (I.)

Signora. " Mrs." (I.)

Signorina. " Miss." (I.)

Sñ., Sn., San., Saint. (S.)

Sor., Sores. Señor, señores. " Mr.," " Messrs.," or Gentlemen. (S.)

Sr., Sres. Señor, Señores. *See* above.

Sra., Sras. Señora, Señoras. Mrs., Mesdames. (S.)

Srta., S^{rta}. Señorita. Miss. (S.)

SS. AA. Sus Altezas. Their Highnesses. (S.)

SS. MM. Sus Majestades. Their Majesties. (S.)

St. Sainte. Saint. (F.)

Sta. Saint (*fem.*). (S.)

Ste. Sainte. Saint (*fem.*). (F.)

Su. *See* **S.**

Sua. *See* **S.**

T.

ten., tente. teniente. Lieutenant. (S.)

V.

V. Venerable. (S., F., Eng.)

V. Venerabilis, venerandus. Venerable. (L.)

V.A. Vice Admiral.

V.G. Vicar General.

V.P. Vice President.

V. Rev. Very Reverend.

BRIEF LIST OF IMPORTANT PLACES OF PUBLICATION AND THEIR ABBREVIATIONS

For places and forms not in this list consult Deschamps, P. C. E., *Dictionnaire de geographie ancienne et moderne*, Paris, 1870 (often sold as *Supplément au (Brunet's) Manuel du libraire et de l'amateur de livres)*; Ebert, F. A., *General bibliographical dictionary*, 4 v., Oxford, 1837; Power, John, *Handy-book about books*, London, 1870, pp. 51–63. (English places): Rogers, W. T., *Manual of bibliography*, London, 1891, pp. 168–82; Brown, J. D., *Manual of practical bibliography*, London, pp.163–72. For location and other information consult any good gazetteer such as *Lippincott's*. Only the nominative form is usually given here.

A.

A.V. Augusta Vindelicorum. Augsburg.

A(a)rhusium. Aarhus.

Aberd. Aberdeen.

Aberdonia. Aberdeen.

Aix-la-Chapelle. Aachen.

Abred., Abredea. Abredonia. Aberdeen.

Agsp. Augspurg. Augsburg.

Alatum Castrum. Edinburgh.

Alb. Albany.

Alba Bulgarica, Alba Græca. Belgrade.

Albani Villa. St. Albans.

Aldenburgum. Altenburg.

Alt., Altd. Altdorf.

Alten., Altenb. Altenburg.

Amst. Amsterdam.

Amstel. Amsteldam, Amstelodamium, Amstelæda-
mum, Amstelredamum. Amsterdam.

Amsterd. Amsterdam.

Aneda. Edinburgh.

Antuerpia. Antwerp.

Antv. Antverpia. Antwerp.

Antw. Antwerpen. Antwerp.

Aqua Bonæ. Bonn.

Aquæ-Grani. Aquis granum. Aix-la-Chapelle.

Arg., Argent. Argentina, Argentina Reni, Argento-
ratum. Strasburg.

Arhusen. Arhuzia. Aarhus.

Arn., Arnheim.

Aschaffbg. Aschaffenburg.

Athenæ Rauracæ. Basle.

Augsb. Augsburg.

Augsp., Augsperg. Augsberg.

Aug. Taur., Augusta Taurinorum. Turin.

Aug. Tib., Augusta Tiberii. Ratisbon (Regensburg).

Aug. Treb., Augusta Trebocorum. Strasburg.

Augusta Trinobantum. London.

Aug. Vind., Augusta Vindelicorum. Augsburg.

Aurelia. Orleans.

Aurelia Allobrogum. Geneva.

Avenium. Avignon.

B.

B. Boston.

Bâle. Basle (Basel).

Balt. Baltimore.

Bamb. Bamberg.

Barcel. Barcelona.

Barchino, Barcino, Barxino. Barcelona.

Bas., Basil. Basileæ. Basilea Rauracorum Basle (Basel).

Basel. Basle.

Bielef. Bielefeld.

Ber., Berl. Berlin.

Bern., Berna. Berne.

Berol., Berolin. Berolinum. Berlin.

Bip. Bipontium. Deux-Ponts, Zweibrücken.

Bisuntia. Besançon.

Bklyn. Brooklyn.

Bln. Berlin.

Bmb. Bamberg.

Bonna. Bonn.

Bon. Bononia. **Bologna.**

Bost. Boston.

Bp. Budapest.

Brangonia. Worcester.

Braunschw. Braunschweig.

Brem. Bremen.

Bresl. Bresla, Bressavia. Breslau.

Brixia. Briscia.

Brsl. Breslau.

Brno. Brünn.

Brschwg. Braunschweig.

Brns., Brs. Braunschweig.

Brugæ, Brugæ Bearniæ, Brügge. Bruges.

Brun., Bruns., Brunsw. Brunonia, Brunsviga. Brunswick.

Brüssel. Brussels.

Brux. Bruxelles, Bruxellæ. Brussels.

Bucharesci. Buchurestum, Bucharest.
Byzancium, Byzantium. Constantinople.

C.

Cadomuna. Caen.
Caesar Augusta. Zaragoza.
Camb., Cb., Cbr. Cambridge.
Camboricum, Cantabrig(i)a, Capitabriga. Cambridge.
Cantab. Cantabrig(i)a. Cambridge.
Ch., Chic. Chicago.
Chra. Christiania.
Cin. Cincinnati.
Cob. Coburg.
Cobl. Coblenz.
Codania. Copenhagen.
Col., Colon. Colonia. Cologne.
Cöln. (Cölln.). Cologne.
Colon. Ag., Colonia Agrippina. Cologne.
Colonia Allobrogum. Geneva.
Colonia Claudia. Cologne.
Colonia Julia Romana. Seville.
Colonia Munatiana. Basle.
Colonia Ubiorum. Cologne.
Copenh., Copng., Coppenh. Copenhagen.
Copenhaven. Copenhagen.
Cpl. Constantinopolis. Constantinople.

D.

Dantiscum. Danzig.
Danz. Danzig.
Darms. Darmstadium. Darmstadt.
Daventria. Deventer.

Delfi, Delphi. Delft.
Den Haag. The Hague.
Dill. Dillingen.
Divio. Dijon.
Divodurum. Metz.
Dortm. Dortmund.
Dr., Dres., Dresd. Dresda. Dresden.
Dresde. Dresden.
Dub., Dubl. Dublinum. Dublin.
Dunedin. Edinburgh.
Düsseld. Düsseldorf.

E.

Eblana. Dublin.
Ebor. Eboracum. York.
Ed., Edin., Edinb. Edinburgh.
Edinburgum, Edinum, Edinburchium. Edinburgh.
Elvetiorum Argentina. Strasburg.
Erf. Erfurt.
Erff. Erfford. (Erfurt.)
Erid. Eridanium. Milan.
Erl. Erlangen.

F.

F.a.M., Ff.a.M. Frankfurt am Main.
F.a.d.O., F.a.O., Ff.a.O., Frf.O. Frankfurt an (der)
Oder.
Fir. Firenze. Florence.
Flor. Florentia. Florence.
Francof. Francofortum. Frankfurt.
Frankf., Frankfurt a. M. Frankfurtium ad Mænum.
Frankfurt am Main.

Frankf., Frankfurt a. O. Frankfurtium ad Oderam. Frankfurt an (der) Oder.

Frf. Frankfurt.

Friberga in Misnia. Freiberg.

Friburgum Brisgoviæ. Freiburg in Brisgau.

Friburgum Helvetiorum. Fribourg in Switzerland.

G.

Ganabum. Orleans.

Gand., Ganda. Gandav(i)um. Ghent.

Gebenna, Gen., Genève. Geneva.

Genf. Geneva.

Genova, Genua. Genoa.

Gent. Ghent.

Gies., Giess. Giessen.

Gl., Glas., Glasg. Glascova, Glascua. Glasgow.

Goett. Göttingen.

Got. Gotinga.

Göt., Gött. Götting. Göttingen.

Götb. Göteborg.

's Gravenh. 's Gravenhage. The Hague.

Greifsw. Greifswald.

Gron. (Grön.) Groninga, Gröninga. Groningen.

H.

(den) Haag. The Hague.

Haarl. Haarlem.

Hafnia. Copenhagen.

Haga, Haga Comitis, Haga Comitum. The Hague.

's Hage. The Hague.

Hagen. Hagenau.

Hala. Halle.

Hall. Halle.

Hamb. Hambourg. Hamburgum. Hamburg.

Hammona. Hamburg.

Hannov. Hannover.

Hanov. Hanovia. Hanau.

Harlemum. Haarlem.

Hav. Havnia. Copenhagen.

Hdlb. Heidelberg.

Helms. Helmstadt.

Heid. Heidelberg.

Helenopolis. Frankfurt-am-Main.

Herb. Herborn.

Hispalis. Seville.

Hlmst. Helmstadt.

Hmb. Hamburg.

Holmia. Stockholm.

I.

Ie., Ien. Iena.

Iéna. Iena.

Ingolst. Ingolstadt.

Insula, Insulæ. Lille.

Ispalis. Seville.

K.

Karlsr. Karlsruhe.

Kbh., Kbhvn. Köbenhavn.

Kgsb. Königsberg.

Khvn. Köbenhavn.

Kjöb. Kjöbenhavn.

Köbenhavn. Copenhagen.

Königsb. Königsberg.

162

Köln. Cologne.
Kop., Kopenh. Kopenhagen.
Kristiania. Christiania.

L.

L. London.
L.B., LB. Lugdinum Batavorum.
Ld., Leid. Leido, Leiden. Leyden.
Leipz. Leipzig.
Lemg., Lemgau. Lemgo.
Ley. Leyden.
Liptzk., Liptzik. Leipzig.
Lisb. Lisboa, Lisbon.
Loewen. Louvain.
Lond. Londinium, Londinum, Londonia. London.
Lond. Goth. Londinum Gothorum. Lund.
Londres. London.
Lov. Lovanium. Louvain.
Lips. Lipsia. Leipzig.
Lps. Lipsia.
Lpz. Leipzig.
Lüb. Lübeck.
Lubecae. Lubicensum. Lübeck.
Lug., Lugd. Lugdinium. Lyons.
Lug. Bat., Lugd. Bat. Lugdinum Batavorum. Leyden.
Lut. Par., Lutet. Lutetia Parisorum. Paris.
Lyon. Lyons.

M.

Madr. Madritum. Madrid.
Magdeb. Magdeburg.
Mainz. Mayence.

Manh. Manheim. Mannheim.
Mannh. Mannheim.
Marb. Marburg.
Marionis. Hamburg.
Mars. Marseille. Marseilles.
Mediol. Mediolanum. Milan.
Merseb. Merseburg.
Mil. Milano. Milan.
Monachium. Munich.
Mosc. Moscovia, Moscua. Moscow.
Mosk. Moskva. Moskau. Moscow.
Mrb. Marburg.
Mün., Münch. München. Munich.

N.

N. O. New Orleans.
N. Y. New York.
Nap. Napoli. Naples.
Neap. Neapolis. Naples.
Neust. Neustadt.
Norica. Nürnberg. Nuremberg.
Norimb. Norimberga. Nuremberg.
Nov. Ebor. Novum Eboracum. New York.
Nrb. Nürnberg.
Nürnb. Nürnberg. Nuremberg.

O.

Ofen. Budapest.
Offenb. Offenbach.
Olisipo, Olysipo. Lisbon.
Ox., Oxf. Oxford.
Ox., Oxon. Oxonia, Oxonium. Oxford.

P.

P., Par. Parisius. Paris.
Padova. Padua.
Panormitum, Panormum. Palermo.
Petrop. Petropolis. St. Petersburg.
Ph., Phil., Phila., Philad. Philadelphia.
Plzna. Pilsen.
Prag. Prague.
Praha. Prague.
Ptb. Petersburg.

Q.

Qdlb. Quedlinburg.

R.

Ratis. Ratisbon.
Regensberg. Ratisbon.
Regiom. Regiomontium. Königsberg.
Reut., Reutl. Reutlingen.
Rom. Roma. Rome.
Rost. Rostock.
Roterod., Roterodamum. Rotterdam.
Rott. Rotterdam.
Rvik. Reykjavik. Reikeivik.

S.

S. F. San Francisco.
Salam. Salamanca.
Saragoss. Saragossa.
San Fran. San Francisco.
Sev. Sevilla. Seville.

165

Salzb., Slb. Salzburg.

St., Stutt. Stuttgart.

St. L. St. Louis.

St. P., St. Pet., St. Ptb. St^e Petersbourg. St. Petersburg.

Stett. Stettin.

Sth., Sthm., Stockh. Stockholm.

Strassb., Strb. Strasbourg. Strassburg.

Strals. Stralsund.

Strasb. Strasbourg. Strassburg.

Stut. Stutgardia. Stuttgart.

Stut., Stutt., Stuttg. Stuttgart.

Sulzb. Sulzbach.

T.

Taurinum. Turin.

Tig. Tigurum. Zurich.

Tor. Torino. Turin.

Traj. Rh. Trajectum (ad) Rhenum.

Triboccorum. Strasburg.

Trj. ad Rh. Trajectum ad Rhenum. Utrecht.

Trj. ad Viad. Trajectum ad Viadrum. Frankfurt-an-Oder.

Trj. Inf. Trajectum Inferius. Utrecht.

Tub., Tüb., Tübgn. Tubinga. Tübingen.

Turicum Helvetiorum, Turigum. Zurich.

U.

Ubii. Cologne.

Ultr. Ultrajectum. Utrecht.

Ulyssipo, Ulyssipolis. Lisbon.

Upps., Uppsal. Uppsala. Upsala.

Ups., Upsal. Upsala.
Utr. Utrecht.

V.

V. Venice.
Val. Valencia.
Vars. Varsavia, Varsovia. Warsaw.
Ven. Venezia, Venise. Venice.
Venedig. Venice.
Venet. Venetiæ. Venice.
Vigorina. Worcester.
Vin., Vind. Vindabona. Vienna.
Vitemb. Vitemberg. Wittenberg.
Vratisl. Vratislavia. Breslau.

W.

W., Wash. Washington.
W., Wien. Vienna.
Warsch. Warschau. Warsaw.
Warszawa. Warsaw.
Weim. Weimar.
West. Westmonasterium. Westminster.
Wiesb. Wiesbaden.
Witt., Wittenb. Wittenberg.
Wmr. Weimar.
Würzb. Würzburg.

Z.

Zena. Genoa.
Zür. Zürich. Zurich.
Zutph. Zutphen.
Zweibr. Zweibrücken, Deux-Ponts.

USEFUL REFERENCE SERIES.   NO. 14.

TECHNICAL TERMS USED IN
BIBLIOGRAPHIES AND BY THE
BOOK AND PRINTING TRADES.

TECHNICAL TERMS

USED IN

BIBLIOGRAPHIES AND BY THE BOOK AND PRINTING TRADES

BY

AXEL MOTH

(FORMING A SUPPLEMENT TO F. K. WALTER'S ABBREVIATIONS AND TECHNICAL TERMS USED IN BOOK CATALOGS AND IN BIBLIOGRAPHIES.)

BOSTON
THE BOSTON BOOK COMPANY
1915

Portions of this Compilation
have been published in The
Bulletin of Bibliography
during 1912 to 1915.

The Riverdale Press, Brookline, Mass., U.S.A.

PREFACE

The present publication forms part of a more extensive unpublished piece of work undertaken a number of years ago, and will now serve as a supplement to F. K. Walter's "Abbreviations and Technical Terms used in Book Catalogues and Bibliographies," published in Boston in 1912.

The original manuscript was planned somewhat differently, and included library terms, now published separately. Changes in the arrangement were made necessary in order to make it uniform with the work it now supplements. Terms already in Mr. Walter's work, are, with a few exceptions, omitted here.

In the compilation numerous works on bibliography, printing, and binding have been consulted, as well as periodicals relating to these subjects.

Several foreign librarians have given me their kind assistance in cases where I was unable to find the terms. Thus a number of Dutch terms were supplied by Dr. H. Greve and Mr. R. van der Meulen, Italian by Dr. Eugenio Rossi, Spanish by Mrs. Figarola Caneda, and Swedish by Dr. Isak Collijn.

Mr. F. K. Walter, who is the compiler of the Latin list, a field left untouched by me,

v

has given valuable assistance in the final preparation of the work by contributions, especially of French and German abbreviations and terms. To him and to the above mentioned librarians I hereby express my sincere thanks. Their contributions have added to what there is of value in the work. For its shortcomings I am solely responsible.

-

CONTENTS

Abbreviations Used

b. bibliography; — **bb.** bookbinding; — **bo.** book-trade; — **e.** engraving; — **pa.** paper; — *pl.* plural; — **pr.** printing; — *Stand. Dict.* Standard Dictionary of the English Language; — *Webster.* Webster's International Dictionary of the English Language.

ENGLISH

A

abstract *or* **summary** *or* **synopsis.**

Dan. Kompendium; *Du.* kort begrip, overzicht; compendium; *Fr.* abrégé; sommaire; *Ger.* Kompendium; *It.* compendio, sommario; *Sp.* compendio, resumen; *Sw.* kompendium.

acrostic.

Dan. Navnedigt, Akrostichon; *Du.* naamdicht; *Fr.* acrostiche; *Ger.* Namengedicht; ·*It.* acrostico; *Sp.* poema acróstico; *Sw.* namndikt, akrostikon.

act. Part of a play.

Dan. Akt; *Du.* bedrijf; *Fr.* acte; *Ger.* Aufzug; *It.* atto; *Sp.* acto; *Sw.* akt.

advance sheets *or* **early copies.** (bo.) Sample sheets of a book, issued in advance as an advertisement.

Dan. Udhængsark; *Du.* schoone bladen; *Fr.* bonnes feuilles, feuilles d'auteur; *Ger.* Aushängebogen; *It.* fogli impaginati; *Sp.* hojas de autor; *Sw.* rentryckt ark.

advertisement.

Dan. Avertissement; *Du.* advertentie, aankondiging; *Fr.* annonce; *Ger.* Inserat, Anzeige, Annonce; *It.* annunzio; *Sp.* aviso; *Sw.* annons.

all published *or* **no more published. (b.)**

Dan. mere udkom ikke; *Du.* alles wat verscheen; *Fr.* tout ce qui a paru; *Ger.* soweit erschienen; *It.* fin qui; non si é pubblicato altro; *Sp.* todo publicado; *Sw.* allt utgifvet.

alliteration. The repetition of the same letter at the beginning of two or more words immediately succeeding each other, or at short intervals. *Webster.*

Dan. Bogstavrim; *Du.* stafrijm; *Fr.* allitération; *Ger.* Stabreim; *It.* alliterazione; *Sp.* aliteración; *Sw.* stafrim, alliteration.

also under the title. (b.)

Dan. ogsaa med Titel; *Du.* ook onder den titel; *Fr.* aussi sous le titre; *Ger.* auch unter dem Titel; *It.* anche sotto il titolo; *Sp.* también con el título; *Sw.* också med titel, äfven med titel.

annotation. A remark, note or commentary on some passage of a book, intended to illustrate its meaning. *Webster.*

Dan. Anmærkning; *Du.* aanteekening; *Fr.* annotation; *Ger.* Anmerkung; *It.* annotazione; *Sp.* anotación; *Sw.* anmärkning.

annotator *or* **commentator.**

Dan. Kommentator, Fortolker; *Du.* aanteekenaar; *Fr.* annotateur, commentateur; *Ger.* Erläuterer, Kommentator; *It.* annotatore, commentatore; *Sp.* anotador. comentador; *Sw.* anmärkare, utläggare, kommentator.

2

annual *or* **yearly.**

Dan. aarlig; *Du.* jaarlijksch; *Fr.* annuel;
Ger. jährlich; *It.* annuale; *Sp.* anual;
Sw. årlig.

annual report. *See* **report, annual.**

appendix *or* **supplement.**

Dan. Bilag, Tillæg, Supplement; *Du.*
aanhangsel, bijvoegsel; *Fr.* appendice,
supplément; *Ger.* Anhang, Beilage, Er-
gänzung, Nachtrag; *It.* appendice, sup-
plemento; *Sp.* apendice, suplemento;
Sw. bihang, supplement, tillägg.

approval, on. (bo.)

Dan. til Eftersyn; *Du.* op zicht, zichtzending; *Fr.* à l'examen; sous condition;
Ger. zur Ansicht, Ansichtssendung; *It.*
sotto condizione; *Sp.* condicionalmente,
en comisión; *Sw.* till påseende, till
benäget påseende.

art of printing.

Dan. Bogtrykkerkunst; *Du.* boekdruk-
kunst; *Fr.* art typographique; *Ger.*
Buchdruckerkunst; *It.* arte dello stampare; *Sp.* arte de la imprenta; *Sw.* boktryckarkonst.

at the author's expense *or* **privately printed.
(bo.)**

Dan. paa eget Forlag, trykt som Manuskript; *Du.* voor rekening van den schrijver, privaat uitgaaf; *Fr.* aux frais de
l'auteur; *Ger.* Selbstverlag des Verfas-
sers, Privatdruck; *It.* a spese dell'
autore; *Sp.* por cuenta del autor; *Sw.*
på eget förlag.

auction. *See* **book auction.**
author.
> *Dan.* Forfatter; *Du.* auteur, schrijver;
> *Fr.* auteur; *Ger.* Verfasser, Schrift-
> steller; *It.* autore; *Sp.* autor; *Sw.* för-
> fattare.

author's expense, at the. *See* **at the author's**
expense.
awarded a prize.
> *Dan.* prisbelönnet, *Du.* bekroond; *Fr.*
> couronné; *Ger.* gekrönt; *It.* premiato;
> *Sp.* premiado; *Sw.* prisbelönt.

B

back, to. (bb.) To prepare the back of a book
with glue, etc. *Webster.*
> *Dan.* sætte Ryg i en Bog; *Du.* den rug
> van een boek maken; *Fr.* endosser;
> *Ger.* mit Rücken versehen; *It.* indossare;
> *Sp.* enlomar; *Sw.* förse med rygg.

back of a book. (bb.)
> *Dan.* Bogryg; *Du.* rug van een boek; *Fr.*
> dos d'un livre; *Ger.* Rücken eines Buches;
> *It.* dorso; costola, schiena; *Sp.* lomo de
> un libro; *Sw.* bokrygg.

back, loose. (bb.)
> *Dan.* lös Ryg; *Du.* losse rug, vrije rug;
> *Fr.* dos brisé, dos souple, reliure à l'alle-
> mande; *Ger.* loser Rücken; *It.* legatura
> flessibile; *Sp.* lomo hueco; *Sw.* lös rygg.

back, spring. (bb.)
> *Dan.* Knepryg; *Du.* veerende rug; *Fr.*
> dos à ressort; *Ger.* Sprungrücken; *It.*

dorso a scatto; *Sp.* lomo de resorte; *Sw.* fjäderrygg.

back, tight. (bb.)

Dan. fast Ryg; *Du.* vaste rug; *Fr.* dos rigide, dos adhèrent, dos ferme; *Ger.* fester Rücken; *It.* dorso rigido; *Sp.* lomo rígido; *Sw.* fast rygg.

backing. (bb.) Preparing of the back of a book with glue, etc. *Webster.*

Dan. Bogrygs Tildannelse; *Du.* het maken van den rug; *Fr.* endossure; *Ger.* Rückenbildung; *It.* indossatura; *Sp.* enlomado; *Sw.* bokryggs förfärdigande.

bands, raised. (bb.) The cords upon which the sheets of a volume are sewn. If the cords are not imbedded in the back of the sheets and thus show as ridges, they are called raised bands.

Dan. ophöjede Bind; *Du.* ribbenband; *Fr.* nerfs, nervures; *Ger.* erhabene Bünde; *It.* correggiuole; *Sp.* nervios; *Sw.* upphöjda bind, höga bind.

bastard-title *or* **half-title** *or* **fly-title.** **(b.)** A short title-page preceding the regular full title-page. *Webster.*

Dan. Smudstitel, Halvtitel; *Du.* Fransche titel, voor-de-handsche titel; *Fr.* fauxtitre; *Ger.* Schmutztitel, Vorsatztitel; *It.* titolo falso, frontispizio falso, frontispizio morto, occhietto; *Sp.* falso frontis, falsa portada; *Sw.* smutstitel.

battered letter. (pr.) *See* **letter, battered.**

Bible.
> *Dan.* Bibel; *Du.* Bijbel; *Fr.* Bible; *Ger.* Bibel; *It.* Bibbia; *Sp.* Biblia; *Sw.* Bibel.

bibliomaniac.
> *Dan.* Biblioman; *Du.* bibliomaan; boekengek; *Fr.* bibliomane; *Ger.* Biblioman, Büchernarr; *It.* bibliómano; *Sp.* bibliomano; *Sw.* biblioman.

bibliophile.
> *Dan.* Bogelsker; *Du.* boekenliefhebber; *Fr.* bibliophile; *Ger.* Bücherfreund; *It.* bibliôfilo; *Sp.* bibliofilo; *Sw.* bibliofil.

bid on a book.
> *Dan.* byde paa en Bog; *Du.* bieden op een boek; *Fr.* mettre une enchère sur un livre; *Ger.* für ein Buch offeriren; *It.* incantare su di un libro; *Sp.* ofrecer en un libro; *Sw.* bjuda på en bok.

bi-monthly. Occurring once in two months. *Webster.*
> *Dan.* hver anden Maaned; *Du.* tweemaandelijksch; *Fr.* paraissant tous les deux mois; *Ger.* zweimonatlich; *It.* bimestrale; *Sp.* bimestral; *Sw.* hvar annan månad.

bind, to. (bb.)
> *Dan.* indbinde; *Du.* inbinden; *Fr.* relier; *Ger.* einbinden; *It.* legare; *Sp.* encuadernar; *Sw.* binda in.

binder *or* **bookbinder.**
> *Dan.* Bogbinder; *Du.* boekbinder; *Fr.* relieur; *Ger.* Buchbinder; *It.* legatore

6

di libri; *Sp.* encuadernador; *Sw.* bokbindare.

binder's title.

> *Dan.* Rygtitel; *Du.* boekbinderstitel, rug-
> titel; *Fr.* titre du relieur; *Ger.* Rücken-
> titel; *It.* titolo del legatore; *Sp.* título
> del encuadernador; *Sw.* ryggtitel.

bindery *or* **bookbinder shop.**

> *Dan.* Bogbinderi; *Du.* boekbinderij; *Fr.*
> atelier de relieur; *Ger.* Buchbinderei;
> *It.* legatoria; *Sp.* taller de encuaderna-
> ción; *Sw.* bokbinderi.

binding.

> *Dan.* Indbinding; *Du.* band; *Fr.* reliure;
> *Ger.* Einband; *It.* legatura; *Sp.* encua-
> dernación; *Sw.* inbindning.

binding, worn.

> *Dan.* slidt Bind; *Du.* versleten band; *Fr.*
> reliure fatiguée; *Ger.* abgenützter Ein-
> band; *It.* legatura logora; *Sp.* encuader-
> nación muy usada; *Sw.* sliten inbind-
> ning.

binding in boards. *See* **boards, in.**

black letter. (pr.) The old English or modern
Gothic letter in which the early English books were printed.

> *Dan.* gammelt engelsk Frakturbogstav;
> *Du.* Duitsche letter; *Fr.* lettre de forme,
> lettre flamande; *Ger.* altenglischer Buch-
> stabe; *It.* carattere gotico; *Sp.* letra
> de tortis; *Sw.* gammal engelsk frak-
> turstil.

blacks. (pr.) A space, quadrat or piece of furniture which rises and is imprinted on the sheet.

Dan. Spis; *Du.* zwarte vlekken; *Fr.* espace montée à l'impression; *Ger.* Spiess; *It.* spazî; *Sw.* spis.

blank book. *See* **book, blank.**

bleed, to. (bb.) To cut into the printed part of a book in trimming. *Stand. Dict.*

Dan. skære en Bog ned saa meget at Teksten lider; *Du.* afsnijden met tekstverminking; *Ger.* mit Textverlust beschneiden; *It.* smarginare; *Sp.* cortar de modo que sufra lo impreso; *Sw.* skära i stil.

blind blocking. *See* **blind tooling.**

blind tooling *or* **blind blocking. (bb.)**

Dan. Blindtryk; *Du.* blinddruk op banden; *Fr.* fers à froid, ornements à froid; *Ger.* Blindpressung, Blinddruck; *It.* ornamenti a secco; *Sp.* estampadura en seco; *Sw.* blindtryck.

block-book. (b.) A book printed from engraved blocks of wood. *Webster.*

Dan. Blokbog; *Du.* houtblokdruk; *Fr.* livre xylographique; *Ger.* Holztafeldruck, Blockbuch; *It.* libro xilografico; *Sp.* libro xilogrâfico; *Sw.* blockbok.

blotting paper.

Dan. Klatpapir, Trækpapir; *Du.* vloeipapier; *Fr.* papier buvard; *Ger.* Löschpapier; *It.* carta sugante, carta asciugante; *Sp.* papel secante; *Sw.* läskpapper.

boards. (bb.) Pasteboard sides for a book cover. *Webster.*

Dan. Pappermer; *Du.* kartonnenband; *Fr.* plats de carton; *Ger.* Pappdeckel; *It.* piatti in cartone; *Sp.* tapas de cartón; *Sw.* papp-pärmar.

boards, in. (bb.) A book with pasteboard covers.

Dan. stifthæftet; *Du.* gecartonneerd; *Fr.* cartonné; *Ger.* kartonniert, steif-broschiert; *It.* incartonato, cartonato; *Sp.* encartonado; *Sw.* styfhäftad, kartonnerad.

boards, wooden. (bb.)

Dan. Træbogpermer; *Du.* houtband; *Fr.* plats de bois; *Ger.* Holzdeckel; *It.* piatti in legno; *Sp.* tapas de madera; *Sw.* träpärmar.

bodkin, (pr.) A sharp pointed instrument for picking type from a form in correcting. *Stand. Dict.*

Dan. Aal; *Du.* correctie-els; *Fr.* pointe; *Ger.* Ahle; *It.* lesina; *Sp.* punzón, punta; *Sw.* ål.

body type. (pr.) The type ordinarily used.

Dan. Brödskrift, Værkskrift; *Du.* broodletters; *Fr.* caractères ordinaires; *Ger.* Brotschriften; *It.* tipi comuni; *Sp.* letra usual; *Sw.* vanlig tryckstil.

bold faced type. *See* **type, bold faced.**

book.

Dan. Bog; *Du.* boek; *Fr.* livre; *Ger.* Buch; *It.* libro; *Sp.* libro; *Sw.* bok.

book, blank.

Dan. ubeskrevet Bog, Skrivebog; *Du.* onbeschreven boek; *Fr.*l ivre blanc; *Ger.* unbeschriebenes Buch; *It.* falso volume, libro bianco; *Sp.* libro en blanco; *Sw.* skrifbok.

book, secondhand.

Dan. brugt Bog; *Du.* tweedehandsch boek; *Fr.* livre d'occasion; *Ger.* antiquarisches Buch; *It.* libro d'occasione; *Sp.* libro de segunda mario; libro de ocasión, libro de lance; *Sw.* använd bok.

book of hours. A Roman Catholic prayer-book containing prayers to be repeated at stated times of the day. *Webster.*

Dan. Tidebog; *Du.* getijdenboek, getij-boek; *Fr.* livre d'heures, paire d'heures, heures; *Ger.* Stundengebete; *It.* libro delle ore; *Sp.* libro de horas; *Sw.* horarium.

book in quires. *See* **book in sheets.**

book in sheets *or* **book in quires.** (bo.) A book not folded or bound. *Amer. Dict. of Pr.*

Dan. Bog i Materie; *Du.* boek in losse bladen; *Fr.* livre en feuilles; *Ger.* rohes Exemplar; *It.* libro in fogli; *Sp.* libro en rama; *Sw.* bok i exemplar, ohäftad bok.

book-auction.

Dan. Bogauktion; *Du.* openbare boek-verkooping, boekenveiling; *Fr.* vente publique de livres; *Ger.* Bücher-Ver-steigerung; *It.* asta libraria, vendita di

libri all' asta; *Sp.* remate de libros, sub-
asta de libros; *Sw.* bokauktion.

bookbinder. *See* **binder.**

bookbinder shop. *See* **bindery.**

book collector.

Dan. Bogsamler; *Du.* boekenverzamelaar;
Fr. collectionneur de livres; *Ger.* Büchersammler; *It.* amatore di libri, collettore
di libri; *Sp.* colector de libros; *Sw.*
boksamlare.

book-compositor. (pr.)

Dan. Værksætter; *Du.* boekzetter; *Fr.*
compositeur de livre; *Ger.* Werksetzer;
It. compositore; *Sp.* cajista de libros.

book-cover. *See* **cover.**

bookdealer. *See* **bookseller.**

book-fair.

Dan. Boghandlermesse; *Du.* boekhandel-
kermes; *Fr.* foire de librairie; *Ger.* Buchhändlermesse; *It.* fiera di libri; *Sp.*
feria de libros; *Sw.* bokhandlaremessa.

book-mark. Any object, as a ribbon, to be
placed between or on the leaves of a
book to mark a place for ready reference.
Stand. Dict.

Dan. Bogmærke; *Du.* boekenlegger,
leeswijzer; *Fr.* signet; *Ger.* Buchzeichen,
Zeichenbändchen; *It.* segno; *Sp.* marcador; *Sw.* bokmärke.

bookplate *or* **ex-libris.** An engraved label,
placed on or in a book to indicate
ownership or proper place in a library.
Stand. Dict.

Dan. Bogplade; *Du.* boekmerk, boekmerkteeken; *Fr.* ex libris; *Ger.* Bücherzeichen, ex libris; *It.* ex libris; *Sp.* ex libris; *Sw.* bokägarmärke.

bookseller *or* **bookdealer.**
Dan. Boghandler; *Du.* boekhandelaar; *Fr.* libraire; *Gr.* Buchhändler; *It.* libraio; *Sp.* librero; *Sw.* bokhandlare.

bookseller, secondhand.
Dan. Antikvarboghandler; *Du.* tweedehands boekhandelaar; *Fr.* bouquiniste, antiquaire; *Ger.* Antiquar, Büchertrödler; *It.* venditore di libri vecchi; *Sp.* vendedor de libros usados; *Sw.* antikvarbokhandlare.

bookseller-catalogue.
Dan. Boghandlerkatalog; *Du.* boekhandelaarscatalogus; *Fr.* catalogue de librairie; *Ger.* Buchhändlerkatalog; *It.* catalogo di libraio; *Sp.* catálogo de librero; *Sw.* bokhandlarekatalog.

bookstore.
Dan. Boghandel, Boglade; *Du.* boekwinkel; *Fr.* librairie; *Ger.* Buchhandlung, Buchladen; *It.* libreria; *Sp.* librería; *Sw.* bokhandel, boklåda.

booktrade.
Dan. Boghandel; *Du.* boekhandel; *Fr.* commerce de livres; *Ger.* Buchhandlung, Buchhandel; *It.* commercio di libri; *Sp.* comercio de libros; *Sw.* bokhandel.

book-work. (pr.) Work on books and pamphlets, as distinguished from job-work or newspaper work. *Stand. Dict.*

Dan. Bogtryk, Værkarbejd; *Du.* boekwerk; *Fr.* composition de livre; *Ger.* Werksatz; *It.* composizione di libri; *Sp.* composición de libros; *Sw.* boktryck.

bookworm. The larva of an insect destructive to books. *Stand. Dict.*

Dan. Bogorm; *Du.* boekworm; *Fr.* ptilin; *Ger.* Bücherwurm; *It.* tarlo, tignuola; *Sp.* polilla que roe los libros; *Sw.* bokmal.

border *or* **margin.**

Dan. Rand, Margen; *Du.* rand; *Fr.* marge; *Ger.* Rand; *It.* margine; *Sp.* margen, orilla; *Sw.* rand.

border, mourning. *See* **mourning border.**

bosses. Protuberant metal ornaments on the boards of a book.

Dan. Metalbeslag; *Du.* metaalbeslag; *Fr.* ferrures; *Ger.* Metallbeschläge; *It.* ferratura sulla legatura; *Sp.* ornamentos metálicos en los costados de la pasta para resguardarla; *Sw.* metallbeslag.

bottom of a page. The blank space at the foot of a page.

Dan. Underslag; *Du.* voet van een bladzijde; *Fr.* bas d'une page; *Ger.* Unterschlag; *It.* calce; *Sp.* pie de una página; *Sw.* underslag.

bottom-line. Last line on the page, preceding the direction-line.

Dan. Slutningslinie; *Du.* slotregel; *Fr.* ligne inférieure; *Ger.* Schlusslinie, Grundlinie; *It.* linea di fondo; *Sp.* ₊línea del pie de la página; *Sw.* slutrad.

bound.

Dan. indbunden; *Du.* gebonden; *Fr.* relié; *Ger.* eingebunden; *It.* legato; *Sp.* encuadernado; *Sw.* inbunden.

box in, to. (pr.) To place rules around a page.

Dan. indramme med Linier; *Du.* omlijs- ten; *Fr.* encadrer avec des filets; *Ger.* einrahmen mit Linien; *It.* incorniciare, inquadrare; *Sp.* encuadrar con reglas, orlar; *Sw.* inrama med linjer.

brackets *or* **squares.** [ ]

Dan. Klammer; *Du.* haken; *Fr.* crochets carrés; *Ger.* eckige Klammer; *It.* paren- tesi quadre; *Sp.* paréntesis angulares, corchetes; *Sw.* klammer, vinkelparentes.

broadside. A sheet of paper printed on one side only.

Dan. Etbladstryk; *Du.* éénblad-druk; *Fr.* feuille de papier imprimée d'un seul côté; *Ger.* Einblattdruck; *It.* foglio di carta stampato solamente da una parte; *Sp.* hoja suelta impresa en una sola cara; *Sw.* ettbladstryck.

brushproof.

Dan. Börsteaftræk; *Du.* proefblad met den borstel getrokken; *Fr.* épreuve à la brosse; *Ger.* Bürstenabzug, Abklatsch; *It.* bozza col rullo; *Sp.* prueba sacada con escobilla.

14

C

calendering. (pa.) Making paper smooth and glossy. *Webster.*

Dan. Glitning; *Du.* satineering; *Fr.* satinage; *Ger.* Satinieren; *It.* satinatura; *Sp.* satinación; *Sw.* satinering.

calf leather.

Dan. Kalveskind; *Du.* kalfsleer; *Fr.* peau de veau; *Ger.* Kalbleder; *It.* vitello; *Sp.* becerrillo, vitela; *Sw.* kalfskinn.

calico.

Dan. Kaliko, Bogbinderlærred; *Du.* katoen; *Fr.* percaline, calicot; *Ger.* Kaliko, Perkal; *It.* percallina; *Sp.* percal, percalina; *Sw.* kalikå.

cancel. A leaf or part of any printed matter or work suppressed or stricken out, also any printed matter substituted for that stricken out.

Dan. omtrykt Blad; *Du.* verbeterblad; *Fr.* feuillet refait, carton refait, défet; *Ger.* Auswechselblatt, Answurfbogen, Karton, Umdruckblatt; *It.* foglietto ristampato a cagione di qualche errore; *Sp.* cartön, cuartilla; *Sw.* kartong.

canceled. (e.) crossed out or obliterated.

Dan. overströget; *Du.* doorgeschrapt; *Fr.* biffé; *Ger.* durchgestrichen; *It.* biffato; *Sp.* borrado; *Sw.* utstruket.

capital letter. *See* **letter, capital.**

15

capitals, small. (pr.) Letters made in imitation of capitals, but of smaller size. *Stand. Dict.*

Dan. Kapitelker, smaa Kapitaler; *Du.* kleine kapitalen; *Fr.* petites capitales; *Ger.* Kapitälchen; *It.* maiuscoletti; *Sp.* versalitas; *Sw.* kapitäler.

case.

Dan. Foderal; *Du.* foedraal; *Fr.* étui; *Ger.* Futteral; *It.* custodia, busta; *Sp.* caja; *Sw.* fodral.

catchword. The word placed at the bottom of each page, under the last line, which is to be printed as the first word on the following page. *Webster.*

Dan. Kustos; *Du.* bladwachter, custode; *Fr.* réclame; *Ger.* Kustode, Eckwortkustode, Blattweiser, Blatthüter; *It.* richiamo; *Sp.* reclamo; *Sw.* kustod.

cento. A composition formed by verses or passages from different authors, arranged in a new order. *Webster.*

Dan. Flikkeværk; *Du.* dichtstuk samengesteld uit de werken van andere dichters; *Fr.* centon; *Ger.* Flickgedicht; *It.* centone; *Sp.* centón; *Sw.* dikt sammanplockad af verser från flere författare.

chapbook. A small book carried about for sale by hawkers. *Webster.*

Dan. Flyveskrift solgt of Kolportörer; *Du.* vlugschrift; *Fr.* brochure vendue par des colporteurs; *Ger.* kolportierte

Flugschrift; *Sp.* folleto vendido por un pacotillero; *Sw.* utkolporterad flyg-skrift.

chapter.

Dan. Kapitel; *Du.* hoofdstuk; *Fr.* chapitre; *Ger.* Kapitel; *It.* capitolo; *Sp.* capítulo; *Sw.* kapitel.

character. *See* **letter.**

chase. (pr.) An iron frame used by printers to confine types when set in columns or pages. *Webster.*

Dan. Formramme; *Du.* vormraam; *Fr.* châssis d'imprimerie; *Ger.* Rahmen; *It.* telaio di stamperia; *Sp.* rama; *Sw.* formram.

cheap edition. *See* **edition, cheap.**

chiaroscuro. (e.) A method of printing engravings, usually wood-engravings, from blocks representing lighter and darker shades, used especially in the 15th and 16th centuries.

Dan. Halvskyggetryk; *Du.* clair-obscuur; *Fr.* impression clair-obscure; *Ger.* Hell-dunkeldruck; *It.* stampa a chiaro-scuro; *Sp.* claroscuro; *Sw.* klärobskyr tryck.

clasp. A small hook to hold together the covers of a book. *Webster.*

Dan. Hægte; *Du.* klamp; *Fr.* fermoir; *Ger.* Schloss, Schliesse; *It.* borchia, fermaglio; *Sp.* broche para cerrar un libro; *Sw.* knäppe.

close matter. (pr.) *See* **matter, close.**

cloth. (bb.)
> *Dan.* Shirting; *Du.* linnen; *Fr.* toile; *Ger.* Leinwand; *It.* tela; *Sp.* tela; *Sw.* klot, linne.

coat of arms. Originally a surcoat charged with heraldic devices, hence the armorial bearings of a person. *Stand. Dict.*
> *Dan.* Vaabenskjold; *Du.* wapenschild; *Fr.* blason, armes; *Ger.* Wappen; *It.* stemma; *Sp.* escudo de armas, escudete; *Sw.* vapenskjöld.

collected works. *See* **works, collected.**

collection.
> *Dan.* Samling; *Du.* verzameling, collectie; *Fr.* collection; *Fr.* recueil, collection; *Ger.* Sammlung; *It.* raccolta; *Sp.* colección; *Sw.* samling.

collective title. *See* **title, collective.**

colon.
> *Dan.* Kolon; *Du.* dubbelpunt; *Fr.* deux points; *Ger.* Kolon, Doppelpunkt; *It.* due punti; *Sp.* colon; *Sw.* kolon.

colophon. An inscription at the end of a book containing the place and year of publication, the printer's name, etc. A colophon is found only in early printed books.
> *Dan.* Kolofon; *Du.* slotschrift; *Fr.* souscription, colophon; *Ger.* Endschrift, Schlusschrift, Explicit, Rubrum, Kolophon; *It.* sottoscrizione; *Sp.* colofón; *Sw.* kolofon.

colored.

Dan. koloreret, kulört; *Du.* gekleurd; *Fr.* enluminé, en couleurs; *Ger.* koloriert, in Farben; *It.* miniato; *Sp.* miniado; *Sw.* färgad, kulört.

colored work *or* **polychromy.**

Dan. Farvetryk; *Du.* kleurendruk; *Fr.* impression en couleurs; *Ger.* Mehrfarbendruck; *It.* stampa a colori; *Sp.* estampa en colores; *Sw.* färgtryck.

column. (pr.) One of two or more vertical series of lines, separated by a rule or blank space. *Stand. Dict.*

Dan. Spalte; *Du.* kolom; *Fr.* colonne; *Ger.* Spalte, Kolonne; *It.* colonna; *Sp.* columna; *Sw.* spalt.

column rule. (pr.) A thin brass strip, type-high, used to mark the division of columns. *Stand. Dict.*

Dan. Spaltelinie; *Du.* streep tusschen twee kolommen; *Fr.* colombelle, filet de milieu; *Ger.* Spaltenlinie; *It.* riga di colonna; *Sp.* raya de columna, corondel; *Sw.* spaltlinje.

combed edges. *See* **edges, combed.**

comma.

Dan. Komma; *Du.* Komma; *Fr.* virgule; *Ger.* Komma; *It.* virgola; *Sp.* coma; *Sw.* komma.

commence even *or* **flush. (pr.)**

Dan. begynde uden Indrykning; *Du.* zonder inspringen beginnen; *Fr.* commencer sans renfoncement; *Ger.* stumpf anfangen; *It.* cominciare in riga, cominciare senza capoverso; *Sp.* comenzar igual; *Sw.* börja utan indrag.

commentator. *See* **annotator.**

compilation.
Dan. Kompilation, Samling; *Du.* compilatie; *Fr.* compilation; *Ger.* Sammlung; *It.* compilamento, compilazione; *Sp.* compilación; *Sw.* kompilation, samling.

compiler.
Dan. Samler, Kompilator; *Du.* verzamelaar; *Fr.* compilateur; *Ger.* Sammler; *It.* compilatore; *Sp.* compilador; *Sw.* kompilator, samlare.

complete.
Dan. komplet; *Du.* compleet; *Fr.* complet; *Ger.* vollständig; *It.* compiuto, perfetto; *Sp.* completo, perfecto; *Sw.* komplett.

complete edition.
Dan. fuldstændig Udgave; *Du.* volledige uitgaaf; *Fr.* édition des oeuvres complètes; *Ger.* Gesamtausgabe; *It.* opere complete, corpo; *Sp.* edición de obras completas; *Sw.* fullständig upplaga.

compose, to. (pr.) To set types or characters in a composing stick, arranging the letters in the proper order.
Dan. sætte; *Du.* zetten; *Fr.* composer; *Ger.* setzen; *It.* comporre; *Sp.* componer; *Sw.* sätta.

composing board *or* **letter board. (pr.)**

Dan. Sættebrædt; *Du.* letterplank,. zetplank der letterzetters; *Fr.* composoir;
Ger. Setzbrett; *It.* bancone; *Sp.* anaquel para tipos; *Sw.* sättbräde.

composing machine *or* **typesetting machine.
(pr.)**

Dan. Sættemaskine; *Du.* zetmachine;
Fr. machine à composer; *Ger.* Setzmaschine; *It.* macchina a comporre; *Sp.*
máquina para componer las letras; *Sw.*
sättmaskin.

composing rule *or* **setting rule. (pr.)** A thin
piece of type-high brass or steel rule,
cut to a required measure, but with a
beak left at one or both of the upper
corners. Used in setting and handling
type. *Stand. Dict.*

Dan. Sættelinie; *Du.* zetlijn; *Fr.* réglette;
Ger. Setzlinie; *It.* filetto; *Sp.* regleta;
Sw. sättlinje.

composing stick, (pr.) A tray or receptacle,
capable of adjustment, so as to vary
the length of a line as required, which
the compositor holds in his left hand, and
in which he arranges in words and lines
the type that he takes from the cases.
Stand. Dict.

Dan. Vinkelhage; *Du.* zethaak, winkelhaak; *Fr.* composteur; *Ger.* Winkelhaken; *It.* compositoio; *Sp.* componedor; *Sw.* vinkelhake.

21

composition, interlined *or* **leaded matter.** (pr.) Composition with leads between the lines.

Dan. skudt Sats; *Du.* zetsel met interlinies; *Fr.* composition interlignée; *Ger.* durchschossener Satz; *It.* composizione interlineata; *Sp.* composición regleteada *Sw.* mellanslagen sats.

composition, spaced. (pr.)

Dan. spærret Sats; *Du.* gespatieerd zetsel; *Fr.* composition espacée; *Ger.* gesperrter Satz, splendider Satz; *It.* composizione spazieggiata; *Sp.* composición espaciada; *Sw.* spärrad sats.

compositor. (pr.) One who sets type.

Dan. Sætter; *Du.* letterzetter; *Fr.* compositeur; *Ger.* Setzer; *It.* compositore; *Sp.* cajista; *Sw.* sättare.

condition, in good. (bo.)

Dan. i god Tilstand; *Du.* in goeden toestand; *Fr.* en bon état; *Ger.* in gutem Zustand; *It.* in buono stato; *Sp.* en buen estado, bien conservado; *Sw.* i godt stånd.

consecutive numbering of pages *or* **continuous pagination.**

Dan. fortlöbende Paginering; *Du.* doorloopende paginatuur; *Fr.* pagination continue; *Ger.* fortlaufende Numerierung; *It.* paginatura continua; *Sp.* paginación ·continua; *Sw.* fortlöpande paginering.

contents.

Dan. Indhold; *Du.* inhoud; *Fr.* contenu, matières; *Ger.* Inhalt; *It.* contenuto; *Sp.* contenido; *Sw.* innehåll.

context.

Dan. Sammenhæng; *Du.* samenhang; *Fr.* contexte; *Ger.* Zusammenhang; *It.* contesto; *Sp.* contexto; *Sw.* sammanhang.

continued, to be.

Dan. fortsat, Fortsættelse fölger; *Du.* wordt vervolgd; *Fr.* à suivre; *Ger.* Fortsetzung folgt; *It.* continua; *Sp.* continuará; *Sw.* fortsatt, fortsättning följer.

continuous pagination. *See* **consecutive numbering of pages.**

copper-engraving. *See* **copperplate-engraving.**

copper-plate engraving. (e.) An impression from an engraved copper-plate. *Stand. Dict.*

Dan. Kobberstik; *Du.* kopergravure; *Fr.* gravure en taille douce; *Ger.* Kupferstich; *It.* incisione in rame; *Sp.* grabado en cobre; *Sw.* kopparstick.

copy. Duplicate of a manuscript.

Dan. Genpart, Kopi; *Du.* kopij; *Fr.* copie; *Ger.* Kopie, Abschrift, Duplikat; *It.* copia; *Sp.* copia; *Sw.* kopia.

copy. A single book or a set of books. *Stand. Dict.*

Dan. Eksemplar; *Du.* exemplaar; *Fr.* exemplaire; *Ger.* Exemplar: *It.* esemplare; *Sp.* ejemplar; *Sw.* exemplar.

copy, fine. (bo.)

Dan. smukt Eksemplar; *Du.* schoon exemplaar; *Fr.* bel exemplaire; *Ger.* schönes Exemplar; *It.* bell' esemplare; *Sp.* ejemplar hermoso; *Sw.* felfritt exemplar.

copyright. The exclusive right secured by law to authors to publish and dispose of their works for a limited time. *Stand. Dict.*

Dan. Forlagsret; *Du.* kopijrecht, auteursrecht; *Fr.* droit d'impression, droits d'auteur; *Ger.* Verlagsrecht; *It.* proprietà letteraria; *Sp.* propiedad de una obra literaria, derechos de autor; *Sw.* förlagsrätt.

corner of a book.

Dan. Hjörnet af en Bog; *Du.* hoek van een boek; *Fr.* coin d'un livre; *Ger.* Ecke eines Buches; *It.* angolo di un libro, punta, cantone; *Sp.* cantonera; *Sw.* hörn af en bok.

correspondence.

Dan. Brevveksling; *Du.* briefwisseling, correspondentie; *Fr.* correspondance; *Ger.* Briefwechsel, Korrespondenz; *It.* carteggio; *Sp.* correspondencia; *Sw.* brefvexling.

cotton paper.

Dan. Bomuldspapir; *Du.* boomwolpapier; *Fr.* papier de coton; *Ger.* Baumwollpapier; *It.* carta bambagina; *Sp.* papel de algodón; *Sw.* bomullspapper.

cover. (bb.)
> *Dan.* Omslag; *Du.* omslag; *Fr.* couverture;
> *Ger.* Umschlag, Deckel; *It.* copertina;
> *Sp.* cubierta; *Sw.* omslag.

cover, publisher's. (bb.)
> *Dan.* Originalomslag; *Du.* oorspronkelijk
> omslag; *Fr.* couverture originale; *Ger.*
> Originalumschlag; *It.* copertina origi-
> nale; *Sp.* cubierta original; *Sw.* original-
> omslag.

cropped. Trimmed close to the print. *Stand. Dict.*
> *Dan.* stærkt beskaaret; *Du.* kort afge-
> sneden; *Fr.* découpé, trop rogné; *Ger.*
> stark beschnitten; *It.* smarginato; *Sp.*
> muy recortado; *Sw.* kort afskuren.

cul de lampe. *See* **tail-piece.**

cuneiform characters. Wedge-shaped characters used by the ancient Assyrians
and Babylonians. *Stand. Dict.*
> *Dan.* Kileskrift; *Du.* spijkerschrift; *Fr.*
> écriture cunéiforme; *Ger.* Keilschrift;
> *It.* caratteri cuneiformi; *Sp.* carácteres
> cuneiformes; *Sw.* kilskrift.

cursive characters. *See* **Italics.**

cut. *See* **engraving.**

cut down. (bb.)
> *Dan.* beskaaret; *Du.* gesnoeid; *Fr.* rogné;
> *Ger.* beschnitten; *It.* raffilato; *Sp.* recor-
> tado; *Sw.* afskuren.

D

dagger *or* **obelisk. (pr.)** A reference mark
[†], so named from its form.

Dan. Obelisk, Daggert, Kors; *Du.* kruisje; *Fr.* croix; *Ger.* Kreuz; *It.* crocétta; *Sp.* cruz; *Sw.* kors.

daily.
Dan. daglig; *Du.* dagelijksch; *Fr.* quotidien; *Ger.* täglich; *It.* quotidiano; *Sp.* cotidiano; *Sw.* daglig.

dash. A mark or line in writing or printing, noting a break or stop in the sentence. *Webster.*
Dan. Tankestreg; *Du.* streepje; *Fr.* trait suspensif; *Ger.* Gedankenstrich; *It.* tratto di penna; *Sp.* rasgo de pluma; *Sw.* tankstreck.

dead heading. *See* **heading, dead.**

dedication. An address or inscription to a patron or friend, prefixed or attached to a literary, musical, or artistic work, as a token of gratitude or respect. *Stand. Dict.*
Dan. Tilegnelse; *Du.* opdracht, toewijding; dedicatie; *Fr.* dédicace; *Ger.* Widmung, Zueignung, Dedikation; *It.* dedica; *Sp.* dedicatoria; *Sw.* tillegnande.

dentelle border. (bb.) A lace-like decoration. *Stand. Dict.*
Dan. kniplingsdannet Forsiring; *Du.* versiering in kantvorm; *Fr.* dentelles; *Ger.* Spitzornament; *It.* merletto, pizzo, dentelle; *Sw.* spetsbordyr.

deposit copy. A copy of a book delivered to certain libraries according to law.

Dan. Pligtexemplar; *Du.* verplicht exemplaar; *Fr.* dépôt légal; *Ger.* Pflichtexemplar; *It.* deposito legale; *Sp.* deposito legal; *Sw.* årstryck, pliktexemplar.

descending letters. *See* **tail-type.**

design *or* **drawing.**

Dan. Tegning; *Du.* teekening; *Fr.* dessin;
Ger. Zeichnung; *It.* disegno; *Sp.* dibujo;
Sw. teckning.

dictionary.

Dan. Ordbog, Leksikon; *Du.* woordenboek; *Fr.* dictionnaire; *Ger.* Wörterbuch; *It.* dizionario; *Sp.* diccionario;
Sw. ordbok.

direction line. The abbreviated title of a book
at the foot of the first page of each sheet.

Dan. Norm; *Du.* titel-signatuur; *Fr.* signature de titre; *Ger.* Norm; *It.* segnatura; *Sp.* línea de reclamo; *Sw.* norm.

directory.

Dan. Vejviser; *Du.* adresboek; *Fr.* almanach des adresses; *Ger.* Adressbuch;
It. elenco degl' indirizzi; *Sp.* directorio,
anuario; *Sw.* adresskalender.

discontinued.

Dan. ophört at udkomme; *Du.* uitgave
gestaakt; *Fr.* cessé de paraître; *Ger.*
eingegangen; *It.* morto; *Sp.* ha dejado
de publicarse; *Sw.* upphört at utkomma.

dissertation *or* **thesis.**

Dan. Disputats; *Du.* academisch proefschrift, dissertatie; *Fr.* thèse; *Ger.*

Thesis, Abhandlung; *It.* tesi; *Sp.* disertación; *Sw.* thes, afhandling.

distribute the types. (pr.)
Dan. lægge af; *Du.* distribueeren; *Fr.* distribuer les types; *Ger.* ablegen; *It.*
scomporre; *Sp.* distribuir los tipos; *Sw.*
lägga af.

division *or* **section.**
Dan. Afdeling, Afsnit; *Du.* afdeeling; *Fr.*
division, section; *Ger.* Abteilung, Abschnitt; *It.* divisione, sezione; *Sp.*
división, sección, párrafo; *Sw.* afdelning.

dog's ear. The corner of a book, turned like
a dog's ear.
Dan. Æselsöre; *Du.* ezelsoor; *Fr.* corne,
oreille d'âne; *Ger.* Eselsohr; *It.* orecchio,
canto ripiegato d'una pagina; *Sp.* hoja
doblada de un libro; *Sw.* hundöra.

dotted prints. (e.) Engravings in which the
design is brought out by white dots and
lines, or sometimes by white dots only,
or by white lines only, on a black
ground.
Fr. manière criblée; *Ger.* Schrotblatt; *Sp.*
grabado crible.

dotted rule. (pr.)
Dan. punkteret Linie; *Du.* gepunteerde
regel; *Fr.* filet pointé; *Ger.* punktierte
Linie; *It.* linea punteggiata; *Sp.* línea
de puntos; *Sw.* punkterad linje.

double. (pr.)

Dan. Bryllup; *Du.* dubbel gezet woord; *Fr.* double; *Ger.* Doppelsatz, Hochzeit; *It.* duplicatura; *Sp.* duplicado; *Sw.* bröllop.

draft, rough. *See* **sketch.**

drama.

Dan. Skuespil; *Du.* tooneelspel; *Fr.* drame; *Ger.* Schauspiel; *It.* dramma; *Sp.* drama; *Sw.* skådespel.

drawing. *See* **design.**

dry point. (e.) (1.) A fine etching-needle used to incise copperplate in fine lines without the use of acid or etching ground. (2.) Work thus engraved. *Stand. Dict.*

Dan. kold Naal, kold Naal Radering; *Du.* droge naald, droge naald ets; *Fr.* pointe sèche; *Ger.* Kaltnadelstich; *It.* punta secca; *Sp.* punta seca; *Sw.* torrnål, kallnål, torrnål radering, kallnål radering.

duck. (bb.) A strong untwilled linen or cotton fabric used in bookbinding. *Stand. Dict.*

Dan. Sejldug; *Du.* zeildoek; *Fr.* canevas; *Ger.* Segeltuch; *It.* tela di vela; *Sp.* tela para velas; *Sw.* segelduk.

E

early copies. *See* **advance sheets.**

edge, lower *or* tail. (bb.)

Dan. Undersnit; *Du.* staart, ondersnee; *Fr.* queue; *Ger.* Schwanz, unterer Schnitt; *It.* il disotto del libro; *Sp.* canto inferior; *Sw.* undersnitt.

edges. (bb.)

Dan. Snit; *Du.* snede, snee; *Fr.* tranches; *Ger.* Schnitt; *It.* taglio del libro; *Sp.* corte, canto; *Sw.* boksnitt.

edges, combed. (bb.)

Dan. Kammarmorsnit; *Du.* kammarmersnee; *Fr.* tranches peignées; *Ger.* Kammarmorschnitt; *It.* taglio marmorizzato al pettine; *Sp.* cortes jaspeados, cantos jaspeados; *Sw.* marmorsnitt.

edges, gilt. (bb.)

Dan. Guldsnit; *Du.* verguld op snede; *Fr.* doré sur tranches, tranches dorées; *Ger.* mit Goldschnitt; *It.* dorato sui fogli, taglio dorato; *Sp.* cantos dorados, cortes dorados; *Sw.* förgyldt snitt.

edges, marbled. (bb.)

Dan. Marmorsnit; *Du.* gemarmerd op snede; *Fr.* tranches marbrées; *Ger.* Marmorschnitt; *It.* marmoreggiato sui fogli; *Sp.* cantos jaspeados; *Sw.* marmorsnitt.

edges, red. (bb.)

Dan. rödt Snit; *Du.* roodgekleurd op snede; *Fr.* tranches rouges; *Ger.* Rotschnitt; *It.* taglio rosso; *Sp.* cantos rojos, cantos encarnados; *Sw.* rödt snitt.

edges, sprinkled. (bb.)

Dan. sprængt Snit; *Du.* gespikkeld op snede; *Fr.* tranches jaspées; *Ger.* gesprenkelter Schnitt; *Sp.* cantos jaspeados; *It.* taglio spruzzato; *Sw.* sprängdt snitt.

edges, tooled. (bb.)

Dan. ciseleret Snit; *Du.* geciseleerde snede; *Fr.* tranches ciselées; *Ger.* ziselierter Schnitt, gepunzter Schnitt; *It.* taglio cesellato; *Sp.* cantos cincelados; *Sw.* ciseleradt snitt.

edited.

Dan. bearbejdet; *Du.* bewerkt; *Fr.* édité; *Ger.* bearbeitet; *It.* edito; *Sp.* hecho, escrito, compuesto; *Sw.* bearbetad.

edition.

Dan. Udgave, Oplag; *Du.* uitgaaf, oplaag, druk; *Fr.* édition, tirage; *Ger.* Ausgabe, Auflage; *It.* edizione, impressione; *Sp.* edición, tirada; *Sw.* upplaga.

edition, cheap.

Dan. billig Udgave; *Du.* goedkoope uitgaaf; *Fr.* édition à bon marché; *Ger.* billige Ausgabe; *It.* edizione economica; *Sp.* edición barata; *Sw.* godtköpsupplaga.

edition, limited.

Dan. lille Oplag; *Du.* beperkte uitgaaf, kleine oplaag; *Fr.* tirage limité; tiré à petit nombre; *Ger.* kleine Auflage; *It.* edizione limitata, tiratura di pochi esemplari; *Sp.* edición de pocos ejemplares, corta edición; *Sw.* liten upplaga.

edition, popular.

Dan. Folkeudgave; *Du.* volksuitgaaf; *Fr.* édition populaire; *It.* edizione popolare; *Sp.* edición popular; *Sw.* folkupplaga.

editor (of a book).

Dan. Udgiver; *Du.* bewerker, uitgever; *Fr.* éditeur; *Ger.* Herausgeber; *It.* editore; *Sp.* editor; *Sw.* utgifvare.

editor (of a newspaper).

Dan. Redaktör; *Du.* redacteur; *Fr.* rédacteur, directeur; *Ger.* Schriftleiter; *It.* redattore; *Sp.* redactor, director; *Sw.* redaktör.

editorial *or* **leader.** An article in a newspaper or magazine presumably written by the editor, and published as an official expression of opinion. *Stand. Dict.*

Dan. ledende Artikel; *Du.* hoofdartikel; *Fr.* article de fond; *Ger.* Leitartikel; *It.* articolo di fondo; *Sp.* editorial; *Sw.* redaktörs ledare.

engraver.

Dan. Gravör; *Du.* plaatsnijder, graveur; *Fr.* graveur; *Ger.* Graveur; *It.* intagliatore; *Sp.* grabador; *Sw.* gravör.

engraving *or* **cut.**

Dan. Stik; *Du.* plaat; *Fr.* gravure; *Ger.* Stich; *It.* incisione; *Sp.* grabado; *Sw.* gravyr.

engraving, copper. *See* **copper-plate engraving.**

engraving, steel. *See* **steel engraving.**

engraving, stipple. *See* **stipple engraving.**

engraving, wood. *See* **wood engraving.**

enlarged.

Dan. foröget; *Du.* vermeerderd; *Fr.* augmenté; *Ger.* vermehrt; *It.* accresciuto,

32

aumentato; *Sp.* aumentado; *Sw.* tillökad.

entitled.

Dan. med Titel; *Du.* getiteld; *Fr.* intitulé;
Ger. mit Titel; *It.* intitolato; *Sp.* titulado; *Sw.* med titel.

etching.

Dan. Radering; *Du.* ets, sterkwaterplaat;
Fr. eau-forte; *Ger.* Radierung; *It.* incisione coll' acqua forte, acqua forte; *Sp.*
grabado al agua fuerte, agua fuerte; *Sw.*
radering.

etching ground. (e.) The coating of wax or
varnish on a plate prepared for etching.
Stand. Dict.

Dan. Radeergrund, Ætsbund; *Du.* ets-
grond; *Fr.* vernis de graveur; *Ger.*
Radiergrund; *It.* strato da incidere;
Sp. barniz de grabadores; *Sw.* etsgrund.

even page. *See* **page, even.**

exclamation point.

Dan. Udraabstegn; *Du.* uitroepingsteeken;
Fr. point d'exclamation; *Ger.* Ausrufszeichen; *It.* punto esclamativo; *Sp.*
puntos de admiración; *Sw.* utropstecken.

expense, at the author's. *See* **at the author's
expense.**

extract.

Dan. Uddrag, Udtog; *Du.* uittreksel; *Fr.*
extrait; *Ger.* Auszug; *It.* estratto; *Sp.*
extracto; *Sw.* utdrag.

F

false line. *See* **line, false.**

fancy letter. *See* **letter, fancy.**

fascicle.

Dan. Levering, Hæfte; *Du.* aflevering; *Fr.* livraison, fascicule; *Ger.* Lieferung, Heft; *It.* dispensa, fascicolo; *Sp.* entrega, fascículo; *Sw.* häfte.

fat. (pr.) Pieces of composition, for instance, running titles, that are kept for future use and are not taken apart till the whole work is finished.

Dan. Svinesteg; *Du.* spek; *Fr.* du bon; *Ger.* Speck; *It.* roba buona, composizione agevole; *Sw.* fortel.

filleted.

Dan. med Linieornamentering; *Du.* gefiletteerd; *Fr.* orné d'un filet; *Ger.* mit einer Leiste dekoriert; *It.* filettato; *Sp.*. fileteado; *Sw.* med linieornamentering.

fine copy. *See* **copy, fine.**

first form. *See* **form, first.**

flush. *See* **commence even.**

flyleaf. A blank leaf at the beginning or end of a book. *Stand. Dict.*

Dan. Forsætsblad; *Du.* blank blad, schutblad; *Fr.* garde, feuille blanche, feuille de garde; *Ger.* Vorsatzblatt, Vorsatz; *It.* foglio bianco, guardia; *Sp.* guarda; *Sw.* försättspapper, försättsblad.

flysheet. A small sheet of paper such as is used for printing hand bills, etc.

Dan. Flyveblad; *Du.* los blad; *Fr.* feuille volante, pièce volante; *Ger.* Flugblatt; *It.* foglio volante; *Sp.* hoja volante; *Sw.* flygblad.

fly-title. *See* **half-title.**

folded.

Dan. sammenfoldet; *Du.* gevouwen; *Fr.* plié; *Ger.* gefaltet; *It.* ripiegato; *Sp.* plegado; *Sw.* inviken, hopviken.

foot-note (b.) A note at the foot of the page.

Dan. Note under Teksten; *Du.* noot; *Fr.* note de pied; *Ger.* Fussnote; *It.* nota in calce; *Sp.* nota al pie; *Sw.* anmärkning nederst på sidan.

for press. (pr.)

Dan. kan rentrykkes, færdig til Trykken; *Du.* voor de pers gereed; *Fr.* bon à tirer; *Ger.* druckfertig; *It.* si stampi, visto: si stampi; *Sp.* listo para ponerle en prensa, puede imprimirse; *Sw.* tryckfärdig.

fore-edge.

Dan. Forsnit; *Du.* voorsnede; *Fr.* gouttière; *Ger.* Vorderschnitt, Schnauze; *It.* davanti del libro, gola del libro, canale del libro; *Sp.* media caña; *Sw.* framsnitt.

form *or* **composition. (pr.)**

Dan. Sats; *Du.* zetsel; *Fr.* composition; *Ger.* Satz, Typenform; *It.* composizione; *Sp.* forma, composición; *Sw.* sats.

form, first. (pr.)

Dan. Sköntryksform, Primaform; *Du.* schoondruk; *Fr.* forme première, côté de première; *Ger.* Schöndruck; *It.* bianca, stampa in bianca; *Sp.* blanco; *Sw.* primaform.

form, second. (pr.)

Dan. Gentrykform, Vidertrykform, Sekundaform; *Du.* weerdruk; *Fr.* seconde forme, côté de seconde; *Ger.* Widerdruck; *It.* volta, stampa in volta; *Sp.* retiración; *Sw.* sekundaform.

fox-skin.

Dan. Ræveskind; *Du.* vossenleer; *Fr.* peau de renard; *Ger.* Fuchsleder; *It.* pelle di volpe; *Sp.* piel de zorra; *Sw.* räfskinn.

fragment.

Dan. Brudstykke; *Du.* fragment; *Fr.* fragment; *Ger.* Bruchstück; *It.* frammento; *Sp.* fragmento; *Sw.* fragment.

frontispiece. A plate or illustration in the front of a book facing or preceding the title page.

Dan. Titelkobber; *Du.* titelplaat, frontispice; *Fr.* frontispice; *Ger.* Titelkupfer; *It.* antiporta figurata, antiporta ornata; *Sp.* frontis grabado; *Sw.* titelplansch.

full face types. *See* **types, bold face.**

furniture. (pr.) Wooden or metal strips of less than type-height, put around and between pages of type to make proper margins, and fill the spaces between the pages and the chase. *Stand. Dict.*

Dan. Forms Stege *pl.*; *Du.* houtblokjes *pl.*; *Fr.* garniture; *Ger.* Stege *pl.*; *It.* marginatura di legno o di piombo; *Sp.* fornitura; *Sw.* steg.

G

galley. (pr.) A flat oblong tray, commonly of brass, flanged on one or both sides and at one end, for holding composed type. *Stand. Dict.*

Dan. Skib; *Du.* galei, zetraam; *It.* galée; *Ger.* Setzschiff; *It.* vantaggio; *Sp.* galera; *Sw.* sättskepp.

galley proof *or* slip-proof. (pr.) An impression taken from type on a galley. *Stand. Dict.*

Dan. Korrekturaftryk i Strimler uden Paginering; *Du.* galei-proef; *Fr.* épreuve en placard; *Ger.* Fahnenabzug; *It.* bozza in colonnini; *Sp.* galerada; *Sw.* afdrag af förrådssättning.

gathering. (bb.) The collecting and placing in consecutive order the signatures of folded sheets of a book or pamphlet.

Dan. Arkenes Ordning; *Du.* bijeenbrengen, vergaren; *Fr.* assemblage; *Ger.* Lage; *It.* assembramento di fogli; *Sp.* alzado; *Sw.* läggens ordning.

general-index.

Dan. Generalregister; *Du.* verzamel-index; *Fr.* index général; *Ger.* Gesamtregister; *It.* indice generale; *Sp.* indice general; *Sw.* generalregister.

gilt.
Dan. forgyldt; *Du.* verguld; *Fr.* doré; *Ger.* vergoldet; *It.* dorato; *Sp.* dorado; *Sw.* förgyld.

gilt edged.
Dan. med Guldsnit; *Du.* verguld op snede, met goudsnede; *Fr.* doré sur tranches, tranches dorées; *Ger.* mit Goldschnitt; *It.* dorato sui fogli; taglio dorato; *Sp.* cantos dorados, cortes dorados; *Sw.* förgyldt snitt.

gilt top.
Dan. överste Snit forgyldt; *Du.* bovensnede verguld, kop verguld; *Fr.* tête dorée; *Ger.* oberer Schnitt vergoldet; *It.* dorato in testa, disopra dorato, taglio superiore dorato; *Sp.* cabeza dorada; *Sw.* förgyld topp.

goatskin.
Dan. Gedeskind; *Du.* geitenleer; *Fr.* peau de chèvre; *Ger.* Ziegenhaut; *It.* pelle di capra; *Sp.* piel de cabra; *Sw.* getskinn.

gold tooling. (bb.) Ornamentation with gold leaf by tooling. *Stand. Dict.*
Dan. Presseforgyldning; *Du.* gouddruk; *Fr.* ornements en or; *Ger.* Goldpressung; *It.* ornamenti in oro; *Sp.* estampadura en oro; *Sw.* pressförgyllning.

gothic letters. *See* **letters, gothic.**

guard. (bb.) One of the slips bound in at the back of an album, scrapbook, etc., to prevent its breaking when receiving an added illustration or leaf. *Stand. Dict.*
Dan, Fals; *Du.* papierstrook; *Fr.* onglet; *Ger.* Falz; *It.* brachetta; *Sp.* escartibana; *Sw.* fals.

H

half binding. A style of binding in which only the back and corners of a volume are covered with leather or cloth.
Dan. Vælskbind, Halvbind; *Du.* halfleeren band, halflinnen band; *Fr.* demireliure; *Ger.* Halbfranzband; *It.* mezza pelle, mezza tela; *Sp.* media pasta; *Sw.* halfband.

half-title *or* **bastard-title** *or* **fly-title.**
Dan. Smudstitel, Halvtitel; *Du.* Fransche titel, voor-de-handsche titel; *Fr.* fauxtitre; *Ger.* Schmutztitel, Vorsatztitel; *It.* titolo falso, frontipizio falso, occhietto; *Sp.* falso frontis, falsa portada; *Sw.* smutstitel.

hand-paper *or* **hand-made paper.**
Dan. Böttepapir, Haandpapir; *Du.* geschept papier; *Fr.* papier vergé, papier à la cuve; *Ger.* Büttenpapier, Handpapier; *It.* carta a mano; *Sp.* papel trabajado á mano; *Sw.* dokument papper, handgjordt papper.

head of a book. (bb.)
Dan. överste Snit; *Du.* kop; *Fr.* tête; *Ger.* Kopf, oberer Schnitt; *It.* disopra

del libro, taglio superiore, testa del libro; *Sp.* cabeza del libro; *Sw.* öfre snitt.

headband. (bb.) A decorative terminal cord or roll forming the end of the inner back of a book. *Stand. Dict.*

Dan. Kapital paa en Bog, Kapitaltöj; *Du.* kapitaalband; *Fr.* tranchefile; *Ger.* Kapitalband; *It.* capitello, tranciafila; *Sp.* cabezada de libro; *Sw.* kapitaling.

heading.

Dan. Overskrift, Rubrik; *Du.* hoofd, opschrift, bovenschrift, rubriek; *Fr.* rubrique; *Ger.* Überschrift, Rubrik; *It.* intestazione, testata; *Sp.* encabezamiento; *Sw.* öfverskrift, rubrik.

heading, dead *or* **paginal number. (pr.)**

Dan. Kolumnetitel, Sidenummer; *Du.* doode kolommentitel, volgnummer der bladzijde; *Fr.* chiffre de la page; *Ger.* toter Kolumnentitel, Kolumnenziffer; *It.* numero d'una pagina; *Sp.* título con solo la paginación; *Sw.* död kolumntitel.

heading, live *or* **running title.**

Dan. levende Kolumnetitel; *Du.* veranderlijke koptitel, levende kolommentitel; *Fr.* titre courant; *Ger.* lebender Kolumnentitel; *It.* titolo corrente; *Sp.* título con palabras, título de página; *Sw.* lefvande kolumntitel.

head-line. (pr.) A line of type set above the text to which it refers, in a book, newspaper, etc. *Stand. Dict.*

Dan. Titellinie; *Du.* bovenregel; *Fr.* ligne de tête; *Ger.* Hauptzeile; *It.* riga di testa; *Sp.* línea de cabeza; *Sw.* hufvudlinje, rubrikrad.

head-margin. The blank space above the first line of the first page.

Dan. Nedrykning paa den förste Side; *Du.* open vak op de eerste bladzijde; *Fr.* blanc du folio recto; *Ger.* Vorschlag, Überschlag; *It.* il bianco della prima pagina sopra la prima riga; *Sp.* espacio en blanco de la primera página sobre el primero renglón; *Sw.* nedryckning på den första sida.

head-piece. The decorative design at the top of a printed page or above a chapter-heading *Stand. Dict.*

Dan. Begyndelsesvignet; *Du.* kopvignette; vignette aan het begin van een hoofdstuk; *Fr.* en-tête, tête de chapitre; *Ger.* Kopfvignette; *It.* capopagina, testata illustrata; *Sp.* cabeza de un capítulo; *Sw.* anfangsvignet.

hogskin. *See* **pigskin.**

hours. *See* **book of hours.**

hyphen.

Dan. Bindestreg; *Du.* koppelteeken; *Fr.* tiret, trait d'union; *Ger.* Bindestrich; *It.* tratto d'unione; *Sp.* guión; *Sw.* bindestreck.

I

illumination. Embellishment of old manuscripts with colors and gold.

Dan. Illuminering; *Du.* verluchting; *Fr.* enluminure; *Ger.* Illuminierung; *It.* miniatura; *Sp.* iluminación; *Sw.* illuminering, färglagd prydnad.

illuminator.

Dan. Illuminator; *Du.* verluchter, kleurder; *Fr.* enlumineur, miniaturiste; *Ger.* Illuminator; *It.* miniatore; *Sp.* iluminador; *Sw.* illuminist.

illustration.

Dan. Afbildning, Illustration; *Du.* afbeelding, illustratie; *Fr.* figure, illustration; *Ger.* Abbildung, Illustration; *It.* figura, illustrazione; *Sp.* ilustración, figura; *Sw.* afbildning, illustration.

imperfect *or* incomplete.

Dan. defekt, ufuldstændig; *Du.* geschonden; *Fr.* imparfait; *Ger.* mangelhaft, unvollständig; *It.* difettoso, imperfetto; *Sp.* defectuoso; *Sw.* ofullständig.

impression. (e.) A print struck off from an engraved plate or stone. *Stand. Dict.*

Dan. Aftryk; *Du.* afdruk; *Fr.* tirage; *Ger.* Abdruck; *It.* tiratura; *Sp.* impresión; *Sw.* aftryck.

imprint. The section of the title-page which gives the name of the publisher, place and date of printing.

Dan. Trykangivelse; *Du.* drukkersopgaaf; *Fr.* adresse bibliographique; *Ger.* Erscheinungsvermerk; *It.* nota tipografica; *Sp.* pie de imprenta; *Sw.* angifvelse af tryckort och förläggare.

42

imprint date *or* **year of publication.**

> *Dan.* Trykkeaar, Udgivelsesaar; *Du.* jaar van druk, jaar van uitgaaf; *Fr.* date d'impression, date de publication; *Ger.* Druckjahr, Erscheinungsjahr; *It.* data di stampa, data di pubblicazione; *Sp.* año de imprenta, año de la edición; *Sw.* tryckår, utgifningsår.

in a lot.

> *Dan.* under Ét; *Du.* en bloc, in eens, ongeteld; *Fr.* à forfait, en bloc; *Ger.* im Ganzen; *It.* in blocco; *Sp.* sin contar, á granel; *Sw.* en bloc.

incomplete. *See* **imperfect.**

incunabula. *pl.* Books printed before or shortly after A.D. 1500.

> *Dan.* Vuggetryk; *Du.* wiegedrukken; eerstelingsdrukken; *Fr.* incunables; *Ger.* Erstlingsdrucke, Wiegendrucke; *It.* incunaboli; *Sp.* libros incunables; *Sw.* inkunabler.

indent, to. (pr.)

> *Dan.* indrykke; *Du.* inspringen; *Fr.* renfoncer; *Ger.* einen Satz einziehen; *It.* indentare; *Sp.* sangrar; *Sw.* indraga.

indention. (pr.) The setting in of a line or body of type by a blank space at the beginning or left hand, as in the first line of a paragraph. *Stand. Dict.*

> *Dan.* Indrykning; *Du.* inspringing; *Fr.* renfoncement; *Ger.* Einzug des Satzes; *It.* rientramento; *Sp.* sangría; *Sw.* indrag.

index *or* **table of contents.**
> *Dan.* Indholdsfortegnelse, Register; *Du.* bladwijzer, inhoudsopgave; *Fr.* table des matières; *Ger.* Inhaltsverzeichnis, Register, Elenchus; *It.* indice, tavola delle materie; *Sp.* indice, tabla de materias; *Sw.* innehållsförteckning, register.

index of names.
> *Dan.* Navnefortegnelse; *Du.* naamregister; *Fr.* table des noms propres; *Ger.* Namenregister; *It.* indice dei nomi proprii; *Sp.* tabla de los nombres; *Sw.* namnförteckning.

ink.
> *Dan.* Blæk; *Du.* inkt; *Fr.* encre; *Ger.* Tinte; *It.* inchiostro; *Sp.* tinta; *Sw.* bläck.

ink, printer's. *See* **printer's ink.**

inset. A printed leaf inserted in a book before binding.
> *Dan.* indsat Blad; *Du.* ingestoken bladzijde, insteek; *Fr.* encart; *Ger.* Einsteckbogen; *It.* quartino, rincarto; *Sp.* encarte; *Sw.* inhäftadt blad.

interleaf. A blank leaf inserted or bound between others, so as to permit written additions. *Stand. Dict.*
> *Dan.* indskudt Blad; *Du.* doorgeschoten blad; *Fr.* feuillet blanc inséré; *Ger.* Durchschussblatt; *It.* foglio bianco inserito; *Sp.* hoja intercalada; *Sw.* insatt blankt papper.

interleaved. Supplied with blank leaves inserted between the other leaves. *Stand. Dict.*

Dan. gennemskudt med hvide Blade; *Du.* doorschoten; *Fr.* interfolié; *Ger.* durchschossen, interfoliiert; *It.* interfogliato; *Sp.* interfoliado; *Sw.* interfolierad.

interrogation point.

Dan. Spörgsmaalstegn; *Du.* vraagteeken; *Fr.* point d'interrogation; *Ger.* Fragezeichen; *It.* punto. interrogativo; *Sp.* punto de interrogación; *Sw.* frågetecken.

introduction.

Dan. Inledning; *Du.* inleiding; *Fr.* introduction; *Ger.* Einleitung; *It.* introduzione; *Sp.* introducción; *Sw.* inledning.

italics *or* **cursive characters.** Style of type in which the letters slope towards the right, invented in Italy about 1500, and now used for emphasis. *Stand. Dict.*

Dan. Kursivskrift; *Du.* cursiefletters; *Fr.* caractères italiques; *Ger.* Kursivschrift, Italique; *It.* caratteri corsivi; *Sp.* letras cursivas, letras italianas, bastardillas, letras venecianas; *Sw.* kursivskrift.

J

job-printer. One who does miscellaneous printing, such as cards, posters, etc. *Stand. Dict.*

Dan. Akcidenstrykker; *Du.* smoutdrukker; *Fr.* imprimeur des ouvrages de ville; *Ger.* Akzidenzdrucker; *It.* stampatore in lavori di fantasia; *Sp.* impresor de remiendos; *Sw.* accidenstryckare.

job-printing. Miscellaneous printing, such as printing of cards, posters, handbills, etc. *Stand. Dict.*

Dan. Akcidenstryk; *Du.* smoutwerk; *Fr.* bilboquet, travail de ville; *Ger.* Akzidenzdruck; *It.* lavori avventizi, lavori di fantasia; *Sp.* remiendo; *Sw.* accidenstryck.

justification. (pr.)

Dan. Tilretning; *Du.* aankooiing; *Fr.* justification; *Ger.* Ausschliessung: *It.* giustezza dei caratteri; *Sp.* justificación; *Sw.* radutslutning.

juvenile literature.

Dan. Börneböger; *Du.* kinderboeken; *Fr.* écrits pour l'enfance; *Ger.* Jugendschriften; *It.* libri per l'infanzia; *Sp.* literatura para la juventud; *Sw.* ungdomsskrifter.

L

label *or* **lettering piece.**

Dan. Boglap; *Du.* rugschild; *Fr.* pièce au dos; *Ger.* Rückenschild; *It.* cartello; cartellino; *Sp.* rótulo; *Sw.* boklapp.

labeled.

Dan. med Boglap; *Du.* met rugschild; *Fr.* avec étiquette; *Ger.* mit Etiquette versehen; *It.* cartellinato; *Sp.* rotulado; *Sw.* med etikett.

large paper. *See* **paper, large.**

lead. (pr.) A thin strip of type-metal or brass, less than type-high, used in type composition to separate lines. *Stand. Dict.*

Dan. Skydelinie; *Du.* interlinie; *Fr.* interligne; *Ger.* Durchschuss; *It.* interlinea; *Sp.* regleta, interlínea; *Sw.* mellanslag.

leaded. (pr.) Type separated by leads. *Stand. Dict.*

Dan. skudt; *Du.* met interlinies; *Fr.* interligné; *Ger.* durchschossen; *It.* interlineato; *Sp.* interlineado; *Sw.* mellanslagen.

leaded matter. *See* **composition, interlined.**

leader. *See* **editorial.**

leaf. A single division of a folded sheet of paper. *Stand. Dict.*

Dan. Blad; *Du.* blad; *Fr.* feuille, feuillet; *Ger.* Blatt; *It.* foglio; *Sp.* hoja, foja; *Sw.* blad.

lean faced types. *See* **types, light faced.**

leather *or* **skin.**

Dan. Læder, Skind; *Du.* leder, leer, vel; *Fr.* peau, cuir; *Ger.* Leder, Haut; *It.* pelle, cuoio; *Sp.* piel, cuero; *Sw.* skinn.

leaves, preliminary.

Dan. indledende unumererede Blade; *Du.* voorwerk; *Fr.* feuilles préliminaires; *Ger.* einleitende unnumerierte Blätter; *It.* principi del libro; *Sp.* hojas preliminares; *Sw.* inledande onumrerade blad.

letter.

Dan. Brev; *Du.* brief; *Fr.* lettre; *Ger.* Brief; *It.* epistola; *Sp.* carta; *Sw.* bref.

letter *or* **character. (pr.)**
>*Dan.* Bogstav, Skrifttegn; *Du.* letter; *Fr.*
>lettre; *Ger.* Buchstabe; *It.* lettera; *Sp.*
>letra, carácter; *Sw.* bokstaf.

letter, battered. (pr.)
>*Dan.* læderet Skriftegn; *Du.* gekwetste
>letter; *Fr.* lettre usée, lettre fatiguée,
>lettre gatée; *Ger.* Defekt-Buchstabe;
>*It.* lettera guasta, lettera logora; *Sp.*
>letra machucada; *Sw.* defekt-bokstaf.

letter, black. (pr.) *See* **black letter.**

letter, capital. (pr.)
>*Dan.* stort Bogstav, Majuskel; *Du.* hoofd-
>letter; *Fr.* lettre capitale, lettre majus-
>cule; *Ger.* Kapitalbuchstabe, Majuskel;
>*It.* lettera maiuscola; *Sp.* letra mayús-
>cula; *Sw.* stor bokstaf, versal, majuskel.

letter, descending *or* **tail type. (pr.)**
>*Dan.* Bogstav som naar ned under Linien;
>*Du.* staartletter; *Fr.* lettre à queue;
>*Ger.* geschwänzte Schrift; *It.* lettera dis-
>cendente, lettera con asta discendente;
>*Sp.* letra descendente; *Sw.* bokstaf som
>räcker under linjen.

letter, fancy. (pr.)
>*Dan.* forsiret Bogstav; *Du.* sierletter; *Fr.*
>lettre de fantaisie, lettre ornée; *Ger.*
>Zierbuchstabe; *It.* lettera di fantasia;
>*Sp.* letra de adorno, letra de capricho,
>letra florida; *Sw.* utsirad bokstaf.

letter, small. (pr.)
>*Dan.* lille Bogstav, Minuskel; *Du.* kleine
>letter; *Fr.* lettre minuscule; *Ger.* Minus-

kel; *It.* lettera minuscola; *Sp.* letra minúscula; *Sw.* liten bokstaf, minuskel.

letter, turned. (pr.)

Dan. blokeret Bogstav; *Du.* omgekeerde letter, geblokkeerde letter; *Fr.* lettre renversée, lettre bloquée; *Ger.* Fliegenkopf; *It.* lettera capovolta; *Sp.* letra revuelta; *Sw.* upp och nedvänd bokstaf.

letter-board. *See* **composing board.**

letter-head.

Dan. Brevhoved; *Du.* briefhoofd; *Fr.* tête de lettre; *Ger.* Briefkopf; *It.* intestazione di lettera; *Sp.* encabezamiento de carta; *Sw.* brefhufvud.

lettering piece. *See* **label.**

letters, German. *See* **letters, Gothic.**

letters, Gothic *or* **German letters. (pr.)**

Dan. Fraktur, gotiske Bogstaver; *Du.* fractuur letters, Gothische letters; *Fr.* caractères gotiques; *Ger.* Fraktur, gothische Typen; *It.* caratteri gotici; *Sp.* letras góticas; *Sw.* frakturstil.

letters, Roman *or* **antique. (pr.)**

Dan. Antiqua; *Du.* antiqua letters; *Fr.* caractères romains; *Ger.* Antiqua, römische Schrift; *It.* caratteri romani; *Sp.* letras romanas; *Sw.* antiqua.

libel.

Dan. Smædeskrift; *Du.* schotschrift; *Fr.* libelle; *Ger.* Schmähschrift; *It.* libello infamatorio; *Sp.* libelo; *Sw.* smädeskrift.

light faced types. *See* **types, light faced.**

limited edition. *See* **edition, limited.**

line.

Dan. Linie; *Du.* regel; *Fr.* ligne; *Ger.* Zeile; *It.* linea, riga; *Sp.* renglón; *Sw.* linje, rad.

line, false. (pr.) End line of a paragraph at the beginning of a page.

Dan. Horeunge; *Du.* halve regel aan het begin eener bladzijde of kolom; *Fr.* fausse-ligne; *Ger.* Hurenkind; *It.* righino in testa di colonna o di pagina; *Sp.* ultimo renglón de una alínea al comienzo de una página; *Sw.* utgångslinje öfverst på en sida.

line engraving. (e.)

Dan. Liniestik; *Du.* gravure in lijnenmanier; *Fr.* gravure au burin; *Ger.* Grabstichelmanier, Linienmanier; *It.* intaglio di bulino; *Sp.* grabado al buril; *Sw.* gravering med grafstickel, buringravyr.

list price *or* published price.

Dan. Bogladepris; *Du.* prijs van uitgaaf; *Fr.* prix fort; *Ger.* Ladenpreis; *It.* prezzo lordo; *Sp.* precio de catálogo; *Sw.* bokládspris.

lithograph. A print produced from a flat lithographic stone on which a drawing, design or transfer has been made in a soapy ink or by other suitable process. *Stand. Dict.*

Dan. Stentryk; Litografi; *Du.* steendrukplaat; *Fr.* lithographie; *Ger.* Lithographie, Steindruck; *It.* litografia; *Sp.* litografía; *Sw.* stentryck, litografi.

live heading. *See* **heading, live.**

loose back. *See* **back, loose.**

lot, in a. *See* **in a lot.**

lower case. (pr.)

 Dan. Typer tagne fra Skriftkassens neder-
 ste Del, som indeholder de smaa Bogstaver; *Du.* onderkast letters; *Fr.* bas de
 casse; *Ger.* Typen aus dem Unterkasten; *It.* cassa bassa; *Sp.* caja baja; *Sw.*
 stilar tagna från kastens nedersta fack,
 som innchåller de små bokstäfverna.

lower edge. *See* **edge, lower.**

M

make up. (pr.) To arrange composed type
 into columns or pages. *Stand. Dict.*

 Dan. ombrække; *Du.* opmaken; *Fr.*
 mettre en pages; *Ger.* umbrechen; *It.*
 impaginare; *Sp.* ajustar, ordenar la
 composición por páginas de una obra;
 Sw. bryta om.

maker up. (pr.) One who arranges composed
 type in columns or pages. *Stand. Dict.*

 Dan. Ombrækker; *Du.* metteur en pages;
 Fr. metteur en pages; *Ger.* metteur en
 pages; *It.* impaginatore; *Sp.* ajustador,
 compaginador; *Sw.* ombrytare.

manuscript.

 Dan. Haandskrift; *Du.* handschrift; *Fr.*
 manuscrit; *Ger.* Handschrift; *It.* mano-
 scritto; *Sp.* manuscrito; *Sw.* handskrift.

manuscript note.

 Dan. haandskreven Anmærkning; *Du.*

manuscript noot; *Fr.* note à la main; *Ger.* Manuskript-Anmerkung; *It.* nota manoscritta; *Sp.* nota manuscrita; *Sw.* marginal notering.

map.

Dan. Landkort; *Du.* landkaart; *Fr.* carte géographique; *Ger.* Landkarte; *It.* carta geografica; *Sp.* mapa geográfico; *Sw.* karta.

map of the world.

Dan. Verdenskort; *Du.* wereldkaart; *Fr.* mappe-monde; *Ger.* Weltkarte; *It.* mappamondo; *Sp.* mapamundi; *Sw.* verldskarta.

marble edged. *See* **edged, marble.**

marble paper. *See* **paper, marble.**

margin. The blank space on the edge of a printed sheet. *Stand. Dict.*

Dan. Rand, Margin; *Du.* rand, kant, marge; *Fr.* marge; *Ger.* Rand; *It.* margine; *Sp.* margen; *Sw.* rand.

margin border.

Dan. Bort; *Du.* randlijst; *Fr.* bordure; *Ger.* Randleiste; *It.* orlatura di margine; *Sp.* orla de pâgina; *Sw.* bort.

marginal notes.

Dan. Randbemærkninger; *Du.* marginaliën, kantteekeningen; *Fr.* notes marginales, manchettes; *Ger.* Randbemerkungen; *It.* note in margine; *Sp.* notas marginales; *Sw.* randanteckningar.

mark of correction. (pr.) *See* **proofmark.**

mark the pages, to.

 Dan. paginere, numerere Siderne i en Bog;
 Du. pagineeren; *Fr.* numéroter les
 pages; *Ger.* paginieren; *It.* paginare,
 cartolare; *Sp.* paginar; *Sw.* paginera.

matter, close *or* solid matter. (pr.)

 Dan. kompres Sats; *Du.* gedrongen zetsel;
 Fr. composition serrée; *Ger.* kompresser
 Satz; *It.* composizione serrata; *Sp.*
 composición sólida; *Sw.* kompres sats.

matter, leaded *or* interlined composition. (pr.)

 Dan. skudt Sats; *Du.* zetsel met interlinies;
 Fr. composition interlignée; *Ger.* durchschossener Satz; *It.* composizione interlineata; *Sp.* composición regleteada;
 Sw. mellanslagen sats.

matter, solid. *See* **matter, close.**

memoirs.

 Dan. Memoirer, Erindringer; *Du.* gedenkschriften; *Fr.* mémoires; *Ger.* Denk-
 schriften; *It.* memorie; *Sp.* memorias;
 Sw. memoarer.

mezzotint. (e.) A method of copperplate
 engraving in which the entire surface of
 the plate is slightly roughened after
 which the drawing is traced, and then
 the portion intended to show high lights
 or middle lights are scraped and bur-
 nished while the shadows are strengthened. *Stand. Dict.*

 Dan. Sortkunst, sort Manér; *Du.* zwarte
 kunst, schraapmanier; *Fr.* manière noire;
 Ger. Schabmanier, schwarze Kunst;

It. mezzotinto; *Sp.* estampa de humo, media tinta. *Sw.* svartkonstmanér.

mildew *or* **water stain.**

Dan. Fugtighedsplet; *Du.* vochtvlek; *Fr.* tache de moisissure; *Ger.* Wasserfleck; *It.* gora; *Sp.* mancha de agua; *Sw.* mögelfläck.

minutes. The official records of the proceedings of any deliberative body.

Dan. Protokoloptegnelser fra et Möde; *Du.* notulen van eene bijeenkomst; *Fr.* procès verbaux d'une séance; *Ger.* Protokoll; *It.* verbale di un' adunanza; *Sp.* minutas de un cuerpo deliberante; *Sw.* protokollanteckningar.

misprint.

Dan. Trykejl; *Du.* drukfout; *Fr.* faute typographique; *Ger.* Druckfehler; *It.* errore di stampa; *Sp.* falta tipográfica, errata tipográfica; *Sw.* tryckfel.

missal *or* **mass-book.** The book containing the service for the celebration of mass throughout the year.

Dan. Messebog; *Du.* misboek; *Fr.* missel, livre d'office; *Ger.* Messbuch; *It.* messale; *Sp.* misal; *Sw.* mässbok.

moldy *or* **mouldy.**

Dan. muggen; *Du.* beschimmeld; *Fr.* moisi; *Ger.* schimmelig; *It.* muffato; *Sp.* mohoso; *Sw.* möglad.

monogram.

Dan. Navnetræk; *Du.* naamcijfer; *Fr.* monogramme; *Ger.* Monogram; *It.*

monogramma; *Sp.* monograma; *Sw.* monogram.

monthly.

Dan. maanedlig; *Du.* maandelijksch; *Fr.* mensuel; *Ger.* monatlich; *It.* mensuale, mensile, d'ogni mese; *Sp.* mensual; *Sw.* månatlig.

monthly publication.

Dan. Maanedsblad; *Du.* maandblad; *Fr.* publication mensuelle; *Ger.* Monatsblatt; *It.* pubblicazione mensile; *Sp.* publicación mensual; *Sw.* månadsblad.

monthly report.

*Dan.*Maanedsberetning;*Du.*maandelijksch verslag; *Fr.* compte rendu mensuel; *Ger.* Monatsbericht; *It.* relazione mensile; *Sp.* memoria mensual; *Sw.* månatlig berättelse.

morocco. Leather made from goatskins tanned with sumac, named after the city of Morocco.

Dan. Maroquin; *Du.* marokijnleer; *Fr.* maroquin; *Ger.* Marokkoleder; *It.* marrocchino; *Sp.* tafilete; *Sw.* marokäng.

mouldy. *See* **moldy.**

mounted. Attached to a backing.

Dan. opklæbet; *Du.* opgeplakt, gemonteerd; *Fr.* monté; *Ger.* aufgezogen; *It.* montato; *Sp.* pegado; *Sw.* uppklistrad.

mourning border.

Dan. Sörgerand; *Du.* rouwrand; *Fr.* filet noir; *Ger.* Trauerrand; *It.* margine di lutto; *Sp.* raya de luto; *Sw.* sorgkant.

mutilated.

Dan. beskadiget; *Du.* geschonden, beschadigd; *Fr.* mutilé, endommagé; *Ger.* beschädigt; *It.* mutilato; *Sp.* mutilado; *Sw.* skadadt.

N

newspaper.

Dan. Avis; *Du.* nieuwsblad, courant, krant; *Fr.* journal; *Ger.* Zeitung; *It.* giornale; *Sp.* diario, periódico; *Sw.* tidning.

newspaper, weekly.

Dan. Ugeblad; *Du.* weekblad; *Fr.* journal hebdomadaire; *Ger.* Wochenblatt; *It.* periodico ebdomadario; *Sp.* periódico semanal; *Sw.* veckoblad.

newspaper clipping.

Dan. Avisudklip; *Du.* courantenuitknipsel; *Fr.* découpure de journaux; *Ger.* Zeitungsausschnitt; *It.* taglio di giornale; *Sp.* recorte de periódico; *Sw.* tidningsurklip.

no date.

Dan. uden Aar; *Du.* zonder jaar; *Fr.* sans date, sans millésime; *Ger.* ohne Jahr; *It.* senz' anno, senza data, senza millesimo; *Sp.* sin data, sin fecha; *Sw.* utan år.

no more published. *See* **all published.**

no place.

Dan. uden Trykkested; *Du.* zonder plaats; *Fr.* sans lieu; *Ger.* ohne Ort; *It.* senza luogo; *Sp.* sin lugar; *Sw.* utan ort.

no title-page.

> *Dan.* uden Titelblad; *Du.* zonder titelblad; *Fr.* sans feuille de titre; *Ger.* ohne Titelblatt; *It.* senza frontispizio; *Sp.* sin portada; *Sw.* utan titelblad.

not for sale.

> *Dan.* ikke i Boghandelen; *Du.* niet in den handel; *Fr.* non mis en vente, pas dans le commerce; *Ger.* nicht im Handel; *It.* fuori vendita, fuori commercio; *Sp.* no se vende; *Sw.* ej i bokhandeln.

note.

> *Dan.* Anmærkning; *Du.* aanmerking, noot; *Fr.* note; *Ger.* Anmerkung; *It.* nota; *Sp.* nota; *Sw.* anmärkning.

novel.

> *Dan.* Roman; *Du.* roman, novelle; *Fr.* roman; *Ger.* Roman, Novelle; *It.* romanzo; *Sp.* novela; *Sw.* roman.

now published.

> *Dan.* lige udkommen; *Du.* zoo juist verschenen; *Fr.* vient de paraître; *Ger.* soeben erschienen; *It.* novità; *Sp.* acaba de publicarse; *Sw.* nyss utkommen.

number the pages, to. *See* **mark the pages.**

O

oblong.

> *Dan.* aflang; *Du.* dwars; *Fr.* oblong; *Ger.* länglich; *It.* oblungo; *Sp.* apaisado; *Sw.* aflång.

odd page. *See* **page, odd.**

on approval. (bo.) *See* **approval, on.**

out. (pr.) Omission of a word or phrase made by the compositor.

Dan. Begravelse; *Du.* weggelaten zetsel; *Fr.* bourdon; *Ger.* Leiche; *It.* pesce, lasciato, lasciatura; *Sp.* olvido; *Sw.* lik.

out of print.

Dan. udsolgt; *Du.* uitverkocht; *Fr.* épuisé; *Ger.* vergriffen; *It.* esaurito; *Sp.* agotado, vendido; *Sw.* utgången ur bokhandeln.

P

page.

Dan. Side; *Du.* bladzijde; *Fr.* page; *Ger.* Seite; *It.* pagina, faccia; *Sp.* pagina, plana; *Sw.* sida.

page, even *or* verso. The left-hand page of a book.

Dan. Bagside, Verso; *Du.* achterzijde, even bladzijde, verso; *Fr.* page paire, verso; *Ger.* Rückseite, gerade Kolumne, Verso; *It.* verso della pagina; *Sp.* pâgina par, verso; *Sw.* vänster sida, verso.

page, odd *or* recto. The right-hand page of a book.

Dan. Forside, Recto; *Du.* oneven bladzijde, voorzijde, recto; *Fr.* belle-page, page impaire, recto; *Ger.* Vorseite, ungerade Kolumne, Recto; *It.* prima pagina, retto, recto; *Sp.* pâgina impar, recto; *Sw.* höger sida, recto.

page-cord. Twine used to tie around a page of type to keep it assembled. *Stand. Dict.*

Dan. Kolumnesnor, Klummesnor; *Du.* pagina-touwtje; *Fr.* ficelle; *Ger.* Kolumnenschnur; *It.* funicella, spago; *Sp.* cuerda, bramante; *Sw.* kolumnsnöre.

paginal number. *See* **heading, dead.**

pagination.

Dan. Paginering; *Du.* pagineering; *Fr.* pagination; *Ger.* Paginierung; *It.* paginatura; *Sp.* paginación; *Sw.* paginering.

pamphlet.

Dan. Brochure, Flyveskrift, Pjece; *Du.* brochure, vlugschrift, pamflet; *Fr.* brochure; *Ger.* Broschüre, Flugschrift; *It.* opuscolo; *Sp.* folleto, librejo, pamfleto, opusculo; *Sw.* broschyr, flygskrift, pamflett.

panel. (bb.) A section of the back of a bound book, between two bands.

Dan. Rygfelt; *Du.* paneel; *Fr.* compartiment, entre-nerfs; *Ger.* Feld des Rückens; *It.* distanza fra le carreggiuole; *Sp.* tejuelo; *Sw.* ryggfält.

paper.

Dan. Papir; *Du.* papier; *Fr.* papier; *Ger.* Papier; *It.* carta; *Sp.* papel; *Sw.* papper.

paper, blotting.

Dan. Klatpapir, Trækpapir; *Du.* vloeipapier; *Fr.* papier buvard; *Ger.* Löschpapier; *It.* carta asciugante, carta sugante; *Sp.* papel secante; *Sw.* läsk-papper.

paper, large *or* **tall copy.**

Du. groot papier; *Fr.* grand papier; *Ger.* Grosspapier; *It.* carta grande; *Sp.* gran papel.

paper, marble.

Dan. marmoreret Papir; *Du.* marmer-papier; *Fr.* papier marbré; *Ger.* marmoriertes Papier; *It.* carta marmo-reggiata; *Sp.* papel jaspeado; *Sw.* marmoreradt papper.

paper cover *or* **jacket.**

Dan. Papir-Omslag; *Du.* papier-omslag; *Fr.* couverture de papier; *Ger.* Papier-Umschlag; *It.* copertina di carta; *Sp.* cubierta de papel; *Sw.* pappersomslag.

paper cover, in. *See* **stitched.**

paper cutter *or* **paper knife.**

Dan. Papirkniv; *Du.* papiermes; *Fr.* coupe-papier; *Ger.* Papiermesser; *It.* taglia-carte; *Sp.* corta-papeles; *Sw.* pappers-knif.

paper knife. *See* **paper cutter.**

paragraph.

Dan. ny Linie; *Du.* alinea; *Fr.* alinéa; *Ger.* Absatz; *It.* capoverso, alinea; *Sp.* pár-rafo nuevo; *Sw.* ny rad.

parchment. The skin of sheep or goats pre-pared and polished with pumice stone for writing, engraving, etc.

Dan. Pergament; *Du.* perkament; *Fr.* parchemin; *Ger.* Pergament; *It.* per-

gamena; *Sp.* pergamino; *Sw.* pergament.

part.

Dan. Del; *Du.* gedeelte; *Fr.* partie; *Ger.*
Teil; *It.* parte; *Sp.* parte; *Sw.* del.

pasteboard.

Dan. Pap; *Du.* stroobord, bordpapier; *Fr.*
carton de collage; *Ger.* Pappe; *It.* cartone; *Sp.* cartón fuerte; *Sw.* papp.

pastoral letter.

Dan. Hyrdebrev; *Du.* herderlijke brief;
Fr. lettre pastorale; *Ger.* Pastoralbrief;
It. lettera pastorale; *Sp.* carta pastoral;
Sw. herdabref.

period.

Dan. Punktum; *Du.* punt; *Fr.* point; *Ger.*
Punkt; *It.* punto; *Sp.* punto; *Sw.*
punkt.

periodical.

Dan. Tidsskrift; *Du.* tijdschrift; *Fr.*
écrit périodique; *Ger.* Zeitschrift; *It.*
opera periodica; *Sp.* periódico; *Sw.*
tidskrift.

picture book.

Dan. Billedværk; *Du.* prentenboek; *Fr.*
livre d'images; *Ger.* Bilderbuch; *It.*
libro d'imagini; *Sp.* libro de láminas;
Sw. bilderbok.

pie *or* **pi.** Type that has been upset or other-
wise disarranged, so that it cannot be
readily used until assorted. *Stand. Dict.*

Dan. Svibelfisk; *Du.* pastei; *Fr.* paté;
Ger. Eierkuchen, Zwibelfisch; *It.* pas-

ticcio di caratteri; *Sp.* pastel; *Sw.* svibelfisk.

pieced out *or* repaired.
>*Dan.* repareret, lappet; *Du.* hersteld, bij-
geplakt; *Fr.* rapiécé; *Ger.* ausgebessert;
It. rattoppato; *Sp.* remendado, pegado;
Sw. lagad.

pigskin *or* hogskin.
>*Dan.* Svinelæder; *Du.* varkensleer; *Fr.*
peau de truie; *Ger.* Schweinsleder; *It.*
pelle di porco; *Sp.* piel de cerdo; *Sw.*
svinskinn.

placard. *See* **poster.**

place of printing. *See* **printing, place of.**

place of publication. *See* **publication, place of.**

plate.
>*Dan.* Stik; *Du.* plaat, snede; *Fr.* gravure,
planche; *Ger.* Stich; *It.* incisione, intaglio, tavola; *Sp.* grabado; *Sw.* gravyr,
plansch.

playing cards.
>*Dan.* Spillekort; *Du.* speelkaarten; *Fr.*
cartes à jouer; *Ger.* Spielkarten; *It.*
carte da giuoco; *Sp.* barajas; *Sw.* spelkort.

pocket edition.
>*Dan.* Lommeudgave; *Du.* zakuitgaaf; *Fr.*
édition de poche, édition portative; *Ger.*
Taschenausgabe; *It.* edizione portatile;
Sp. edición de bolsillo; *Sw.* upplaga i
fickformat.

poem.
>*Dan.* Digt; *Du.* gedicht; *Fr.* poème; *Ger.*

Gedicht; *It.* poema; *Sp.* poema; *Sw.* dikt.

popular edition. *See* **edition, popular.**

portrait.

Dan. Portræt; *Du.* portret; *Fr.* portrait; *Ger.* Portrait; *It.* ritratto; *Sp.* retrato; *Sw.* porträtt.

poster *or* **placard.** An advertising sheet of considerable size, usually printed and often illustrated.

Dan. Plakat, Opslag; *Du.* aanplakbiljet; *Fr.* affiche, placard; *Ger.* Plakat, Anschlag; *It.* avviso; *Sp.* cartel; *Sw.* anslag.

posthumous works. *See* **works, posthumous.**

prayer-book.

Dan. Bönnebog; *Du.* gebedenboek; *Fr.* livre de prières; *Ger.* Gebetbuch; *It.* libro di preghiere; *Sp.* devocionario, libro de devociones; *Sw.* bönbok.

preface.

Dan. Fortale, Forord; *Du.* voorrede, voorbericht, voorwoord; *Fr.* préface, avant-propos; *Ger.* Vorrede, Vorwort; *It.* prefazione; *Sp.* prefación; *Sw.* förtal.

prefix.

Dan. Forstavelse; *Du.* voorvoegsel; *Fr.* préfixe; *Ger.* Vorsilbe; *It.* prefisso; *Sp.* prefijo; *Sw.* förestafvelse.

preliminary leaves. *See* **leaves, preliminary.**

prepared *or* **edited.**

Dan. bearbejdet; *Du.* bewerkt; *Fr.* édité; *Ger.* bearbeitet; *It.* edito; *Sp.* compuesto, hecho, escrito; *Sw.* bearbetad.

presentation copy.

Dan. Gaveeksemplar, Frieksemplar; *Du.* presentexemplaar; *Fr.* exemplaire d'hommage, livre d'hommage, envoi d'auteur; *Ger.* Geschenkexemplar; *It.* esemplare di omaggio, invio dell' autore, omaggio dell' autore; *Sp.* ejemplar regalado; *Sw.* gåfvo-exemplar, friexemplar.

press. (pr.)

Dan. Presse; *Du.* drukpers; *Fr.* presse; *Ger.* Presse; *It.* torchio; *Sp.* prensa; *Sw.* press.

press, in the.

Dan. i Trykken; *Du.* ter perse; *Fr.* sous presse; *Ger.* im Druck; *It.* sotto il torchio; *Sp.* en prensa; *Sw.* under tryckning.

press, revolving.

Dan. Cylinderpresse; *Du.* cylinderpers; *Fr.* presse à cylindre; *Ger.* Cylinderpresse; *It.* torchio a cilindro; *Sp.* prensa de cilindro; *Sw.* cylinderpress.

press-proof.

Dan. sidste Korrektur; *Du.* persrevisie; *Fr.* dernière épreuve, tierce; *Ger.* Pressrevision, Superrevision; *It.* ultima bozza; *Sp.* última prueba, prueba de prensa; *Sw.* reviderark.

price.

Dan. Pris; *Du.* prijs; *Fr.* prix; *Ger.* Preis; *It.* prezzo; *Sp.* precio; *Sw.* pris.

print, to.

Dan. trykke; *Du.* drukken; *Fr.* imprimer;

Ger. drucken; *It.* stampare; *Sp.* imprimir, estampar; *Sw.* trycka.

printer.

Dan. Bogtrykker; *Du.* boekdrukker; *Fr.* imprimeur; *Ger.* Drucker; *It.* stampatore; *Sp.* impresor; *Sw.* boktryckare.

printer's ink.

Dan. Bogtrykkersværte; *Du.* drukinkt; *Fr.* encre d'imprimeur; *Ger.* Druckfarbe; *It.* inchiostro da stampa; *Sp.* tinta de imprenta; *Sw.* trycksvärta.

printer's mark.

Dan. Bogtrykkermærke; *Du.* drukkersmerk; *Fr.* marque d'imprimeur, marque typographique, devise; *Ger.* Druckermarke, Druckerzeichen; Druckersignet; *It.* marca tipografica, insegna, segno; *Sp.* marca del impresor; *Sw.* boktryckares märke.

printing, art of. *See* **art of printing.**

printing, place of.

Dan. Trykkested; *Du.* plaats van druk; *Fr.* lieu d'impression; *Ger.* Druckort; *It.* luogo di stampa; *Sp.* lugar de imprenta; *Sw.* tryckort.

printing office.

Dan. Bogtrykkeri; *Du.* boekdrukkerij; *Fr.* imprimerie; *Ger.* Druckerei; *It.* stamperia; *Sp.* imprenta; *Sw.* boktryckeri, tryckeri.

privately printed. *See* **at the author's expense.**

prize, awarded a.

Dan. prisbelönnet; *Du.* bekroond; *Fr.* couronné; *Ger.* gekrönt; *It.* premiato, coronato; *Sp.* premiado, coronado; *Sw.* prisbelönt.

prize-essay.

Dan. Prisskrift; *Du.* prijsschrift; *Fr.* ouvrage couronné; *Ger.* Preisschrift; *It.* opera coronata; *Sp.* obra coronada; *Sw.* prisskrift.

proceedings. The published record of the action taken, or the things done at a meeting of an association. *Stand. Dict.*

Dan. Forhandlinger; *Du.* verslagen; *Fr.* bulletins; *Ger.* Sitzungsberichte; *It.* atti, resoconti; *Sp.* actas; *Sw.* förhandlingar.

proof before letters. (e.) An impression taken before the title or inscription is engraved.

Dan. för Skriften; *Du.* vóór de letter; *Fr.* avant la lettre, épreuve d'artiste; *Ger.* Abdruck eines Stiches vor der Schrift; *It.* prova avanti lettera; *Sp.* prueba de artista; prueba antes de la letra; *Sw.* afdrag utan text.

proofmark, *or* **mark of correction.**

Dan. Korrekturtegn; *Du.* correctieteeken; *Fr.* marque de correction; *Ger.* Korrekturzeichen; *It.* segno di correzione; *Sp.* signo de corrección; *Sw.* korrekturtecken.

proof-reader. One who reads and marks corrections in printer's proofs.

Dan. Korrekturlæser; *Du.* proeflezer, corrector; *Fr.* correcteur; *Ger.* Korrektor; *It.* correttore; *Sp.* corrector de pruebas; *Sw.* korrekturläsare.

proof-reading. Reading and making corrections in printer's proofs.

Dan. Korrekturlæsning; *Du.* correctie van drukproeven; *Fr.* correction; *Ger.* Korrektur; *It.* correzione delle prove; *Sp.* corrección de pruebas; *Sw.* korrekturläsning.

proof-sheet. A sheet of paper on which a proof has been taken. The margin is wide for marking corrections.

Dan. Korrekturark; *Du.* drukproef, proefblad; *Fr.* épreuve; *Ger.* Korrekturbogen, Probebogen; *It.* prova, bozza; *Sp.* prueba, pliego de prueba; *Sw.* korrekturark, profark.

publication, place of.

Dan. Udgivelsessted; *Du.* plaats van uitgaaf; *Fr.* lieu de publication; *Ger.* Erscheinungsort; *It.* luogo di pubblicazione, luogo dell' edizione; *Sp.* lugar de edición; *Sw.* utgifningsort.

publication, year of. *See* **imprint date.**

punctuation.

Dan. Interpunktion; *Du.* punctuatie; *Fr.* ponctuation; *Ger.* Interpunktion; *It.* punteggiatura; *Sp.* puntuación; *Sw.* interpunktion.

Q

quadrat. (pr.) A piece of type metal lower than the letters, used in spacing between words and filling out blank lines. *Stand. Dict.*

Dan. Kvadrat; *Du.* kwadraat; *Fr.* cadrat; *Ger.* Gevierte; *It.* quadretto; *Sp.* cuadrado; *Sw.* kvadrat.

quarterly.

Dan. fjerdingaarlig; *Du.* driemaandelijksch; *Fr.* trimestriel; *Ger.* vierteljährlich; *It.* trimestrale; *Sp.* trimestral; *Sw.* utkommande kvartalvis.

quire. (pa.) A collection of twenty-four sheets of paper of the same size and quality, either not folded or having a single fold.

Dan. Bog Papir; *Du.* boek papier; *Fr.* main de papier; *Ger.* Buch Papier; *It.* quaderno di fogli; *Sp.* mano de papel; *Sw.* bok papper.

quotation marks.

Dan. Anförselstegn, Gaaseöjne; *Du.* aanspraakteeken, aanhalingsteeken; *Fr.* guillemets; *Ger.* Anführungszeichen; *It.* virgolette; *Sp.* virgulillas; *Sw.* anföringstecken, citationstecken.

R

rare *or* **scarce.**

Dan. sjælden; *Du.* zeldzaam; *Fr.* rare; *Ger.* selten; *It.* raro; *Sp.* raro; *Sw.* sällsynt, rar.

ream. (pa.) A quantity of paper, usually twenty quires.

Dan. Riis; *Du.* riem; *Fr.* rame; *Ger.* Ries; *It.* risma; *Sp.* resma; *Sw.* ris.

rebind, to. (bb.)

Dan. inbinde paany; *Du.* herbinden; *Fr.* relier de nouveau; *Ger.* neubinden; *It.* legare di nuovo, rilegare; *Sp.* reencuadernar; *Sw.* inbinda ånyo.

recto. *See* **page, odd.**

red edged. *See* **edged, red.**

reference book.

Dan. Haandbog; *Du.* handboek; *Fr.* livre de référence; *Ger.* Nachschlagebuch, Promptuarium, Handbuch; *It.* libro di consultazione, manuale; *Sp.* libro de referencia; *Sw.* handbok, uppslagsbok.

remainders. (bo.) Copies of a book remaining in the publisher's stock when sales have ceased.

Dan. Restoplag; *Du.* oplage restanten; *Fr.* restant de l'édition; *Ger.* Auflagereste, Remittenden; *It.* copie invendute, il fondo; *Sp.* restante de la edición; *Sw.* restupplaga.

repaired. *See* **pieced out.**

report. An official statement of facts, oral or written.

Dan. Beretning; *Du.* verslag; *Fr.* compterendu; *Ger.* Bericht; *It.* rendiconto, resoconto; *Sp.* memoria; *Sw.* berättelse, redogörelse.

report, annual.

Dan. Aarsberetning; *Du.* jaarverslag; *Fr.* compte-rendu annuel, rapport annuel; *Ger.* Jahresbericht; *It.* resoconto annuale, rendiconto annuale; *Sp.* memoria anual; *Sw.* årsbrättelse, årsredogörelse.

report, monthly.

Dan. Maanedsberetning; *Du.* maandelijksch verslag; *Fr.* compte rendu mensuel; *Ger.* Monatsbericht; *It.* rendiconto mensile, resoconto mensile; *Sp.* memoria mensual; *Sw.* månatlig berättelse, månatlig redogörelse.

reprint.

Dan. Særtryk, Separataftryk; *Du.* overdruk, herdruk; *Fr.* réimpression, tirage à part; *Ger.* Neudruck, Sonderdruck, Separatabdruck; *It.* ristampa, tiratura a parte; *Sp.* reimpresión, tirada especial; *Sw.* särtryck, separattryck.

reprint (unauthorized).

Dan. Eftertryk; *Du.* nadruk; *Fr.* réimpression illégale, contrefaçon; *Ger.* Nachdruck; *It.* contraffazione tipografica, ristampa furtiva; *Sp.* reimpresión ilegal; *Sw.* eftertryck.

review.

Dan. Revue; *Du.* revue; *Fr.* revue; *Ger.* Revue; *It.* rivista; *Sp.* revista; *Sw.* revy.

revolving press. *See* **press, revolving.**

rewritten.

    Dan. omarbejdet; *Du.* omgewerkt; *Fr.* refondu; *Ger.* umgearbeitet; *It.* riscritto; *Sp.* refundido; *Sw.* omarbetad.

rounding. (bb.) The process of making the back of a book round.

    Dan. Ombankning; *Du.* rugrondingswerk; *Fr.* arrondissage; *Ger.* Umklopfen; *Sp.* la acciön de redondear un lomo de libro.

rubricated. Marked with red.

    Dan. med Rödtryk; *Du.* gerubriceerd; *Fr.* rubriqué; *Ger.* rubriziert; *It.* marcato di rosso, rubricato; *Sp.* impreso en rojo; *Sw.* med rödtryck.

running title. *See* **heading, live.**

Russia leather. Fragrant goat- or sheep-leather, which is made by a special dressing-process and resists moisture and ravages of insects. *Stand. Dict.*

    Dan. Ruslæder; *Du.* Russisch leer, juchtleer; *Fr.* cuir de Russie; *Ger.* Juchtenleder; *It.* cuoio di Russia; *Sp.* cuero de Moscovia; *Sw.* ryssläder.

S

scarce. *See* **rare.**

scrapbook. A blank book in which extracts or pictures cut from books and papers may be pasted.

    Dan. Udklipsalbum; *Du.* uitknipselboek; *Fr.* album de découpures; *Ger.* Exzerptenbuch; *It.* album di ritagli, estratti

tagliati; *Sp.* album de recortes; *Sw.*
utklippsalbum.

second form. (pr.) *See* **form, second.**

secondhand book. *See* **book, secondhand.**

secondhand bookseller. *See* **bookseller, secondhand.**

selected works. *See* **works, selected.**

selection.

> *Dan.* Udvalg; *Du.* keur; *Fr.* choix; *Ger.* Auswahl; *It.* scelta; *Sp.* selección; *Sw.* urval.

semicolon.

> *Dan.* Semikolon; *Du.* komma-punt; *Fr.* point et virgule; *Ger.* Semikolon; *It.* punto e virgola; *Sp.* punto y coma; *Sw.* semikolon.

semi-monthly. Appearing every half month.

> *Dan.* to Gange om Maaneden; *Du.* half-maandelijksch; *Fr.* bimensuel; *Ger.* halbmonatlich; *It.* quindicinale; *Sp.* quincenal; *Sw.* två gånger i månaden.

series.

> *Dan.* Række; *Du.* reeks; *Fr.* série; *Ger.* Folge, Reihe; *It.* serie; *Sp.* serie; *Sw.* följd.

sermon.

> *Dan.* Prædiken; *Du.* preek; *Ger.* Predigt; *It.* sermone; *Sp.* sermón; *Sw.* predikan.

setting rule. *See* **composing rule.**

sewing board. (bb.)

> *Dan.* Hæftelade; *Du.* naaibank; *Fr.* cousoir; *Ger.* Heftlade; *It.* tavoletta de' legatori di libri; *Sp.* telar; *Sw.* häftlåda.

shagreen *or* **chagrin.** A kind of untanned leather prepared in Russia and the East from the skins of horses, asses, camels, etc., and covered with small round granulations produced by pressing small seeds into the skin when it is moist, shaving the skin down to the level of depressions thus made, and then making the compressed parts swell by soaking. *Stand. Dict.*

Dan. Chagrinlæder; *Du.* segrijnleer; *Fr.* chagrin; *Ger.* Chagrinleder; *It.* zigrino, pelle ruvida; *Sp.* chagrén; piel de zapa; *Sw.* sjagräng.

shank *or* **body of a letter. (pr.)**

Dan. Kegle; *Du.* kegel; *Fr.* corps de lettre; *Ger.* Schriftkegel; *It.* corpo d'un carattere; *Sp.* cuerpo del tipo; *Sw.* kägel.

sheepskin.

Dan. Lammeskind; *Du.* schapenleer; *Fr.* peau d'agneau; *Ger.* Schafleder; *It.* pelle di pecora; *Sp.* piel de carnero; *Sw.* fårskinn.

sheet.

Dan. Ark; *Du.* vel; *Fr.* feuille; *Ger.* Bogen; *It.* foglio; *Sp.* pliego; *Sw.* ark.

signature. A letter or figure placed at the bottom of the first page of each sheet of a book as a direction to the binder in folding the sheets. *Stand. Dict.*

Dan. Arksignatur; *Du.* signatuur; *Fr.* signature; *Ger.* Signatur; *It.* segnatura; *Sp.* signatura; *Sw.* arksignatur.

size.
>   *Dan.* Format; *Du.* formaat; *Fr.* format;
>   *Ger.* Format; *It.* forma, formato, sesto;
>   *Sp.* tamaño; *Sw.* format.

sketch *or* **rough draft.**
>   *Dan.* Afrids, Skizze; *Du.* schets; *Fr.*
>   esquisse, croquis; *Ger.* Abriss, Skizze;
>   *It.* schizzo, abbozzo; *Sp.* esquicio, esbozo;
>   *Sw.* skiss.

skin. *See* **leather.**

slip-proof. *See* **galley proof.**

slug. (pr.) A thick strip of metal less than
>   type high.
>   *Dan.* Udslutning; *Du.* sluitstuk; *Fr.*
>   lingot; *Ger.* Ausschlusstück; *It.* margine
>   di piombo; *Sp.* lingote; *Sw.* utslutning.

small caps. *See* **capitals, small.**

small letter. *See* **letter, small.**

small tools. *See* **tools, small.**

society (learned) publications.
>   *Dan.* lærd Selskabs Skrifter; *Du.* genoot-
>   schapswerken; *Fr.* publications des aca-
>   démies; *Ger.* Gesellschaftsschriften; *It.*
>   pubblicazioni delle accademie; *Sp.*
>   trabajos de academias; *Sw.* lärdt sälls-
>   kaps skrifter.

solid matter. (pr.) *See* **matter, close.**

spring back. *See* **back, spring.**

sprinkled edges. *See* **edges, sprinkled.**

squares. *See* **brackets.**

stain.
>   *Dan.* Smudsplet; *Du.* vlek; *Fr.* souillure;
>   *Ger.* Schmutzfleck; *It.* macchia; *Sp.*
>   mancha; *Sw.* smutsfläck.

stained.

> *Dan.* plettet; *Du.* gevlekt; *Fr.* souillé;
> *Ger.* fleckig; *It.* macchiato; *Sp.* man-
> chado; *Sw.* nedsmutsad, nedfläckad.

stamped paper.

> *Dan.* Stempelpapir; *Du.* zegelpapier; *Fr.*
> papier timbré; *Ger.* Stempelpapier;
> *It.* carta bollata; *Sp.* papel sellado,
> papel estampado; *Sw.* stämpelpapper.

state. (e.)

> *Dan.* Stadium; *Du.* staat; *Fr.* état; *Ger.*
> Zustand, Plattenzustand; *It.* stato; *Sp.*
> estadio; *Sw.* stadium.

steel-engraving. An impression taken from
an engraved steel plate. *Stand. Dict.*

> *Dan.* Staalstik; *Du.* staalgravure; *Fr.*
> gravure sur acier; *Ger.* Stahlstich; *It.*
> incisione in acciaio; *Sp.* grabado en
> acero; *Sw.* stålstick.

stipple engraving. (e.) A method of engraving in which the lights and shades
are produced by dots instead of lines
or hatchings. *Stand. Dict.*

> *Dan.* Punktmanèr; *Du.* punteermanier;
> *Fr.* pointillage; *Ger.* Punktiermanier; *It.*
> punteggiatura; *Sp.* grabado á puntos;
> *Sw.* punktérmanér.

stitched. Leaves of pamphlets fastened with
thread or wire drawn through previously
pierced holes are called stitched.

> *Dan.* hæftet; *Du.* ingenaaid; *Fr.* broché;
> *Ger.* broschiert, geheftet; *It.* legato in
> rustico; *Sp.* cosido à la rustica, en rustica;
> *Sw.* häftad.

subscriber.

Dan. Abonnent; *Du.* inteekenaar; *Fr.* abonné; *Ger.* Subskribent; *It.* abbonato; *Sp.* subscriptor; *Sw.* abonnent.

subscription.

Dan. Abonnement; *Du.* abonnement; inteekening; *Fr.* abonnement; *Ger.* Abonnement; *It.* abbonamento; *Sp.* suscripción; *Sw.* abonnement.

subtitle. A secondary or subordinate title of a book.

Dan. Undertitel; *Du.* ondertitel; *Fr.* soustitre; *Ger.* Untertitel, Sondertitel; *It.* sottotitolo; *Sp.* sototítulo; *Sw.* undertitel.

summary. *See* **abstract.**

superiors. (p.) Type standing at the top of a line, often used as a sign of reference. *Stand. Dict.*

Dan. Notetegn; *Du.* boven-letters; *Fr.* lettrines; *Ger.* Verweisungsbuchstaben; *It.* letterine di chiamata; *Sp.* letras voladas, letras superiores; *Sw.* notsiffra.

supplement. *See* **appendix.**

suppressed.

Dan. beslaglagt; *Du.* in beslag genomen; *Fr.* saisi; *Ger.* mit Beschlag belegt; *It.* sequestrato; *Sp.* recogido por orden del gobierno ó tribunal; *Sw.* beslaglagd.

synopsis. *See* **abstract.**

T

table of contents.

Dan. Indholdsfortegnelse; *Du.* blad-wijzer; *Fr.* table des matières; *Ger.* Inhaltsverzeichnis; *It.* indice, tavola delle materie; *Sp.* tabla de materias, indice; *Sw.* innehållsförteckning.

table of errata.

Dan. Trykfejlsliste; *Du.* lijst van druk-fouten; *Fr.* errata; *Ger.* Druckfehler-verzeichnis; *It.* tavola degli errori, errata; *Sp.* fe de erratas; *Sw.* tryckfels-förteckning.

tail of a book *or* **lower edge.**

Dan. Undersnit; *Du.* staart, ondersnee; *Fr.* queue; *Ger.* unterer Schnitt, Schwanz; *It.* il disotto; *Sp.* canto inferior de un libro; *Sw.* undersnitt.

tail-piece *or* **cul de lampe.** An ornament at the bottom of a short page or at the end of a book. *Stand. Dict.*

Dan. Finale; *Du.* vignette aan het slot van een hoofdstuk; *Fr.* fleuron, cul de lampe; *Ger.* Schlussvignette, Zierleiste; *It.* finale, fregio, vignetta; *Sp.* final; *Sw.* slutvignett.

tail-type. (pr.)

Dan. Bogstav som naar ned under Linien; *Du.* staartletter; *Fr.* lettre à queue; *Ger.* geschwänzte Schrift; *It.* lettera discendente; lettera con asta discen-

77

dente; *Sp.* letra descendente; *Sw.* bokstaf som räcker under linjen.

tale.
> *Dan.* Fortælling; *Du.* verhaal, vertelling;
> *Fr.* conte; *Ger.* Erzählung; *It.* novella;
> *Sp.* cuento; *Sw.* saga.

tall copy. *See* **paper, large.**

thesis. *See* **dissertation.**

tie in, to. (bb.)
> *Dan.* hæfte Arkene; *Du.* kordeeren; *Fr.*
> fouetter; *Ger.* einschnüren; *It.* allacciare;
> *Sp.* encordelar; *Sw.* häfta ark.

tight back. *See* **back, tight.**

time table.
> *Dan.* Fartplan; *Du.* reisgids, spoorboekje;
> *Fr.* indicateur; *Ger.* Fahrplan; *It.* ora-
> rio; *Sp.* itinerario, cuadro de marcha de
> trenes; *Sw.* tidtabell.

tissue-paper.
> *Dan.* Silkepapir; *Du.* vloeipapier; *Fr.*
> papier Joseph, papier de soie; *Ger.*
> Seidenpapier; *It.* carta velina; *Sp.* papel
> de seda, papel José; *Sw.* silkespapper.

title.
> *Dan.* Titel; *Du.* titel; *Fr.* titre; *Ger.* Titel;
> *It.* titolo; *Sp.* título; *Sw.* titel.

title, collective.
> *Dan.* Hovedtitel; *Du.* hoofdtitel; *Fr.*
> grand titre; *Ger.* Gesamttitel; Haupt-
> titel; *It.* titolo collettivo; *Sp.* título
> general; *Sw.* gemensam titel.

title, running. *See* **heading, live.**

title-page.

Dan. Titelblad; *Du.* titelblad; *Fr.* feuille de titre; *Ger.* Titelblatt; *It.* frontispizio, titolo; *Sp.* carátula, portada; *Sw.* titelblad.

title-page lacking.

Dan. Titelblad mangler; *Du.* titelblad ontbreekt; *Fr.* le titre manque; *Ger.* Titel fehlt; *It.* manca il frontispizio; *Sp.* falta de portada; *Sw.* titelblad saknas.

tooled edges. *See* **edges, tooled.**

tools, small. (bb.)

Dan. Smaajern; *Du.* kleine stempels; *Fr.* petits fers; *Ger.* feine Stempel; *It.* piccoli ferri; *Sp.* hierros pequeños; *Sw.* små stämplar.

top, gilt.

Dan. överste Snit forgyldt; *Du.* bovensnede verguld, kop verguld; *Fr.* tête dorée; *Ger.* oberer Schnitt vergoldet; *It.* dorato in testa, disopra dorato, taglio superiore dorato; *Sp.* cabeza dorada; *Sw.* förgyld topp.

transactions.

Dan. Forhandlinger; *Du.* handelingen; *Fr.* travaux, transactions; *Ger.* Abhandlungen; *It.* atti; *Sp.* trabajos; *Sw.* handlingar.

translated.

Dan. oversat; *Du.* overgezet, vertaald; *Fr.* traduit; *Ger.* übersetzt; *It.* tradotto; *Sp.* traducido; *Sw.* öfversatt.

translator.
> *Dan.* Oversætter; *Du.* vertaler; *Fr.* traducteur; *Ger.* Uebersetzer; *It.* tradutt ore; *Sp.* traductor; *Sw.* öfversättare.

transliteration. Spelling in the characters of another alphabet.
> *Dan.* Omskrivning; *Du.* omlettering; *Fr.* translittération; *Ger.* Umschreibung; *It.* traslitterazione; *Sp.* representación de las letras de una lengua por las letras de otra; *Sw.* omskrifning.

turn over the leaves of a book.
> *Dan.* gennemblade; *Du.* doorbladeren; *Fr.* feuilleter; *Ger.* durchblättern; *It.* carteggiare; *Sp.* hojear; *Sw.* genombläddra.

turned letter. *See* **letter, turned.**

type. (pr.)
> *Dan.* Type; *Du.* drukletter; *Fr.* type; *Ger.* Typus; *It.* tipo; *Sp.* tipo; *Sw.* bokstafstil, typ.

type-case. A case containing type.
> *Dan.* Skriftkasse; *Du.* letterkas, letterkast; *Fr.* casse; *Ger.* Schriftkasten; *It.* cassa da caratteri; *Sp.* caja; *Sw.* kast.

type-case, box in a.
> *Dan.* Afdeling i en Skriftkasse; *Du.* letterkastvakje; *Fr.* cassetin; *Ger.* Schriftkastenfach; *It.* cassettino; *Sp.* cajetín; *Sw.* kastfack.

type-setting machine. *See* **composing machine.**

types, bold faced *or* **black faced type** *or* **heavy faced type.**

Dan. fede Typer; *Du.* vette letters; *Fr.* caractères gras; *Ger.* fette Schrift; *It.* caratteri pieni; *Sp.* letras negras, tipos negros; *Sw.* fet stil.

types, light faced *or* **lean faced types.**

Dan. tynd Skrift; *Du.* magere letters; *Fr.* caractères maigres; *Ger.* magere Schrift; *It.* scrittura magra, caratteri magri; *Sp.* tipos delgados, tipos de poco cuerpo; *Sw.* mager stil.

U

unbound.

Dan. uindbunden; *Du.* ongebonden; *Fr.* non relié; *Ger.* ungebunden; *It.* non rilegato; *Sp.* no encuadernado; *Sw.* obunden.

uncut.

Dan. ubeskaaret; *Du.* ongesneden; *Fr.* non rogné; *Ger.* unbeschnitten; *It.* intonso; *Sp.* no cortado; *Sw.* ej afskuren.

underlined. *See* **underscored.**

underscored *or* **underlined.**

Dan. understreget; *Du.* onderstreept; *Fr.* souligné; *Ger.* unterstrichen; *It.* sottolineato; *Sp.* subrayado; *Sw.* understruken.

underscoring *or* **underlining.**

Dan. Understregning; *Du.* onderstreeping; *Fr.* soulignure; *Ger.* Unterstreichung;

It. parola sottolineata; *Sp.* subrayado; *Sw.* understrykning.

upper case. (pr.)

Dan. Typer tagne fra Skriftkassens överste Del; *Du.* bovenkast letters; *Fr.* haut de casse; *Ger.* Typen aus dem Kapitalkasten; *It.* cassa alta; *Sp.* caja alta; *Sw.* stilar från kastens öfversta fack.

V

vellum paper *or* **parchment paper.**

Dan. Velinpapir; *Du.* velijnpapier, perkamentpapier; *Fr.* papier vélin; *Ger.* Velinpapier; *It.* carta velina; *Sp.* papel avitelado; *Sw.* velinpapper.

volume.

Dan. Bind; *Du.* deel; *Fr.* tome, volume; *Ger.* Band; *It.* tomo, volume; *Sp.* tomo, volumen; *Sw.* band, volym.

W

waste-paper.

Dan. Makulatur; *Du.* scheurpapier; *Fr.* maculature, rebut; *Ger.* Makulatur; *It.* fogliaccio; *Sp.* papel de embalaje; *Sw.* makulatur.

waste-paper. (pr.)

Dan. Udskudsark; *Du.* misdruk; *Fr.* braies; *Ger.* Makulaturbogen; *It.* brache; *Sp.* maculatura; *Sw.* makulaturark.

water lines. (pa.) Lines in the paper about 25–30 millimeters apart which intersect at right angles other very closely spaced lines, the so-called wiremarks.

Dan. Vandlinier; *Du.* waterlijnen; *Fr.* pontuseaux; *Ger.* Wasserlinien; *It.* colonelli; *Sp.* puntizones; *Sw.* vattenlinjer.

water mark. A mark produced in paper by pressure of a projecting design on the dandy roll, in the mold, etc. *Webster.*

Dan. Vandmærke; *Du.* watermerk; *Fr.* filigrane, marque d'eau; *Ger.* Wasserzeichen; *It.* filigrana; *Sp.* marca de agua, filigrana; *Sw.* vattenstämpel.

water-stain *or* **mildew.**

Dan. Fugtighedsplet; *Du.* vochtvlek; *Fr.* tache de moisissure; *Ger.* Wasserfleck, Moderfleck; *It.* gora; *Sp.* mancha de agua, mancha de humedad; *Sw.* mögelfläck, vattenfläck.

weekly.

Dan. ugentlig; *Du.* wekelijksch; *Fr.* hebdomadaire; *Ger.* wöchentlich; *It.* d'ogni settimana, settimanale; *Sp.* semanal, hebdomadario; *Sw.* veckligen.

weekly newspaper. *See* **newspaper, weekly.**

wiremarks. (pa.) Very closely spaced lines in paper caused by the brass wires attached to the mold. They intersect the water lines at right angles.

Dan. Tværstriber; *Du.* vormdraden; *Fr.* vergeures; *Ger.* Formstreifen, Formdraht; *It.* vergature; *Sp.* líneas del verjurado; *Sw.* randing i papper.

with explanatory notes.

Dan. forklaret; *Du.* met toelichtingen; *Fr.* expliqué, élucidé; *Ger.* erläutert; *It.* con note esplicative; *Sp.* con notas explicativas; *Sw.* med förklaringar.

witness. Leaves of a book left uncut by the binder to show that he has spared the margin as much as possible.

Fr. témoin; *Ger.* Randzeuge; *It.* testimonio.

wood-engraving. (e.)

Dan. Træsnit; *Du.* houtsnede; *Fr.* gravure sur bois; *Ger.* Holzschnitt; *It.* incisione in legno; *Sp.* grabado en madera; *Sw.* träsnitt.

wooden boards.

Dan. Træbogpærmer; *Du.* houtband; *Fr.* plats de bois; *Ger.* Holzdeckel; *It.* piatti in legno; *Sp.* tapas de madera; *Sw.* träpärmar.

word.

Dan. Ord; *Du.* woord; *Fr.* mot; *Ger.* Wort; *It.* parola; *Sp.* palabra; *Sw.* ord.

work.

Dan. Værk; *Du.* werk; *Fr.* œuvre, ouvrage; *Ger.* Werk; *It.* opera; *Sp.* obra; *Sw.* verk.

works, collected.

Dan. samlede Værker; *Du.* verzamelde werken, volledige werken; *Fr.* œuvres complètes; *Ger.* sämtliche Werke; *It.*

opere complete, corpo; *Sp.* obras completas; *Sw.* samlade arbeten.

works, posthumous.
Dan. efterladte Skrifter; *Du.* nagelaten werken; *Fr.* œuvres posthumes; *Ger.* nachgelassene Werke; *It.* opere postume; *Sp.* obras póstumas; *Sw.* efterlemnade skrifter.

works, selected.
Dan. udvalgte Værker; *Du.* uitgelezen werken; *Fr.* œuvres choisies; *Ger.* ausgewählte Werke; *It.* opere scelte; *Sp.* obras escogidas; *Sw.* utvalda skrifter.

wormhole.
Dan. Ormehul; *Du.* wormgat; *Fr.* piqure; *Ger.* Wurmstich; *It.* tarlatura; *Sp.* picadura de polilla; *Sw.* maskhål.

wormholed.
Dan. ormstukken; *Du.* wormstekig; *Fr.* vermoulu, piqué de vers; *Ger.* wurmstichig; *It.* tarlato, tarmato; *Sp.* apolillado; *Sw.* maskstungen.

worn binding. *See* **binding, worn.**

wrapper *or* **cover.**
Dan. Omslag; *Du.* omslag; *Fr.* couverture; *Ger.* Umschlag; Deckel; *It.* copertina; *Sp.* cubierta; *Sw.* omslag.

wriing.
Dan. Skrift; *Du.* geschrift; *Fr.* écriture; *Ger.* Schrift; *It.* scrittura; *Sp.* escritura; *Sw.* skrift.

wrong letter. *See* **letter, wrong.**

Y

year.

   Dan. Aargang; *Du.* jaargang; *Fr.* année;
   Ger. Jahrgang; *It.* annata, anno; *Sp.*
   año; *Sw.* årgång.

yearly. *See* **annual.**

DANISH

A

A. Aar.

Aal. (pr.) bodkin.

Aar. year.

Aarböger. (b.) annals.

Aarg. Aargang.

Aargang. (b.) year, annual volume.

aarlig. annual, yearly.

Aarsberetning. annual report.

Abonnent. subscriber.

Adgangskort. card of admission.

Afbildning. illustration.

Afgangsark *or* **Makulatur** *or* **Udskudsark. (pr.)** waste sheets.

Aflægning. (pr.) distribution of type.

aflang. (b.) oblong.

Afrids *or* **Skizze.** sketch, rough draft.

Afsnit. (b.) section.

Aftryk. (pr.) impression.

Aftryk, förste. (e.) plain prints.

Aftryk för Skriften. (e.) proof before letters.

Aftryk med Underskrift. (e.) proof with letters.

ægte Bind *or* **ophöjede Tværbind. (bb.)** raised bands.

Akcidenstryk. (pr.) job-printing.

Akcidenstrykker. (pr.) job-printer.

Akt. (b.) act.

Anförselstegn. quotation marks.

Anhang. (b.) appendix.

Anmærkning. (b.) annotation, note.

Anmeldereksemplar. reviewer's copy.

Annonce. *See* **Avertissement.**

Antikvarboghandler. secondhand book-seller.

Ark. (b.) sheet.

Arkenes Ordning *or* **Arkenes Optagning. (bb.)** gathering.

Arksignatur. (b.) signature.

Artikel, ledende *or* **Leder.** editorial.

Æselsöre. (b.) dog's ear.

Ætsbund *or* **Radeergrund. (e.)** etching ground.

Avertissement *or* **Annonce.** advertisement.

Avis. newspaper.

Avisudklip. newspaper clipping.

B

Bagside. (b.) even page, verso.

Balle Papir. ten reams of paper.

Begravelse. (pr.) out, *i.e.*, omission of a word or phrase by the compositor.

Begyndelsesbogstav. initial.

Begyndelsesvignet. (b.) head-piece.

Beretning. report.

beskaaret. cut down.

beskaaret, stærkt. cropped.

beskadiget. damaged, mutilated.

beslaglagt. (bo.) suppressed.

Bind, ægte *or* **ophöjede Tværbind. (bb.)** raised bands.

Bind, slidt. worn binding.

Bindestreg. hyphen.

Blad, omtrykt. cancel.

Blæk. ink.

Blindtryk. (bb.) blind tooling.

Blokbog. blockbook.

blokeret Bogstav. (pr.) turned letter.

Blyantstegning. penciling.

Bog, brugt. secondhand book.

Bog, ubeskreven. blank-book.

Bog i Materie. (b.) book in sheets, book in quires.

Bog Papir. quire.

Bogbinder. binder.

Bogbinderi. bookbinder-shop.

Bogbinderlærred. buckram.

Bogelsker *or* **Bibliofil.** bibliophile.

Boghandlermesse. (bo.) book-fair.

Bogladepris. (bo.) list price, published price.

Boglap. (bb.) lettering piece, label.

Boglap, forsynet med. labeled.

Bogliste. catalogue, list of books.

Bogmærke. bookmark.

Bogorm. bookworm.

Bogplade *or* **ex libris. (b.)** bookplate.

Bogryg. back of a book.

Bogryggens Tildannelse. (bb.) backing.

Bogsamler. book-collector.

Bogsamling. library.

Bogsnit. edges.

Bogstav, blokeret. (pr.) turned letter.

Bogstav, forsiret. (pr.) fancy letter.

Bogstav, læderet. (pr.) battered letter.

Bogstav, lille *or* **Minuskel.** small letter.
Bogstav, stort *or* **Majuskel.** capital letter.
Bogstavrim. alliteration.
Bogtryk *or* **Værksats. (pr.)** bookwork.
Bogtrykker. printer.
Bogtrykkermærke. printer's mark.
Bogtrykkersværte. printer's ink.
Bönnebog. prayer-book.
Börneböger. (pl.) juvenile literature.
Börsteaftryk. brushproof.
Bort. margin-border.
Böttepapir. handmade paper.
Brev. letter.
Brevhoved. letter-head.
Brevveksling. correspondence.
Brochure *or* **Flyveskrift** *or* **Pjece. (b.)** pamphlet.
Brödskrift *or* **Værkskrift. (pr.)** body type, ordinary type.
Brokkasse. *See* **Defektkasse.**
Brudstykke. fragment.
brugt Bog. secondhand book.
Bryllup. (pr.) double, *i.e.*, words or sentences by mistake printed twice.
byde paa en Bog. bid on a book.

C

ciseleret Snit. (bb.) tooled edges.
Cylinderpresse. (pr.) revolving press.

D

Dagblad. daily newspaper.
Daggert *or* **Obelisk** *or* **Kors. (b.)** dagger.

daglig. daily.

Defektkasse *or* **Brokkasse. (pr.)** hell, *i.e.*, a box into which a printer throws his broken types.

Disputats *or* **akademisk Afhandling.** dissertation, thesis.

Divisorium. (pr.) visorium.

Dobbeltnavn. compound name.

Dublet. duplicate.

E

Eftersyn, til. (bo.) on approval.

Eftertryk. unauthorized reprint.

Eksemplar. copy.

Eksemplar, smukt. (bo.) fine copy.

Etbladstryk. (b.) broadside.

Eventyr. fairy tale.

F

Fals. (bb.) guard.

Falseben. (bb.) folding stick.

Falsning. (bb.) folding.

færdig til Trykken *or* **kan rentrykkes. (pr.)** for press.

Fartplan. time-table.

fast Ryg. (bb.) tight back.

fede Typer. (pr.) bold face types, black face types.

Fisk *or* **Svibelfisk. (pr.)** pie; *i.e.*, types mixed.

fjerdingaarlig. quarterly.

Flikkeværk. cento.

Flyveblad. (b.) flysheet.

Flyveskrift *or* **Brochure** *or* **Pjece. (b.)** pamphlet.

Foderal. case.

Folkeudgave. popular edition.

för Skriften. (e.) *See* Aftryk för Skriften.

Foren. Forening.

Forening *or* **Selskab.** society.

forgyldt. (bb.) gilt.

Forhandlinger. proceedings.

Forlag, paa eget. (bo.) at the author's expense, privately published.

Forlægger. publisher.

Forlagsret. copyright.

Format. (b.) size.

Formramme. (pr.) chase.

Forms Stege. (pr.) furniture.

Formtraadsstriber. *pl.* **(pa.)** wiremarks.

Forord *or* **Fortale.** preface.

Forsætsblad *or* **Forsats. (b.)** flyleaf.

Forside. (b.) odd page, recto.

forsiret Bogstav. fancy letter.

Forsnit. (bb.) fore-edge.

Forstavelse. prefix.

Fortale *or* **Forord.** preface.

fortlöbende Paginering. (b.) continuous pagination.

fortsat *or* **Fortsættelse fölger. (b.)** to be continued.

Fortsættelse. continuation.

Fortsættelse fölger. *See* fortsat.

Fraktur. (pr.) gothic characters.

Franskbind. (bb.) half binding with leather back and corners.

Frieksemplar. *See* Gaveeksemplar.

G

Gaaseöjne *or* **Anförselstegn.** quotation marks.

Gaveeksemplar *or* **Frieksemplar.** presentation copy.

Gedeskind. (bb.) goatskin.

Generalregister. (b.) general index.

gennemblade. turn over the leaves of a book.

gennemset. revised.

gennemskudt med hvide Blade. interleaved.

Gentrykform *or* **Vidertrykform** *or* **Sekunda-form. (pr.)** second form.

Glitning. (pa.) calendering.

graveret. engraved.

Gravör. engraver.

Gravstik. (e.) graver.

Guldsnit. (bb.) gilt edges.

H

H. Hæfte.

Haandpresse. (pr.) hand-press.

Haandskrift. handwriting.

Hæfte. fascicle.

Hæftlade. (bb.) sewing-board.

Hægte. (bb.) clasp.

halvaarlig. semi-annual.

Halvtitel *or* **Smudstitel.** half title, bastard title, fly title.

Henvisningstegn. (b.) reference-sign.

Hjörnet af en Bog. corner of a book.

Horeunge. (pr.) false line, *i.e.*, end line of a paragraph at the beginning of a page.

Hoved. heading.

Hovedtitel. (b.) collective title.

Huskorrektur. (pr.) first proof (read in the printing office.)

hver anden Maaned. bi-monthly.

I

i god Tilstand. (bo.) in good condition.

indbinde. to bind.

indbinde paany. to rebind.

Indbinding. binding.

Indholdsfortegnelse. index, table of contents.

Indledning. introduction.

indramme med Linier (pr.) to box in.

indrykke. (pr.) to indent.

Indrykning. (pr.) indentation.

indskudt Blad. (bb.) interleaf.

Indskydning. insertion, interpolation.

J

Justering *or* **Tilretning, (pr.)** justification.

K

K. Kort.

kaldt *or* **med Tilnavn.** called.

Kalvelæder. (bb). calf.

Kammarmorsnit. (bb.) combed edges.

kan rentrykkes *or* **færdig til Trykken. (pr.)** for press.

Kapital *or* **Kapitalbaand. (bb.)** headband.

Kapitaler, smaa *or* **Kapitelker. (pr.)** small capitals.

Kapitel. chapter.

Kapitelker. *See* **Kapitaler, smaa.**

Kegle. (pr.) shank, body of a letter.

Kileskrift. cuneiform letters.

Kladde. draft.

Klammer. brackets.

Klatpapir *or* **Trækpapir.** blotting paper.

Klumme *or* **Kolumne** *or* **Spalte. (b.)** column.

Klummesnor *or* **Kolumnesnor. (pr.)** page-cord.

Knepryg. (bb.) spring back.

kniplingsdannet Forsiring. (bb.) dentelle border.

Kobberstikkabinet. (e.) print-department, printroom.

kold Naal. (e.) dry point.

koloreret. colored.

Kolumnesnor. *See* **Klummesnor.**

Kolumnetitel *or* **Sidenummer. (pr.)** dead heading, page number.

Kolumnetitel, levende. (pr.) live heading, running title.

kompres Sats. (pr.) close matter, solid matter.

Konversationsleksikon. encyclopedia.

Korrekturaftryk i Strimler, uden Paginering. galley proof.

Korrekturark. proof sheet.

Korrekturlæser. proof reader.

Korrekturlæsning. proof reading.

Kors *or* **Obelisk** *or* **Daggert. (pr.)** dagger.

Kort *or* **Landkort.** map.
Kridttegning. crayon.
Kultegning. charcoal drawing.
Kursivskrift. (pr.) italics.
Kustos. (b.) catchword.
Kvadrat. (pr.) quadrat.
kvart. kvartalsvis.
kvartalsvis. quarterly.
Kvartant. quarto edition.

L

Læder *or* **Skind.** leather, skin.
læderet Skrifttegn. (pr.) battered letter.
lægge af. (pr.) distribute the type.
Lammeskind. (bb.) sheepskin.
Lammeskind, brunt. (bb.) basil, bazil.
Landkort. *See* **Kort.**
lappet *or* **repareret. (bb.)** reinforced, re-paired.
ledende Artikel *or* **Leder. (b.)** editorial.
Leder. *See* **ledende Artikel.**
levende Kolumnetitel. *See* **Kolumnetitel, levende.**
lige udkommen. (bo.) now published.
Linie. (b.) line.
Linie, ny, *or* **Paragraf. (b.)** paragraph, alinea.
Linieornamentering. fillet.
Liniestik. (e.) line engraving.
Löbeseddel. handbill.
Lommeudgave. pocket edition.
lös Ryg. (bb.) loose back.
Luksusudgave *or* **Pragtudgave.** edition de luxe.

Lystryk. photolithography.
Lystspil *or* **Komedie.** comedy.

M

maanedlig. monthly.
Maanedsberetning. monthly report.
Makulatur *or* **Afgangsark** *or* **Udskudsark. (pr.)**
  waste-paper.
Manér, sort *or* **Sortkunst.** mezzotint.
marmoreret Papir. marble paper.
Marmorsnit. (bb.) marble edges.
med Tilnavn. called.
mere udkom ikke. (bo.) no more published,
  all published.
Messebog. missal.
Mskrpt. Manuskript. manuscript.
muggen. (bo.) mouldy.
Munk *or* **blegt Tryk. (pr.)** friar.
Munkeskrift. monk's letters.

N

Navnedigt *or* **Akrostichon.** acrostic.
Navnefortegnelse. index of names.
Navnetræk. monogram.
Nedrykning paa den förste Side. (pr.) head-
  margin.
Note under Teksten. footnote.
Notetegn. (pr.) superiors.
Novelle. short story.
ny Linie *or* **Paragraf.** paragraph, alinea.

O

O. A. Oversætterens Anmærkning.

Obelisk *or* **Daggert** *or* **Kors.** (b.) dagger.

ogsaa med Titel. also under the title.

Ombankning. (bb.) rounding.

ombrække. (pr.) make up, impose.

Ombrækker. (pr.) impositor.

omtrykt Blad. (pr.) cancel.

ophöjede Tværbind *or* **ægte Bind.** (bb.) raised bands.

ophört at udkomme. (bo.) discontinued.

Opl. Oplag.

Oplag. edition.

opskaaret. cut open.

Opslag *or* **Plakat.** poster, placard.

Ordbog *or* **Leksikon.** dictionary.

Originalomslag. publisher's cover.

Ormehul. wormhole.

ormstukken. wormholed.

Oversætter. translator.

Oversætterens Anmærkning. translator's note.

Oversigt. synopsis, summary.

Overskrift. heading.

overströget *or* **erklæret ugyldigt.** (e). canceled.

P

paa eget Forlag. (b.) at the author's expense, privately published.

Pap. pasteboard.

Papirkniv. paper-cutter.

Pergament. parchment.

Pjece *or* **Brochure** *or* **Flyveskrift.** pamphlet.

Plakat *or* **Opslag.** poster, placard.

plettet. stained.

Pligteksemplar. deposit copy.

Prædiken. sermon.

Pragtudgave *or* **Luksusudgave.** edition de luxe.

Presseforgyldning. (bb.) gold tooling.

Pris. price.

prisbelönnet. awarded a prize.

Prisskrift. prize essay.

Progr. program.

Protokoloptegnelser. minutes of a meeting.

punkteret Linie. dotted rule.

R

Radeergrund *or* **Ætsbund. (e.)** etching ground.

Radering. (e.) etching.

Ræmike. (pr.) frisket.

Randbemærkning. marginal note.

Ræveskind. (bb.) fox-skin.

Red. *or* **Redakt.** Redaktör.

Red. Anm. Redaktörens Anmærkning.

Redaktör. editor.

Redaktörens Anmærkning. editor's note.

Restoplag. (bo.) remainders.

Ris Papir. ream.

rödt Snit. (bb.) red edges.

Rom. Roman.

Roman. novel.

Ruslæder. (bb.) Russia leather.

Ryg i en Bog, sætte. (bb.) to back.

Ryg, fast. (bb.) tight back.

Ryg, lös. (bb.)   loose back.
Rygfelt. (bb.)   panel.

S

Sagregister.   index.
Samler.   compiler.
sammenfoldet.   folded.
Sammenhæng.   context.
Sært.   Særtryk.
Særtryk *or* **Separataftryk.**   reprint.
Sætning.   sentence.
Sats. (pr.)   form, composition.
Sats, kompres. (pr.)   close   matter,   solid matter.
Sats, skudt. (pr.)   leaded matter.
Sats, spærret. (pr.)   spaced matter.
Sættebrædt. (pr.)   letter-board, composing board.
Sættekasse *or* **Skriftkasse. (pr.)**   type case.
Sættelinie. (pr.)   composing rule, setting rule.
Sættemaskine. (pr.)   composing machine.
Sætter. (pr.)   compositor.
se.   see.
Sejldug. (bb.)   duck.
Sekundasignatur. (b.)   signature with an asterisk.
Selskabsskrifter.   society publications.
Sep.-Aftr.   Separataftryk.
Separataftryk.   *See* **Særtryk.**
Sidenummer *or* **Kolumnetitel. (b.)**   dead heading, page number.
Signaturlinie. (b.)   signature line.
Silkepapir.   tissue paper.
sjælden. (bo.)   rare.

100

Skib. (pr.) galley.

Skind *or* **Læder.** skin, leather.

Skizze. sketch.

Skönskrivning. calligraphy.

Sköntrykform *or* **Primaform.** first form, prime form.

Skrift. writing, types.

Skrift, tynd. (pr.) lightfaced types, leanfaced types.

Skriftkasse *or* **Sættekasse. (pr.)** case, type-case.

Skriftkasse, Afdeling i en. (pr.) box in a type-case.

Skrivepapir. writing paper.

Skrvp. Skrivepapir.

skudt. (pr.) leaded.

Skulder. (pr.) shoulder of a type.

Skydelinie *or* **Reglet. (pr.)** lead.

slidt Bind. worn binding.

Slutningslinie. bottom line.

Slutningsskrift *or* **Kolofon.** colophon.

Smaajern. (bb.) small tools.

Smædeskrift. libel.

Smudsplet. stain.

Smudstitel *or* **Halvtitel.** half-title, bastard-title, fly-title.

smukt Eksemplar. (bo.) fine copy.

Snit. edges.

Snit, ciseleret. (bb.) tooled edges.

Snit, överste. (bb.) head, top.

Snit (överste), forgyldt. (bb.) gilt top.

Snit, rödt. (bb.) red edges.

Snit, sprængt. (bb.) sprinkled edges.

Sörgerand. mourning border.

Sörgespil. tragedy.

Sortkunst *or* **sort Manér. (e.)** mezzotint.

spærret Sats. (pr.) spaced composition.

Spatie. (pr.) space.

Speil. (bb.) paste-down, *i.e.*, leaf that is pasted to the inside of the cover of a book.

Spies. (pr.) blacks, *i.e.*, a space, quadrat or piece of furniture that rises and is imprinted on the sheets.

Spillekort. playing cards.

Spörgsmaalstegn. interrogation point.

sprængt Snit. *See* **Snit, sprængt.**

Sproglære. grammar.

Staalstik. (e.) steel engraving.

Stadium. (e.) state.

Stavelse. syllable.

Stempelpapir. stamped paper.

Stik. (e.) cut, plate, engraving.

Stjerne. (b.) asterisk.

Svibelfisk *or* **Fisk.(pr.)** pie, *i.e.*, types mixed.

Svinelæder. (bb.) pig-skin.

Svinesteg. (pr.) fat, *i.e.*, pieces of composition, for instance, running titles that are kept for future use and not taken apart till the whole work is finished.

T

Tab. Tabel.

Tabel. table.

Tankestreg. dash.

Tavle. plate.

Tb. Tabel.

Tidebog. book of hours.

til Eftersyn. (bo.) on approval.

Tilegnelse. dedication.

Tilföjelse. note, addition.

Tilnavn, med. called.

Tilretning *or* **Justering. (pr.)** justification.

Tilstand, i god. (bo.) in good condition.

Titel, med. entitled.

Titel, uden. anepigraphous, without title.

Titelblad mangler. (bo.) title-page lacking.

Titelkobber. frontispiece.

Titellinie. headline.

Titeludgave. a so-called new edition in every way unchanged, except for the title-page.

to Gange om Maaneden. semi-monthly.

Træbogpermer. *pl.* **(bb.)** wooden boards.

Trækpapir. *See* **Klatpapir.**

trefarvet Tryk. (pr.) three-color print.

Tryk med ophöjede Linier. (pr.) anastatic printing.

Trykfejl. misprint.

Trykfejlsliste. table of errata.

Trykkeaar. imprint date.

Trykken, i. in the press.

Trykkested. place of printing.

Trykkested, uden. no place.

Tuschmanér. aquatint.

Tværbind, ophöjede *or* **ægte Bind. (bb.)** raised bands.

Tværfolio. oblong folio.

Tvl. Tavle.

tynd Skrift. (pr.) lightfaced types, lean-faced types.

Typer, fede. (pr.) boldfaced types, heavy-faced types.

U

u. A. uden Aar, uden Aarstal.

ubeskaaret. uncut.

Uddrag *or* **Udtog.** extract, excerpt.

uden Aar *or* **uden Aarstal.** no date.

uden Trykkested *and* **uden Udgivelsessted.** no place.

Udgangslinie. (pr.) last line of a paragraph.

Udgivelsessted. place of publication.

Udgivelsessted, uden. *See* **uden Trykkested.**

Udhængsark. advance-sheets.

Udklipsalbum *or* **Excerptebog.** scrapbook.

Udraabstegn. exclamation point.

Udskudsark *or* **Afgangsark** *or* **Makulatur.** (pr.) waste-sheets.

Udslutning. (pr.) slug.

udsolgt. (bo.) out of print.

Udtog *or* **Uddrag.** extract, excerpt.

Udv. Udvalg, udvalgt.

Udvalg. selection.

udvalgt. selected.

Ugeblad. weekly newspaper.

ugentlig. weekly.

uindbunden. unbound.

under et. (bo.) by the lot.

Underslag. (pr.) blank space at end of a page.

Undersnit. (bb.) tail, *i.e.*, lower edge of a book.

understreget. underscored.

undertegnet. signed.

104

V

Vælskbind. (bb.) half-sheep.

Vandlinier. *pl.* **(pa.)** waterlines.

Vandmærke. (pa.) watermark.

Værksats *or* **Bogtryk. (pr.)** bookwork.

Værksætter. (pr.) book compositor.

Værkskrift *or* **Brödskrift. (pr.)** body type, the usual type.

Vejviser. directory.

Verdenskort. map of the world.

Vidertrykform *or* **Gentrykform** *or* **Modtryk** *or* **Sekundaform. (pr.)** second form.

Vinkelhage. (pr.) composing stick.

Vuggetryk. incunabula.

DUTCH

A

aanhalingsteeken *or* **aanspraakteeken.** quotation mark.

aanhangsel *or* **bijvoegsel.** appendix, supplement.

aankooiing *or* **vereffening der kolommen. (pr.)** justification.

aanplakbiljet. poster, placard.

aanspraakteeken. *See* **aanhalingsteeken.**

aanteekenaar. annotator, commentator.

aanteekening. annotation.

academisch proefschrift *or* **dissertatie.** dissertation, thesis.

achterkant *or* **achterzijde** *or* **even bladzijde (b.)** even page, verso.

adresboek. directory.

advertentie. advertisement.

afbeelding. illustration.

afdruk. impression.

afdruk vóór de letter. (e.) proof before letters.

afgesneden, kort. cropped.

afkappingsteeken. apostrophe.

afsnijden met tekstverminking. bleed.

antiquaarboekhandelaar. secondhand book seller.

auteursrecht *or* **kopijrecht.** copyright.

B

baal papier. ten reams.

band. binding, cover.

band, versleten. worn binding.

bedrijf. act.

beginletter. initial.

begrip, kort *or* **overzicht.** synopsis, summary.

bekroond. awarded a prize.

beoordeelaar. critic.

beperkte uitgaaf. limited edition.

beschadigd. *See* **geschonden.**

beschimmeld. mouldy.

beschrijvende tekst. descriptive text.

bewerker. editor.

bewerkt. edited, prepared.

bieden op een boek. bid on a book.

bij vooruitbetaling. (bo.) prepaid.

Bijbel. Bible.

bijeenbrengen, vergaren (bb.) gathering.

bijgeplakt *or* **hersteld.** repaired.

bijvoegsel *or* **aanhangsel.** appendix, supplement.

blad, los. fly-sheet.

bladen, schoone. *pl.* **(bo.)** advance sheets.

bladwachter *or* **custode. (b.)** catchword.

bladz. bladzijde.

bladzijde, oneven *or* **vóórzijde.** odd page recto.

blanco vellen. blank leaves.

blijspel. comedy.

blind druk op banden. (bb.) blind tooling.

bloemlezing. anthology.

boek, onbeschreven. blank book.

boek, tweedehandsch. secondhand book.

boek in losse bladen. book in sheets, book in quires.

boek papier. quire.

boekaankondiging. announcement of a book.

boekbeoordeeling *or* **boekrecensie.** book review.

boekbinder. binder.

boekbinderij. bookbinder shop.

boekbinderstitel *or* **rugtitel.** binder's title.

boekdrukkerij *or* **drukkerij.** printing office.

boekengek *or* **bibliomaan.** bibliomaniac.

boekenliefhebber. bibliophile.

boekenveiling. *See* **boekverkooping, openbare.**

boekhandel. booktrade.

boekje *or* **boekske.** small volume.

boekmerk *or* **boekmerkteeken.** bookplate, ex libris.

boekske. *See* **boekje.**

boekverkooping, openbare *or* **boekenveiling.** book-auction.

boekwerk (pr.) bookwork.

boekwinkel. bookstore.

boekworm. bookworm.

boekzetter. (pr.) book compositor.

bont. vari-colored.

boomwolpapier. cotton-paper.

bordpapier *or* **carton** *or* **stroobord.** pasteboard.

bovengen. bovengenoemd.

bovengenoemd. mentioned above.

bovenkast-letters. (pr.) upper case.

bovenletters. (pr.) superiors.

bovenregel. headline.

bovensnede verguld *or* **kop verguld. (bb.)**
  gilt top.

briefhoofd. letter-head.

briefwisseling. correspondence.

broodletters. (pr.) body-type, ordinary type.

C

collectie *or* **verzameling.** collection.

commissie-boekhandelaar. general bookseller.

compilatie. compilation.

correctie van drukproeven. proof reading.

correctie-els. (pr.) bodkin.

correctieteeken. marks of correction, proof-
  reading signs.

courant *or* **krant** *or* **nieuwsblad.** newspaper.

couranten uitknipsel. newspaper clipping.

cursief letters. (pr.) italics.

cylinder pers. (pr.) revolving press.

D

dagelijksch. daily.

dagteekening *or* **datum.** date.

dissertatie *or* **akademisch proefschrift.** thesis,
  dissertation.

doorbladeren. turn over the leaves of a
  book.

doorgeschrapt. canceled, crossed out.

doorloopende paginatuur. continuous pagination.

doorschoten. interleaved.

doortrek papier *or* **kalkeer papier.** tracing paper.

draadhechtmachine. wire stitching machine.

drie-kleuren druk. three-color print.

driemaandelijksch. quarterly.

droge naald, (e.) dry-point.

druk, jaar van. imprint year.

druk, plaats van. imprint place.

drukfeil. *See* **drukfout.**

drukfout *or* **drukfeil.** misprint.

drukfouten, lijst van. list of errata.

drukinkt. printer's ink.

drukkersopgaaf. imprint.

drukletter. type.

drukpers. press.

drukproef *or* **proefdruk** *or* **proefblad.** proof sheet.

drukwerk. printed matter.

dubbel gezet woord (pr.) double.

dubbel punt. colon.

Duitsche letter. (pr.) black letter.

dwars. oblong.

E

éénblad-druk. broadside.

éénkolommig. in one column.

eerstelingsdrukken *or* **wiegedrukken.** incunabula.

ets, weeke-grond. (e.) soft ground etching.

etsgrond. (e.) etching ground.

etsijzer *or* **etsnaald.** etching needle.

etsnaald. *See* **etsijzer.**

exemplaar, mooi. (bo.) fine copy.

ezelsoor. (b.) dog's ear.

F

formaat. size.

fractuurletters *or* **Gothische letters.** Gothic characters.

Fransche titel *or* **voor-de-handsche titel.** half title, bastard title, fly title.

G

gaaf. (bo.) in good condition.

galei. (pr.) galley.

galei-proef. galley-proof.

gebedenboek. prayer-book.

geblokkeerde letter *or* **omgekeerde letter.** **(pr.)** turned letter.

gebrocheerd *or* **ingenaaid. (bb.)** stitched.

gecartonneerd. (bb.) in boards.

gecastigeerd *or* **gedauphineerd.** expurgated.

geciseleerde snede. (bb.) tooled edges.

gecompileerd. compiled.

gedauphineerd. *See* **gecastigeerd.**

gedenkschriften. memoirs.

gedrongen tekstzetsel. (pr.) solid matter.

gefiletteerd. filleted.

gegraveerd. engraved.

geitenleder. goat-skin.

gekwetste letters. battered type.

gemarmerd papier. marble paper.

gemarmerd op snede. marble-edged.

gemonteerd *or* **opgeplakt.** mounted.

genaamd. called.

genootschapswerken. society publications.

gepunteerde regel. dotted rule.

gerubriceerd. rubricated.

geschept papier. hand-made paper.

geschonden *or* **verminkt** *or* **beschadigd.** mutilated, damaged.

geschrift. writing.

gesnoeid. (bb.) cut down.

gespikkeld op snede. sprinkled edges.

getijboek. book of hours.

getiteld. entitled.

gevlekt. stained.

gevouwen. folded.

gewatteerd lederen band. padded leather binding.

Gothische letters *or* **fractuurletters.** Gothic characters.

gouddruk *or* **vergulde ornamenteering.** gold tooling.

goudsnede *or* **verguld op snede.** gilt-edged.

gravure in lijnenmanier. (e.) line engraving.

gravure in punteermanier *or* **gepunteerde gravure. (e.)** stipple engraving.

H

haakjes. parentheses.

haken. brackets.

half Fransche band. half-calf binding.

halfjaarlijksch. half yearly.

halfmaandelijksch. semi-monthly.

handboek. manual, handbook.

handelingen. transactions.

handleiding. guide.

handpapier. handmade paper.

handpers. (pr.) hand-press.

hel. (pr.) hell, *i.e.*, a box into which a printer throws his broken types.

herbinden. rebind.

hersteld *or* **bijgeplakt.** reinforced, repaired.

herzien. revised.

hoek van een boek. corner of a book.

hoofdartikel. editorial.

hoofdletter *or* **kapitaal.** capital letter.

hoofdstuk *or* **kapittel.** chapter.

hoofdtitel. collective title.

houtband. wooden boards.

houtblokdruk. (b.) blockbook.

houtblokjes *or* **loodblokjes. (pr.)** furniture.

i

in ééns *or* **ongeteld** *or* **en bloc. (bo.)** by the lot.

in beslag genomen. suppressed.

incompleet. imperfect, incomplete.

inhoud. contents.

inhoudsopgaaf. table of contents.

inleiding. introduction.

inspringen. indentation.

invoeging. insertion, interpolation.

J

jaar van druk. imprint year.

jaarboeken *or* **jaarboekjes.** *pl.* annals.

jaarboekjes. *See* **jaarboeken.**
jaarverslag. annual report.
jufferboek *or* **mopje.** 17th century book of songs or erotic poetry.

K

kalfslederband. calf-binding.
kalkeerpapier. *See* **doortrek papier.**
kammarmersnede. combed edges.
kantteekeningen *or* **marginaliën.** *pl.* marginal notes.
kapitaal *or* **hoofdletter. (pr.)** capital letter.
kapitaalband. (bb.) head-band.
kapitalen, kleine. (pr.) small capitals.
kartonnenband. binding in boards.
kegel. (pr.) shank, body of a letter.
keur. selection.
kinderboeken. juvenile literature.
klamp. clasp.
kleine kapitalen. (pr.) small capitals.
kleine letter. (pr.) small letter, lower case.
kleine stempels. (bb.) small tools.
kolommentitel, doode, *or* **volgnummer van de bladzijde.** dead heading, page-number.
kolommentitel, levende *or* **veranderlijke koptitel.** live heading, running title.
komma-punt. semicolon.
koorden *or* **ribkoorden. (bb.)** raised bands.
kop. (bb.) head of a book.
kop van een lettertype. (pr.) shoulder of a type.
koper ets. (e.) copper etching.

koperdrukplaat *or* **kopergravure. (e.)** copper-engraving.

kopij. copy.

kopijrecht *or* **auteursrecht.** copyright.

koppelteeken. hyphen.

koptitel, veranderlijke. *See* **kolommentitel, levende.**

kopvignet *or* **en-tête** *or* **vignet aan het begin van een hoofdstuk.** headpiece.

kordeeren. (bb.) tie in.

krant *or* **courant.** newspaper.

kruisje. dagger, cross.

kwadraat (pr.) quadrat.

L

lectuur voor kinderen. *See* **kinderboeken.**

leder *or* **leer.** leather, skin.

leerboek. textbook.

leesboek. reading book.

leeswijzer *or* **boekenlegger.** bookmark.

letter, bovenkast. (pr.) upper case.

letter, Duitsche. (pr.) black letter.

letter, geblokkeerde. (pr.) turned letter.

letter, gekwetste. (pr.) battered type.

letter, onderkast. (pr.) lower case.

letter, vreemde. (pr.) wrong font.

lettergreep. syllable.

letterkas *or* **letterkast. (pr.)** type-case.

letterkast vakje. (pr.) box of a type case.

letterkeer. anagram.

letterplank *or* **zetplank der letterzetters. (pr.)** composing board.

letters, magere. (pr.)   lightfaced types, lean-faced types.

letters, vette. (pr.)   boldfaced types.

letterspijs. (pr.)   type metal.

lettertypen, dubbele. (pr.)   ligature.

letterzetter. (pr.)   compositor.

levende kolommentitel.   *See* **kolommentitel, levende.**

lichtdruk.   photolithography.

lijst van drukfouten.   list of errata.

los blad.   fly sheet.

losse bladen.   *See* **boek in losse bladen.**

losse rug. (bb.)   loose back.

luxe-uitgaaf *or* **prachtuitgaaf.**   edition de luxe.

M

maandblad.   monthly publication.

maandelijksch.   monthly.

magere letters.   *See* letters, magere.

marmerpapier.   marble paper.

mededeelingen *or* **verslagen.**   proceedings.

m.   met.

met.   with.

met toelichtingen.   with explanatory notes.

metaalbeslag. (bb.)   bosses.

misdruk. (pr.)   waste sheet.

monnik. (pr.)   friar, *i.e.*, any part of the page which has not received the ink.

monnikenschrift.   monks' letters.

mooi exemplaar. (bo.)   fine copy.

mopje.   *See* **jufferboek.**

N

naaibank. (bb.) sewing-board.

naamcijfer. monogram.

naamdicht. acrostic.

naamloos. anonymous.

naamregister. index of names.

nadruk. unauthorized reprint.

nagelaten werken. posthumous works.

narede *or* **nawoord** *or* **slotwoord.** epilogue.

nieuwsblad. *See* **courant.**

noot. note.

notitieboek. note-book.

notulen van eene bijeenkomst. minutes of a
meeting.

O

omgekeerde letter *or* **geblokkeerde letter.**
(pr.) turned letter.

omlettering. transliteration.

omlijsten. (pr.) box in.

onafgesneden. uncut.

onbeschreven boek. blank book.

onderkast letters. (pr.) lower case.

onderschot. (b.) the blank space at the end
of a page.

ondersnede *or* **staart.** lower edge of a book,
tail.

onderstreeping. underscoring.

onderstreept. underscored.

ondertitel. subtitle.

oneven bladzijde *or* **vóórzijde.** odd page
recto.

ongeteld *or* **in ééns** *or* **en bloc. (bo.)**   by the lot.

ook onder den titel. also under the title.

op zicht. (bo.) on approval.

opdracht *or* **toewijding.** dedication.

openbare verkooping. auction sale.

opengesneden. cut.

opgeplakt *or* **gemonteerd.** mounted.

opmaken. (pr.) make up.

ordenen *or* **rangschikken.** file.

overgezet *or* **vertaald.** translated.

overzicht *or* **kort begrip.** synopsis, summary.

P

pagina touwtje. (bb.) page-cord.

pagineering. pagination.

palaeotypen *or* **wiegedrukken** *or* **eerstelings-drukken.** incunabula.

pamflet *or* **brochure.** pamphlet.

paneel. (bb.) panel.

papier, geschept. handmade paper.

papiermes. paper-cutter.

pastei. (pr.) pie, *i.e.*, types mixed.

plaat, uitslaande *or* **gevouwen plaat.** folded plate.

plaatsnijder *or* **graveur.** engraver.

prachtuitgaaf *or* **luxe-uitgaaf.** edition de luxe.

prentenboek. picture-book.

presentexemplaar. presentation copy.

prijs van uitgaaf. (bo.) published price, list price.

prijscatalogus, priced catalogue.

prijsschrift. prize essay.

privaat uitgaaf. privately published.

proefblad *or* **drukproef** *or* **proefdruk.** proof sheet.

proefblad met den borstel getrokken. brush proof.

proeflezer *or* **corrector.** proof reader.

punt. period.

R

randlijst. margin border.

rangschikken *or* **ordenen.** file.

reisgids *or* **spoorboekje.** time-table.

rekenboek. textbook of arithmetic.

rekening. bill.

rekening van den schrijver, voor. at the author's expense, privately published.

ribbenband. (bb.) raised bands.

riem. (pa.) ream.

rij. row, file.

roodgekleurd op snede. red-edged.

rouwrand. (pr.) mourning border.

rug, het maken van den (bb.) backing.

rug, losse *or* **vrije. (bb.)** loose back.

rug, vaste. (bb.) tight back.

rug, veerende. (bb.) spring back.

rugrondingswerk. (bb.) rounding.

rugschild. (bb.) lettering piece.

rugtitel *or* **boekbinderstitel.** binder's title.

ruiling. exchange.

ruim tekstzetsel *or* **gespatieerd tekstzetsel. (pr.)** spaced composition.

Russisch leder. (bb.) Russia leather.

S

schapenleder, gelooid. basil, bazil.

schets. sketch.

scheurpapier. waste paper.

schoondruk. (pr.) first form.

schoone bladen. *pl.* **(bo.)** advance sheets.

schoonschrijven. calligraphy. ˙

schotschrift. lampoon.

schraapmanier *or* **zwarte kunst. (e.)** mezzo-tint.

schrijfboek. blank book.

segrijnleder. shagreen.

sierletter. (pr.) fancy letter.

slap omslag. (bb.) flexible binding.

sleutelboek *or* **livre à clef.** a book in which the proper names of persons or localities are disguised by the author.

slotregel. bottom-line.

slotschrift. colophon.

slotwoord, *See* **narede.**

sluitstuk. (pr.) slug.

smaadschrift. libel.

smetten *or* **vlekken. (pr.)** set off.

smoutwerk. (pr.) job-printing.

snede *or* **snee** *or* **plaat. (en.)** cut, engraving, plate, edges.

snede, geciseleerde. (bb.) tooled edges.

snede, gemarmerde. (bb.) marble-edged.

snede, gespikkelde. (bb.) sprinkled edges.

snede, roodgekleurd op. (bb.) red-edged.

snee. *See* **snede.**

snelpers. (pr.) fly-press.

speelkaarten. playing cards.

spelboek. spelling book.

spijkerschrift. cuneiform letters.

spoorboekje *or* **reisgids.** time-table.

sprookje. fairy tale.

staart *or* **ondersnee.** lower edge of a book, tail.

staartletter. (pr.) tail-type, descending letter.

staat. (e.) state.

steendruk. (e.) lithograph.

stempelband. ornamental stamped binding.

stempeling. stamping.

stempels, kleine. small tools.

sterkwaterplaat, *or* **ets. (e.)** etching.

sterretje. asterisk.

stijflinnen. (bb.) buckram.

streepje. dash.

stroobord. *See* **bordpapier.**

T

teekening. drawing.

titel, Fransche *or* **voor-de-handsche titel.** half-title, bastard-title, fly-title.

titelblad ontbreekt. title-page lacking.

titel-signatuur. direction line.

toestand, in goeden. in good condition.

toewijding *or* **opdracht.** dedication.

tooneel. scene.

tooneelspel. drama.

treurspel. tragedy.

tusschenblad. interleaf.

tweedehandsch boek. secondhand book.
tweemaandelijksch. bi-monthly.

U

uitgaaf, beperkte. limited edition.
uitgelezen werken. selected works.
uitknipselboek. scrapbook.
uitroepingsteeken. exclamation point.
uitsl. uitslaand.
uitslaand. folded.
uittreksel. extract.

V

varkensleder. pigskin.
veerende rug. (bb). spring back.
veiling. *See* **boekenveiling.**
verbeterblad. (pr.) cancel.
verguld op snede *or* **goudsnede.** gilt-edged.
verplaatsbaar. adjustable.
verschoten. faded.
vertaald *or* **overgezet.** translated.
vertelling *or* **verhaal.** tale.
vervolgd, wordt. to be continued.
verzameling. *See* **collectie.**
vette letters. (pr.) bold-faced type.
vignet aan het begin van een hoofdstuk *or* **kopvignet.** head-piece.
vignet aan het slot van een hoofdstuk. tail-piece.
vlek. stain.
vlekken *or* **smetten.** set off.
vlekken, zwarte. (pr.) blacks.
vloeipapier. tissue paper, blotting paper.

vlugschrift *or* **brochure** *or* **pamflet.** pamphlet.

volgnummer der bladzijde *or* **doode kolom-mentitel.** dead heading, page number.

volksuitgaaf. popular edition.

vóór alle letters. (e.) plain prints.

voor-de-handsche titel *or* **Fransche titel.** half-title, bastard-title, fly-title.

vóór de letter *or* **afdruk vóór de letter. (e.)** proof before letters.

voor de pers gereed. (pr.) for press.

voor rekening van den schrijver. at the author's expense, privately published.

voorbericht. *See* **voorrede.**

voorkant. *See* **voorzijde.**

voorrede *or* **voorbericht** *or* **voorwoord.** preface.

voorsnee *or* **voorsnede. (bb.)** fore-edge.

vooruitbetaling, bij.ˑ (bo.) prepaid.

voorvoegsel. prefix.

voorwerk. preliminary leaves and pages.

voorzijde *or* **voorkant** *or* **oneven bladzijde.** odd page, recto.

vormdraden. (pa.) wire marks.

vormraam. (pr.) chase.

vossenleder. (bb.) foxskin.

vouwbeen. folding stick.

vouwen. (bb.) folding.

vraagteeken. interrogation mark.

W

waterlijnen. (pa.) water lines.

watermerk. (pa.) water mark.

weekblad. weekly newspaper.

weeke-grond ets. (e.) soft ground proof.

weerdruk. (pr.) second form.

wekelijksch. weekly.

wereldkaart. map of the world.

wiegedrukken *or* **eerstelingsdrukken.** incunabula.

winkelhaak *or* **zethaak. (pr.)** composing stick.

woordenboek. dictionary.

wormgat. wormhole.

wormstekig. wormholed.

Z

z. ald. zie aldaar.

zegelpapier. stamped paper.

zeildoek. duck.

zethaak. *See* **winkelhaak.**

zetlinie. (pr.) composing rule.

zetmachine. (pr.) typesetting machine.

zetplank *or* **letterplank. (pr.)** letterboard, composing board.

zetsel. (pr.) form, composition.

zetsel, gedrongen. (pr.) close matter, solid matter.

zetsel, gespatieerd *or* **ruim zetsel. (pr.)** spaced matter.

zetsel met interlinies. (pr.) leaded matter.

zetsel weggelaten. (pr.) out.

zicht, op. on approval.

zichtzending. books sent on approval.

zie. see.

zie aldaar. see there.

zink ets. zinc etching.

zoo juist verschenen. (bo.) now published.

zwarte kunst *or* **schraapmanier. (e.)** mezzotint.

zwarte vlekken. (pr.) blacks.

FRENCH

A

a.   armes.

à l'examen *or* **sous condition. (bo.)**   on approval.

à forfait *or* **en bloc. (bo.)**   by the lot.

a. l.   avant la lettre.

à plein dos. (bb.)   tight back.

à suivre.   to be continued.

a. t. l.   avant toute lettre.

abonné.   subscriber.

accomp. d. n.   accompagné de notes.

accompagné de notes.   with notes.

acte.   act.

adr.   adresse.

adresse bibliographique.   imprint.

affiche.   poster, placard.

ajouté. (pr.)   new matter.

album de découpures.   scrap-book.

almanach des adresses.   directory.

an.   année.

anépigraphe.   without title.

annales.   annals.

année.   year.

annonce.   advertisement.

anopistographe.   manuscripts or books written and printed on the recto only.

ant.   antiqué.

antiqué.   tooled.

appel de note. (pr.) a number, letter or asterisk referring from the text to a footnote.

approche. (pr.) space between type.

armes. coat of arms.

armoriée. *See* **reliure armoriée,**

arraphique. (bb.) *See* **reliure arraphique.**

arrondissage. (bb.) rounding,

article de fond. editorial.

assemblage. (bb.) gathering.

atelier de relieur. bindery.

au comptant. cash payment.

augm. augmenté.

augmenté. enlarged.

aussi sous le titre. also under the title.

aut. auteur.

auteur. author.

aux frais de l'auteur. at the author's expense, privately printed.

av. let. avec lettre.

avant la lettre *or* **avant lettre** *or* **épreuve d'artiste. (e.)** proof before letter.

avant la retouche. (e.) before the retouch.

avant toute lettre. (e.) plain prints.

avec lettre. (e.) print with signature, title, etc.

avec la lettre tracée. (e.) with etched letters.

B

bardeau. (pr.) hell, *i.e.*, a receptacle for broken and battered type.

bas. basane.

bas de casse. (pr.) lower case.

bas d'une page. bottom of a page.

basane. basil, bazil.

bavochure. (pr.) foul print.

bavure. (e.) foul print.

beauc. beaucoup.

beaucoup. many.

belle page *or* **page impaire** *or* **page de droit** *or* **recto.** odd page, recto.

biffé. (e.) canceled, crossed out.

bilboquet *or* **travail de ville. (pr.)** job printing.

bimensuel. semi-monthly.

bis. second part, *e.g.*, tome 3 bis is v. 3, part 2.

blanc du folio recto. (b.) head margin.

blancs. (pr.) spaces, quadrats, etc.

blason. coat of arms, emblazonry, heraldry.

blocage. (pr.) letter intentionally turned upside down and temporarily used in place of another letter.

bois. (pr.) furniture.

bois habillé. (e.) *See* **gravure habillée.**

bon, du. (pr.) fat, *i.e.*, pieces of composition, for instance, running titles that are kept for future use and not taken apart till the whole work is finished.

bon à tirer. (pr.) for press.

bonnes feuilles. (bo.) advance sheets.

bord. bordure.

bordure. (b.) border, frame.

bougran. buckram.

bouquin. old book, book of small value sold second-hand.

bourdon. (pr.) out, *i.e.*, omission of a word or phrase by the compositor.

braies. *pl.* **(pr.)** waste sheets.

bulletins. *pl.* proceedings.

burin. (e.) graver, *i.e.*, a sharp instrument used for engraving on copper.

C

c. coin.

cachet. seal.

cadrat. (pr.) quadrat.

capitale. (pr.) capital letter.

capitales, petites. *pl.* small capitals.

car. moyens. caractères moyens.

caractères gras. (pr.) bold-faced type.

caractères maigres. (pr.) light-faced type.

caractères moyens. (pr.) medium-sized letters.

caractères ordinaires. (pr.) body type, ordinary type.

carré. square.

carte d'entrée. card of admission.

carte géographique. map.

cartes à jouer. playing cards.

carton de collage. paste-board.

carton refait *or* **feuillet refait** *or* **défet.** cancel.

casse. (pr.) type case.

cassetin. (pr.) section of a type case.

censure. censorship.

cessé de paraître. (bo.) discontinued.

ch. chagrin.

chagrin. shagreen.

chapitre. chapter.

charnière *or* **mors. (bb.)** joint.

charte. chart, map.

chasse. (pr.) excess of manuscript in proportion to a printed page.

chasse. (bb.) projecting edge of cover.

châssis d'imprimerie. (pr.) chase.

chiffre. monogram, cipher.

chiffre de la page. page number.

choix. selection.

clair-obscur. (e.) chiaroscuro.

clous aux coins. studded metal corners.

co-auteur. joint author.

coin. corner.

collé. pasted, mounted.

collé. (pa.) sized.

colombelle *or* **filet de milieu. (pr.)** column rule.

comète. (bb.) artificial headband.

commencer sans renfoncement. (pr.) commence even.

commerce de livres. book trade.

comp. compartiment.

compartiment *or* **entre-nerfs** *or* **entre-nervures. (bb.)** panel.

complément *or* **fascicule supplémentaire.** supplement number.

complétage. completing imperfect books.

compositeur. (pr.) compositor.

compositeur de livre. (pr.) book compositor.

composition espacée. (pr.) spaced matter.

composition interlignée. (pr.) leaded matter

composition serrée. (pr.) close matter.

composoir. (pr.) composing board.

composteur. (pr.) composing stick.

comptant, au. (bo.) cash payment.

compte-rendu. report.

conte. tale, short story.

contenu. contents.

contre-épreuve. (e.) proof taken from fresh proof (by offset) giving reverse of first proof.

contrefaçon. unauthorized reprint.

coquille. (pr.) wrong font.

corne *or* **oreille d'âne. (b.)** dog's ear.

corps de lettre. (pr.) type body.

correcteur. proof-reader.

correction. proof-reading.

côté de première *or* **forme première. (pr.)** first form.

côté de seconde *or* **seconde forme. (pr.)** second form.

couchure. (bb.) the action of placing gold leaves on the back, the boards and the edges of a book.

coupé. leaves cut.

coupée au trait carré. (e.) cut to the square line.

coupe-papier. paper-knife.

court de marges. (b.) narrow margin.

cousoir. (bb.) sewing-board.

couture. (bb.) sewing.

couture métallique. wire stitching.

couverture muette. plain cover.

couverture originale. publisher's cover.

creux, gravure en. intaglio.

criblé, gravure au. *See* **gravure en manière criblée.**

crochets. *pl.* brackets.

croix. (pr.) dagger.

ct. cartonné.

cuir ciselé. designs cut in a flat surface of leather, background being slightly sunk and covered with minute punchings, so that the design appeared in relief.

D

dactylographie. typewriting.

date d'impression. imprint date.

décor. décoration.

découpage. (bb.) cropping.

découpure d'un journal. newspaper clipping.

découpures, album de. scrapbook.

déd. dédicace.

dédicace. dedication.

défet *or* **carton refait** *or* **feuillet refait.** cancel.

défraîchi. faded, shopworn.

demi-reliure amateur. leather back and corners, paper or cloth sides, gilt top and trimmed edges.

dentelle. (bb.) a lace-like decoration.

département des estampes. print department.

dern. dernier, dernière.

dernier. last.

détérioré. damaged.

deux points. colon.

devise *or* **marque d'imprimeur.** printer's mark.

distribuer les types. (pr.) distribute the type.

dit. called.

dos adhérent *or* **dos ferme.** (bb.) stiff back.

dos refait. (bb.) back repaired.

dos à ressort. (bb.) spring back.

dos souple *or* **dos brisé** *or* **reliure à l'allemande.** (bb.) loose back.

double. duplicate.

doublon. (pr.) double, *i.e.*, words or phrases printed twice by mistake.

droit d'impression *or* **droits d'auteur.** copyright.

du bon. (pr.) *See* **bon, du.**

E

échange. exchange.

écrasé. (bb.) crushed.

écrit périodique. periodical.

écrits pour l'enfance. juvenile literature.

édition à bon marché. cheap edition.

édition fausse. a so-called new edition unchanged except for the title-page.

édition de poche *or* **édition portative.** pocket edition.

élucidé *or* **expliqué.** explained.

émail. (bb.) enamel.

emboîtage. (bb.) cased binding, *i.e.*, not "laced in."

en basane. bound in basil.

en bloc *or* **à forfait. (bo.)** by the lot.

encad. encadré.

encadré. framed.

encadrem. encadrement.

encadrement. framing, frame.

encadrer avec des filets. (pr.) to box in, to frame.

encart. inset.

encarter. insert a cancel.

encollage. (pa.) sizing.

encre. ink.

encre d'imprimeur. printer's ink.

endommagé. damaged.

endosser. (bb.) to back.

endossure. (bb.) backing.

enfance, écrits pour l'. *See* **écrits pour l'enfance.**

enjolivé. ornamented.

enlumineur *or* **miniaturiste.** illuminator.

entre-nerfs *or* **entre-nervures** *or* **compartiment. (bb.)** panel.

envoi d'auteur. *See* **exemplaire d'hommage.**

ép. époque.

époque. period.

épr. épreuve.

épreuve. (pr.) proof-sheet.

epreuve d'artiste *or* **avant la lettre.(e.)** artist's proof, proof before letter.

épreuve avec la lettre. (e.) proof with letter.

épreuve boueuse. (e.) excessively black proof from a too heavily inked plate.

épreuve à la brosse. brush-proof.

épreuve chargée. foul proof.

épreuve d'essai. (e.) trial proof.

épreuve neigeuse. (e.) cloudy, white-spotted proof.

épreuve non terminée. (e.) unfinished proof.

épreuve en placard. (pr.) galley proof.

épreuve peu chargée. (pr.) clean proof.

épreuve terminée. (e.) finished proof.

épuré. expurgated.

erreurs, avec. with a list of errata.

escompte. discount.

espace. (pr.) space.

espace montée à l'impression. (pr.) blacks.

espacer. (pr.) to space.

estampille. mark, inscription or signature put on books to indicate to what library they belong.

ét. état.

état. (e.) state.

exemplaire d'hommage *or* **envoi d'auteur.** presentation copy.

exemplaire numéroté. numbered copy.

exemplaire reglé. copy with text underlined, usually with red lines.

extrait. extract.

F

fausse-page *or* **page blanche.** blank page.

faute typographique. misprint.

faux vergé. (pa.) machine made "laid" paper.

ferrures. (bb.) bosses.

feuille blanche *or* **garde** *or* **feuille de garde.** fly-leaf.

feuille de garde. *See* **feuille blanche.**

feuille de titre. title-page.

feuilles d'auteur *or* **bonnes feuilles. (bo.)** advance sheets.

feuilles préliminaires. (b.) preliminary leaves.

feuillet refait *or* **carton refait** *or* **défet. (b.)** cancel.

feuilleter. (bb.) to turn over the leaves of a book.

ficelle. (pr.) page-cord.

filet de milieu *or* **colombelle. (pr.)** column rule.

filet noir. (pr.) mourning border.

filet pointé. (pr.) dotted rule.

foire de librairie. book-fair.

foncé. dark.

forfait, à. (bo.) by the lot.

format Charpentier (18-jésus). a common French book size, 11.7 x 18.3 cm.

forme première *or* **côté de première. (pr.)** first form.

forme seconde *or* **côté de seconde. (pr.)** second form.

fouetter. (bb.) to tie in.

frisquette. (pr.) frisket.

froissée. (e.) rubbed.

C

galée. (pr.) galley.

garde *or* **feuille de garde** *or* **feuille blanche.** fly-leaf.

garniture. (pr.) furniture.

136

gillotage. (e.) *See* **gravure au trait.**

gouttière. (bb.) fore-edge.

grand format. any book over 35 cm.

granite. (bb.) binding colored to resemble granite.

gravure sur acier. (e.) steel engraving.

gravure au burin. (e.) line engraving.

gravure en creux. (e.) intaglio.

gravure habillée *or* **habillage** *or* **bois habillé. (e.)** illustration surrounded by text.

gravure en manière criblée *or* **gravure au criblé. (e.)** dotted prints.

gravure à pleine page. (e.) full page engraving.

gravure pliée *or* **planche pliée. (e.)** folded plate.

gravure au pointillé. (e.) stipple engraving.

gravure en simili *or* **similigravure. (e.)** half tone.

gravure au trait *or* **gillotage** *or* **zincogravure. (e.)** zinc etching.

grecquer. (bb.) to make a track in the back of the assembled folded sections of a book to receive the bands that connect the sections and the covers, and to which the thread that holds the leaves is secured.

grise. *See* **lettre grise.**

guillemets. quotation marks.

H

habillage. *See* **gravure habillée.**

haut de casse. (pr.) upper case.

hebdomadaire. weekly.

heures. *See* **livre d'heures.**

Ī

imp. imprimé, imprimeur.
impr. imprimé, imprimeur.
impression anastatique. anastatic printing.
impression clair–obscure. chiaroscuro.
imprimé. printed
imprimeur des ouvrages de ville. job printer.
inc. incisé, inclusif, incomplet.
incisé. engraved.
incun. incunables.
incunables. incunabula.
indicateur. time-table.
in-plano. (b.) unfolded plate.
interc. intercalé.
intercalation. insertion, interpolation.
intercalé. inserted, interpolated.
interligne. (pr.) lead.
interligné. (pr.) leaded.
intitulé. entitled.

J

jaunissure. fox mark.

L

l. lavé.
lavé. cleaned, washed.
lettre armoriée. letter in several colors, as if emblazoned.
lettre blanche. (pr.) outline letter.
lettre bloquée *or* **lettre renversée. (pr.)** turned letter.

lettre capitale *or* **lettre majuscule. (pr.)** capital letter.

lettre de civilité. (pr.) type imitating written letters.

lettre coulée. (pr.) script.

lettre de fantaisie. (pr.) fancy letter.

lettre fatiguée *or* **lettre usée** *or* **lettre gatée. (pr.)** battered letter.

lettre flamande. *See* **lettre de forme.**

lettre de forme *or* **lettre flamande. (pr.)** black letter.

lettre gatée. *See* **lettre fatiguée.**

lettre grise. (pr.) large initial letter at head of chapters and books.

lettre majuscule. *See* **lettre capitale.**

lettre minuscule *or* **petit caractère. (pr.)** small letter.

lettre ornée. (pr.) ornate (florid) letter.

lettre à queue. (pr.) tail type, descending letter.

lettre renversée. *See* **lettre bloquée.**

lettre de somme. (pr.) bastard Italian type, bastard Roman type.

lettre tourneure. (pr.) ornamental initial used in the 15th century.

lettre usée. *See* **lettre fatiguée.**

lettrine. (pr.) (1) reference letter. (2) decorated initial letter.

libelle. libel.

libr. libraire.

libraire d'assortiment *or* **libraire de détail.** general bookseller.

lieu d'impression. place of printing.

lieu de publication. place of publication.

ligne fausse. false line, *i.e.*, last line of a paragraph at the beginning of a page.

ligne inférieure. *See* **ligne de queue.**

ligne de pied. foot-line, *i.e.*, the line containing only the signature and volume number.

ligne de queue *or* **ligne inférieure.** last line of text on page, bottom line.

ligne de tête. head-line.

ligne à voleur. (**pr.**) a line too widely spaced.

listel. (**pr.**) decorative line surrounding text.

livre blanc. blank book.

livre à clef. a book in which the proper names of persons or localities are disguised by the author.

livre en feuilles. book in sheets.

livre d'heures *or* **paire d'heures** *or* **heures.** book of hours.

livre d'images. picture book.

livre d'office *or* **missel.** missal.

livre de prières. prayer-book.

livre de référence. reference book.

livre xylographique. blockbook.

livret. booklet.

M

machine à composer. (**pr.**) composing machine.

machine typographique *or* **presse mécanique.** (**pr.**) fly-press.

maculature *or* **rebut.** (**pr.**) waste sheets, off-setting of wet printed sheets.

maculer. (**pr.**) to set off.

maison de reliure. bindery.

majuscule. *See* **lettre majuscule.**

manière criblée. *See* **gravure en manière criblée.**

manière noire. (**e.**) mezzotint.

mappe-monde. map of the world.

marbrure. (**bb.**) marbling.

maroquin écrasé. (**bb.**) crushed morocco.

maroquin foncé. (**bb.**) dark morocco.

marque de correction. (**pr.**) proofreader's mark of correction.

marque d'eau. (**pa.**) water mark.

marque d'imprimeur *or* **marque typographique.** printer's mark.

marque de libraire. publisher's mark.

mascaron. (**bb.**) grotesque ornament resembling a mask.

matières. *pl. or* **contenu.** contents.

mauvais état. (**bo.**) poor condition.

mettre une enchère sur un livre. bid on a book.

mettre en pages *or* **remanier.** (**pr.**) make up.

milieu. (**bb.**) ornamental center.

minuscule. *See* **lettre minuscule.**

missel *or* **livre d'office.** missal.

moine. (**pr.**) friar, *i.e.*, any part of a page which has not received the ink.

moisi. mouldy.

monté. mounted.

monté sur onglets. (**bb.**) guarded.

mors. *See* **charnière.**

mosaïque. *See* **reliure mosaïque.**

moyen format. from 25 to 35 cm. high.

N

n. c. non coupé.

n. c. *or* **n. ch.** non chiffré.

n. rog. non rogné.

nerfs *or* **nervures. (bb.)** raised bands.

nerfs postiches. (bb.) false bands.

nom de plume *or* **pseudonyme.** pen-name, pseudonym.

non mis en vente *or* **pas dans le commerce.** not for sale.

not. ms. note manuscrite.

note à la main *or* **note manuscrite.** manuscript note.

note de pied. footnote.

nouvelle *or* **conte.** short story.

O

œuvres choisies. selected works.

œuvres posthumes. posthumous works.

onglet. (bb.) guard.

opusc. opuscule.

opuscule. tract, treatise.

oreille d'âne *or* **corne.** dog's ear.

ouv. cour. ouvrage couronné.

ouvrage couronné. prize essay.

P

p. partie, parties.

p. d. port du.

p. f. petit format.

p. p. port payé.

page blanche *or* **fausse-page.** blank page.

page de droit. *See* page impaire.

page impaire *or* **belle page** *or* **page de droit** *or* **recto.** odd page, recto.

page paire. even page, verso.

paire d'heures. *See* **livre d'heures.**

panne. (bb.) old form of binding with projecting ridge of leather, by which the book could be carried.

papier buvard. blotting paper.

papier de coton. cotton paper.

papier à la cuve *or* **papier à la forme.** Holland paper, handmade paper.

papier glacé. glazed paper.

papier Joseph. very fine tissue paper.

papier léger comme la plume. feather-weight paper.

papier marbré. marbled paper.

papier satiné. calendered paper.

papier serpente. soft tissue paper used to protect illustrations.

papier de soie. tissue paper.

papier timbré. stamped paper.

papillotage. (pr.) set off.

paraissant tous les deux mois. bi-monthly.

pas dans le commerce. *See* **non mis en vente.**

paté. (pr.) pie, *i.e.*, mixed type.

peau d'agneau *or* **peau de mouton. (bb.)** sheepskin.

peau de chèvre. (bb.) goatskin.

peau de mouton. (bb.) *See* peau d'agneau.

peau de porc. (bb.) pigskin.

peau de renard. (bb.) foxskin.

peau de veau. (bb.) calfskin.

pet. car. petits caractères.

petit format. below 25 cm. in height.

petits caractères *or* **lettres minuscules.** small
letters.

pièce au dos *or* **pièce de titre.** lettering
piece.

pièce volante. fly-sheet.

piq. d. v. piqure de ver.

piqure de ver. wormhole.

pl. plat, planche.

planche. plate.

plaq. plaquette.

plaquette. Pamphlet of 1 to 24 pages.

plat de dessous *or* **plat inférieur** *or* **plat
verso. (bb.)** back cover.

plat inférieur. *See* **plat de dessous.**

plat recto *or* **premier plat. (bb.)** front cover.

plat verso. *See* **plat de dessous.**

plats de bois. (bb.) wooden boards.

plein dos, à. (bb.) with tight back.

plein-or. (bb.) gold tooling from large tools.

pleine de barbes. (e.) full of burrs.

pliage. folding.

plié. folded.

plus bas. see below.

point. *abbr.* pointillé.

point. period.

point d'exclamation. exclamation point.

point d'interrogation. interrogation point.

point et virgule. semicolon.

pointe. (pr.) bodkin.

pointe sèche. (e.) dry point.

pointillé. *See* **gravure au pointillé.**

port du. (bo.) transportation charges extra.

port payé. (bo.) transportation charges paid.

premier tirage. (e.) early proof.

presse à cylindre. (pr.) revolving press.

presse manuelle. (pr.) hand-press.

presse mécanique *or* **machine typographique. (pr.)** fly-press.

procès-verbaux d'une séance. minutes of a meeting.

ptilin. bookworm.

publié. edited, published.

Q

qqf. quelquefois.

quelquefois. sometimes.

queue d'un livre. lower edge, tail.

quotidien. daily.

R

r. n. r. rouge non rogné.

racinage. (bb.) tree binding.

rapiécé *or* **réparé** *or* **restauré.** repaired.

rapport *or* **compte-rendu.** report.

rature. erasure.

rebut *or* **maculature. (pr.)** waste sheets.

recueil factice *or* **volume de mélanges.** pamphlet volume.

rédacteur *or* **directeur.** editor of a periodical.

refondu. re-written.

registre. (1) in early books a table showing the signatures composing the book. (2) alphabetical table of 1st word of chapters.

rel. et. br. reliés et brochés.

relier de nouveau. to rebind.

reliés et brochés. (bo.) some bound, some unbound.

relieur, atelier de. bindery.

reliure à l'allemande. *See* **dos souple.**

reliure anglaise. flexible binding in full cloth or leather, with colored edges.

reliure arraphique. binding without any sewing (case binding.)

reliure d'art. art binding, de luxe binding.

reliure à charnière. old binding with wooden boards and hinged clasps.

reliure à l'éventail. binding with fan-like tooling.

reliure à la grecque. (bb.) binding without raised bands.

reliure jumelle. (bb.) volumes or parts bound together front to back, fore-edge of first touching back of second and so on.

reliure monastique. (bb.) stamped pig-skin or calf binding, ususally with ecclesiastical ornaments.

reliure mosaïque. (bb.) binding with back and sides decorated with inlaid or over-laid leathers of different colors.

reliure parlante. (bb.) binding with design symbolic of contents of the book.

reliure en portefeuille. (bb.) binding with flap, like a pocket-book.

reliure à la salamandre. (bb.) binding style of the time of Francis I., with emblem of a salamander.

reliure à la toison. (bb.) binding with small tool representing a sheep suspended by a band, applied at the corners and back of the book.

remanier. (pr.) to remodel a page.

renfoncement. (pr.) indentation.

renfoncer. (pr.) to indent.

renv. renvoi.

renvoi. cross reference.

rép. réparé.

réparé *or* **restauré** *or* **rapiécé.** repaired.

répé. répétition.

répétition. repetition.

rest. restauré.

restant de l'édition. (bo.) remainders.

restauré. *See* **réparé.**

rétiration. (pr.) printing of the second side.

rouge, non rogné. red edges, uncut.

rubriqué. rubricated.

S

s. sur.

s. a. sans année.

s. b. sur bois.

s. f. sans frais.

s. parch. sur parchemin.

s. t. sans titre.

saisi. suppressed.

salamandre, reliure à la. *See* **reliure à la salamandre.**

sans année. *See* **sans millésime.**

sans feuille de titre. no title-page.

sans frais. (bo.) gratis.

sans millésime *or* **sans année** *or* **sans date.** no date.

sans titre, no title.

satinage. (pa.) calendering.

seconde forme. *See* **côté de seconde.**

sigles. *pl.* abbreviations and contractions in manuscripts and early printed books.

signature de titre. (b.) direction line.

signe d'alinéa. (pr.) sign indicating new paragraph.

signet. bookmark.

similigravure. (e.) half tone.

soi-disant. calling himself.

souillé. stained.

souillure. stain.

souligné. underscored.

soulignure. underscoring.

sous condition. (bo.) on approval.

souscription. colophon.

suite. (1) continuation. (2) set of books.

suiv. suivant.

suivant. following.

suivre, à. to be continued.

sur parchemin. on parchment.

suscription. the opening sentence of early printed books without title-page. "Incipit."

T

t. s. v. pl. tournez s'il vous plaît.

148

table des matières. table of contents.

table des noms propres. index of names.

tache de moisissure. water-stain.

talus. (pr.) shoulder of a type.

témoins. (bb.) pages which show by folded corners or edges how much the book has been trimmed in binding or rebinding.

tête de chapitre *or* **en-tête.** head-piece.

tête de lettre. letter-head.

thèse. thesis.

tierce. (pr.) final proof, page or plate proof.

timbre d'une bibliothèque. library stamp.

tirage limité. limited edition.

tit. cou. titre courant.

titre, grand. collective title.

titre courant. running title.

titre du relieur. binder's title.

to. tome.

toile à registre. (bb.) black bookcloth.

toison, reliure à la. *See* reliure à la toison.

tomaison. indication of volume number on each sheet.

tome. volume.

tr. ant. tranche antiquée.

tr. éb. tranche ébarbée.

tr. jasp. tranche jaspée.

trad. traduit, traduction.

traduction. translation.

traduit. translated.

trait d'union *or* **tiret.** hyphen.

trait suspensif. dash.

tranche antiquée. (bb.) tooled edges.

tranche ébarbée. (bb.) trimmed edges.

tranche jaspée. (bb.) sprinkled edges.

tranchefile. (bb.) headband.

travail de ville. *See* bilboquet.

travaux *or* **transactions.** transactions.

trimestriel. quarterly.

V

veau fauve. (bb.) calf leather which has retained its natural color.

vente publique de livres. book-auction.

vermoulu *or* **piqué de vers.** wormholed.

vernis de graveur. (e.) etching ground.

virgule. comma.

voyez. see.

Z

zincogravure *or* **gravure au trait** *or* **gillotage.** (e.) zinc etching.

GERMAN

A

A. Auflage.

Abdruck vor aller Schrift. (e.) plain prints.

abgebraucht *or* **gebraucht.** (bo.) second-hand.

abgedr. abgedruckt.

abgedruckt. printed, reprinted.

abgenützter Einband. *See* **Einband, abgenützter.**

abgesetzt. (bo.) sold.

abgezogen. (e.) printed.

ablegen. (pr.) distribute the type.

Abriss. sketch, rough draft.

Absatz *or* **Paragraph.** (b.) paragraph.

Abschlag, auf. (bo.) *See* **auf Abschlag.**

Abteilung. section, part.

Abtlg. Abteilung.

ahd. althochdeutsch.

Akzidenzdruck. (pr.) job-printing.

Akzidenzdrucker. (pr.) job-printer.

althochdeutsch. Old High German, *i.e.*, the German language in use from the seventh to the beginning of the twelfth century.

Anfangsbuchstabe *or* **Initiale.** initial.

Anführungszeichen. quotation marks.

angeb. angeboten, angebunden.

angeboten. offered for sale.

angebunden. bound with.

Anh. Anhang.

Anhang. appendix.

anopistographisch. printed on one side only.

Anschlag *or* **Plakat.** poster, placard.

Anthologie *or* **Blumenlese** *or* **Blütenlese.** anthology.

Antiqua *or* römische **Schrift.** (**pr.**) Roman characters.

Anz. Anzeige.

Anzeige *or* **Inserat.** advertisement.

Atlasband. satin binding.

Ätzzeichnung. (**e.**) etching.

auf Abschlag. (**bo.**) on account.

aufgeklebt. *See* **aufgezogen.**

aufgeschnitten. cut open.

aufgezogen *or* **aufgeklebt.** mounted.

Auflage. edition.

Auflagereste *or* **Remittenden.** (**bo.**) remainders.

Aufschneidseite *or* **Vorderschnitt** *or* **Schnauze.** fore-edge.

Aufzug *or* **Akt.** act.

Auktion. *See* **Bücher-Versteigerung.**

ausg. ausgewählt.

Ausgabe letzter Hand. (**bo.**) last edition revised by the author.

ausgeb. ausgebessert.

ausgebessert. (**bb.**) repaired.

ausgeschn. ausgeschnitten.

ausgeschnitten. cut out.

ausgewählte Werke. selected works.

Aushängebogen. (**bo.**) advance sheets.

Ausrufszeichen. exclamation point.

Ausschliessung. (pr.) justification.

Ausschlusstück. (pr.) slug.

Ausschn. Ausschnitt.

Ausschnitt. clipping.

Auswahl. selection.

Auswechselblatt *or* **Karton** *or* **Auswurfbogen** *or* **Umdruckblatt** *or* **Defektbogen.** (b.) cancel, *i. e.*, a leaf or any part of printed matter omitted or suppressed, also any printed matter substituted for that stricken out.

Auswechselblatt einfügen. to insert a cancel.

Auswurfbogen. *See* **Auswechselblatt.**

Autotypie. (e.) half tone.

B

Bandangabe. volume number or other volume indication.

Baumwollpapier. cotton paper.

bearbeitet. edited.

Bearbeitung. edition.

bed. verm. bedeutend vermehrt.

bedeutend vermehrt. much enlarged.

Beibl. Beiblatt.

Beiblatt. supplement to a periodical.

beigedr. beigedruckt.

beigedruckt. printed with.

Beistrich. comma.

Bericht. report.

Besatz. (bb.) border.

beschädigt. mutilated.

Beschlag. *See* **mit Beschlag gelegt.**

beschn. beschnitten. cut down.

beschnitten, stark. cropped.

Besitzervermerk. bookplate.

Bettelmantel. *See* **Flickgedicht.**

bezgw., bezw. beziehungsweise.

beziehungsweise. respectively.

Bilderbuch. picture book.

Bindestrich. hyphen.

blasser Druck. (pr.) gray impression.

blattgross. full page.

Blatthüter. *See* **Blattweiser.**

Blattweiser *or* **Blatthüter** *or* **Eckwortkustode** *or* **Kustode. (b.)** catchword.

Blinddr. Blinddruck.

Blinddruck *or* **Blindpressung. (bb.)** blind tooling.

Blindpressung. *See* **Blinddruck.**

Blockbuch. blockbook.

Blumenlese. *See* **Anthologie.**

Blumenzierat. fleuron.

Blütenlese. *See* **Anthologie.**

Bogenbezeichnung. *See* **Bogensignatur.**

Bogensignatur *or* **Bogenbezeichnung. (b.)** signature.

Briefkopf. letter-head.

Briefwechsel. correspondence.

Broschüre *or* **Flugschrift.** pamphlet.

Brotschriften. *pl.* **(pr.)** body type.

Bruchstück. fragment.

Buch, antiquarisches. (bo.) secondhand book.

Buch, unbeschriebenes. blank book.

Buch Papier. quire.

Bücherfreund *or* **Bibliophil.** bibliophile.
Büchernarr *or* **Biblioman.** bibliomaniac.
Büchersammler. book collector.
Büchertrödler. secondhand bookseller.
Bücherversteigerung *or* **Bücher-Auktion**
  book auction.
Bücherwurm. bookworm.
Buchhändler. bookseller.
Buchhändlermesse. book-fair.
Buchladen *or* **Buchhandlung.** bookstore.
Buchschnitt. edges of a book.
Buchst. Buchstabe.
Buchstabe. letter, character, type.
Buchstabe, altenglischer. black letter.
Buchumschlag. loose paper cover.
Bünde, erhabene. (bb.) raised bands.
Buntdruck *or* **Mehrfarbendruck.** polychromy.
Bürstenabzug. (e.) brush proof.

C

Cimelien. (b.) precious, rare books.

D

d. R. W. (d. Rw.). deutsche Reichswährung.
Dam.-E. Damasteinband.
Damasteinband. damask binding.
Darst. Darstellung.
Darstellung. description, explanation.
Decke. board.
Deckel. (pr.) tympan.
Deckel *or* **Umschlag.** (bb.) cover.
defekt. defective, damaged.
Defektbogen. *See* **Auswechselblatt.**

155

Defekt-Buchstabe. (pr.) battered letter.

Dickdruckpapier. feather weight paper.

Doppelsatz *or* **Hochzeit. (pr.)** double, *i.e.*, words or sentences printed twice by mistake.

Doublette. duplicate.

Dreifarbendruck. three-color print.

dreispaltig. (b.) in three columns.

Druck, im. in the press.

drucken. to print.

Druckermarke *or* **Druckersignet** *or* **Drucker-vermerk** *or* **Druckerzeichen.** printer's mark.

Druckersignet. *See* **Druckermarke.**

Druckervermerk. *See* **Druckermarke.**

Druckerzeichen. *See* **Druckermarke.**

Druckfarbe. printer's ink.

Druckf.-V. Druckfehlerverzeichnis.

Druckfehler. misprint.

Druckfehlerverzeichnis. table of errata.

Druckfertig. (pr.) for press.

durchblättern. turn over the leaves of a book.

durchgestrichen. (e.) canceled.

durchschossen *or* **interfoliiert. (b.)** interleaved.

durchschossen. (pr.) leaded.

Durchschuss *or* **Reglette. (pr.)** lead, reglet.

Durchschussblatt. (b.) interleaf.

E

eckige Klammer. *See* **Klammer, eckige.**

Eckwortkustode. *See* **Blattweiser.**

Eierkuchen *or* **Zwiebelfisch.** (**pr.**) pie, *i. e.* types mixed.

Einband, abgenützter. worn binding.

einbinden. to bind.

Einfassung. border.

eingebunden. bound.

eingegangen. (**bo.**) out of print.

einrahmen mit Linien. (**pr.**) to box in.

Einschaltung. insertion, interpolation.

einschl. einschliesslich.

einschliesslich. inclusive.

einschnüren. (**bb.**) to tie in.

einspaltig. in one column.

Einzbl. Einzelblatt.

Einzelblatt. single sheet.

einzig. single, unique.

Einzug des Satzes. (**pr.**) indentation.

Endschrift *or* **Schlusschrift** *or* **Kolophon.** (**b.**) colophon.

Erg.-H. Ergänzungsheft.

Ergänzungsheft. supplement.

erhabene Bünde. (**bb.**) *See* **Bünde, erhabene.**

erkl. erklärt.

erklärt. explained, illustrated.

Erscheinungsvermerk *or* **Impressum.** imprint.

Erstlingsdrucke *or* **Wiegendrucke,** *or* **Inkunabeln.** (**b.**) incunabula.

Eselsohr. dog's ear.

Etui *or* **Futteral** *or* **Papphülse.** case.

Excerptenbuch. scrapbook.

Exemplar, rohes. book in sheets.

F

Fahnenabzug *or* **Fahnen.** (**pr.**)　galley proof, slip-proof.

Fahrplan.　time-table.

Faktur.　invoice.

falsche Signatur. (**b.**)　*See* **Signatur, falsche.**

Famosschrift *or* **Schmähschrift.**　libel.

Feld des Rückens. (**bb.**)　panel.

fester Rücken.　*See* **Rücken, fester.**

fette Schrift.　*See* **Schrift, fette.**

Ff.　Fortsetzung folgt.

fingerfleckig.　with fingermarks.

fl.　fleckig.

fleckig.　stained.

Flickgedicht *or* **Bettelmantel.**　cento., *i.e.* a writing composed of selections from various authors.

Fliegenkopf. (**pr.**)　turned letter.

Flugschrift *or* **Broschüre.**　pamphlet.

Folge *or* **Reihe.**　series.

Foliant.　folio edition.

foliieren.　to page.

Formstreifen. (**pa.**)　wiremarks.

fortlaufende Paginierung.　consecutive numbering of pages.

Forts.　Fortsetzung.

Fortsetzung.　continuation.

Fortsetzung folgt.　to be continued.

Freiexemplar.　free copy.

Fuchsleder.　fox-skin.

Furchenschrift.　boustrophedon.

Futt.　Futteral.

Futteral. *See* **Etui.**

G

Gänsefüsschen *or* **Anführungszeichen.** quotation marks.

Ganzen, im. (bo.) by the lot.

Ganzfranzband. full calf binding.

ganzseitig. full page.

Garnitur. (pr.) series of type.

gbdn. gebunden.

Gebetbuch. prayer-book.

gebr. gebraucht.

gebraucht. used, secondhand.

gebunden. bound.

Gedankenstrich. dash.

Gedicht. poem.

gefaltet. folded.

gekrönt. awarded a prize.

gepunzter Schnitt. (bb.) tooled edges.

gereinigt *or* **kastriert.** expurgated.

ges. gesammelt, gesucht.

gesammelt. collected.

Gesamttitel *or* **Haupttitel.** (b.) collective title.

Gesellschaftsschriften. society publications.

gesperrter Satz. *See* **Satz, gesperrter.**

gesprenkelter Schnitt. *See* **Schnitt, gesprenkelter.**

gest. gestochen.

gestochen. engraved.

gesucht. in demand.

Gevierte. (pr.) quadrat.

gewidmet. dedicated.

gez. gezeichnet.

gezeichnet. drawn.

goldgeprägt. (bb.) stamped with gold.

Goldschn. Goldschnitt.

Goldschnitt. gilt edges.

Grabstichel. (e.) graver.

Grabstichelmanier *or* **Linienmanier. (e.)** line engraving.

Graveur. engraver.

Grosspapier. (b.) large paper.

Grundlinie *or* **Schlusslinie.** bottom line.

Grundriss. plan, outline.

H

Habilitationsschrift. dissertation submitted for the purpose of acquiring the right of lecturing at a university.

halbmonatlich. semi-monthly.

Halbsaffianband. half-morocco binding.

handerzeugtes Papier. *See* **Papier, handerzeugtes.**

Handexemplar. "Marked copy" in which notes or alterations are made, often for basis of a new edition.

handgeschöpftes Papier. *See* **Papier, handerzeugtes.**

Handschrift. manuscript.

Haupttitel. *See* **Gesamttitel.**

Hauptzeile. (b.) headline.

Haut *or* **Leder.** leather, skin.

Hds. Handschrift.

Heftlade. (bb.) sewing-board.

Helldunkeldruck. black-white printing.

hinterl. hinterlassen.

hinterlassene Schriften. posthumous works.

Hirschleder. (bb.) buckskin.

Hlnw., Hlw., Hlwnd. Halbleinwand.

Hlz. Holzband.

Hochdeutsch. High German, *i.e.*, the modern German language.

Hochzeit *or* **Doppelsatz.** (pr.) double, *i.e.*, words or sentences printed twice by mistake.

Holzfaserpapier. woodpulp paper.

Holztafeldruck *or* **Blockbuch.** block-book.

Hülse. *See* **Papphülse.**

Hurenkind, *or* **Bastard.** (pr.) false line, *i.e.* end line of a paragraph at the beginning of a page.

I

im Druck. in the press.

im Ganzen *or* **nicht gezählt.** (bo.) by the lot.

Imit. Imitation.

Impressum. *See* **Erscheinungsvermerk.**

Initiale. *See* **Anfangsbuchstabe.**

Inkunabeln *or* **Wiegendrucke** *or* **Erstlingsdrucke.** incunabula.

Inserat *or* **Anzeige** *or* **Annonce.** advertisement.

interfoliiert. *See* **durchschossen.**

Interpunktion. punctuation.

J

Jchtbd., Jchtn., Jchtnb. Juchtenband.
Jubiläumsausgabe. anniversary edition.
Juchtenband. Russia leather binding.
Jugendschriften. juvenile literature.

K

Kalbleder. calf leather.
Kaliko *or* **Perkal. (bb.)** calico.
Kaltnadelstich. (e.) dry point.
Kammarmorschnitt. combed edges.
Kante. corner.
Kapitalband. (bb.) headband.
Kapitalbuchstabe *or* **Majuskel. (pr.)** capital letter.
Kapitälchen. (pr.) small capitals.
Kapitalkasten, Typen aus dem. (pr.) upper case.
Kapitelüberschrift. chapter heading.
Kartonnage. cardboard.
kastriert. *See* **gereinigt.**
Kattunband. cloth binding.
Kegel. *See* **Schriftkegel.**
Keilschrift. cuneiform letters.
Klammer. parenthesis.
Klammer, eckige. brackets.
kol. koloriert.
Kol. Kolumne.
Kolon *or* **Doppelpunkt.** colon.
Kolophon *or* **Schlusschrift** *or* **Endschrift.** colophon.

koloriert. colored.

Kolumne *or* **Spalte.** column.

Kolumne, gerade *or* **Rückseite.** (**pr.**) even page, verso.

Kolumne, ungerade *or* **Vorderseite** (**pr.**) odd page, recto.

Kolumnenschnur. (**pr.**) page cord.

Kolumnentitel, lebender *or* **Kopftitel.** running title, live heading.

Kolumnentitel, toter *or* **Kolumnenziffer.** (**pr.**) dead heading, page number.

Kolumnenziffer. *See* **Kolumnentitel, toter.**

komm. kommentiert.

kommentiert. explained.

komp. komplett.

komplett. complete.

kompresser Satz. *See* **Satz, kompresser.**

Kopf *or* **oberer Schnitt.** (**bb.**) head, top.

Kopftitel. *See* **Kolumnentitel, lebender.**

Kopfvignette. (**b.**) headpiece.

Korrektor *or* **Faktor.** proof reader.

Korrekturbogen *or* **Probebogen.** proof sheets.

Korrekturzeichen. proof reader's marks.

Kreidezeichnungsstich. (**e.**) crayon.

Kreuz. (**pr.**) dagger.

Kttbd. Kattunband.

Kustode. *See* **Blattweiser.**

L

Lage. (**b.**) gathering.

Lagenregister. (**b.**) register of signatures.

lebender Kolumnentitel. *See* **Kolumnentitel, lebender.**

Lehrb. Lehrbuch.

Lehrbuch. textbook.

Leiche. (pr.) out, *i.e.*, omission of a word or a phrase by the compositor.

Leinenkartonnage. (bb.) cloth boards.

Leiste auf dem Einbande. (bb.) fillet.

Leitartikel. editorial.

Lesezeichen. bookmark.

Lexikon-Oktav. large octavo.

Lichtkupferstich. heliogravure.

Lief. Lieferung.

lieferbar. available.

Lieferung. fascicle.

Linienmanier *or* **Grabstichelmanier. (e.)** line engraving.

Löschpapier. blotting paper.

loser Rücken. (bb.) *See* **Rücken, loser.**

M

magere Schrift. (pr.) *See* **Schrift, magere.**

Mähr. Mährchen.

Mährchen. *See* Märchen.

Majuskel *or* **Versalbuchstabe** *or* **Kapitalbuchstabe.** capital letter.

marm. marmoriert.

marmoriert. marbled.

Makulaturbogen. (pr.) waste sheets.

mangelhaft *or* **defekt.** incomplete, imperfect.

Märchen *or* **Mährchen.** fairy tale.

marmoriertes Papier. *See* **Papier, marmoriertes.**

Material, neues. (pr.) new matter.

Mehrfarbendruck *or* **Buntdruck.** polychromy.

Messbuch. missal.

Messingbeschlag. (bb.) brass bosses.

Messkatalog. old semi-annual booksellers' catalogue issued at Easter and Michaelmas.

Minuskel *or* **kleine Buchstabe.** small letter.

mit Beschlag gelegt. suppressed.

mit vollem Rand. margin uncut.

mitget. mitgeteilt.

mitgeteilt. contributed.

Mittelfeld. (bb.) central panel.

mittelhochdeutsch. Middle High German, *i.e.*, the German language in use from the twelfth to the fifteenth century.

monatlich. monthly.

Monatsbericht. monthly report.

Mönch. (pr.) friar, *i.e.*, any part of the page which has not received the ink.

Mönchschrift. monk's letters.

N

n. gez. nicht gezählt.

n. i. H. nicht im Handel.

Nachw. Nachwort.

Nachwort. epilogue.

Namengedicht *or* **Akrostichon.** acrostic.

Namenszug. signature.

Nebentitel. additional title.

neubinden. to rebind.

Neudruck. reprint.

nicht gezählt. (bo.) by the lot.

nicht im Handel. (bo.) not for sale.

Norm. (b.) direction line.

Notensternchen *or* **Stern. (b.)** asterisk.

O

o. F. ohne Fortsetzung.

o. O., Dr. u. J. ohne Ort, Druckernamen und Jahr.

ö. W. österreichische Währung.

offerieren (für ein Buch). bid on a book.

ohne Fortsetzung. No more.

ohne Titelblatt. no title-page.

orn. ornamentirt.

Originalumschlag. original paper-cover.

österreichische Währung. Austrian currency.

P

Papier, handerzeugtes *or* **handgeschöpftes Papier** *or* **Büttenpapier.** hand-made paper.

Papier, marmoriertes. marble paper.

Papiermesser. paper-cutter.

Pappe. pasteboard.

Papphülse *or* **Futteral** *or* **Etui.** case.

Pasquill *or* **Schmähschrift** *or* **Famosschrift.** libel.

Pflichtexemplar. deposit copy.

Plattdeutsch. Low German, *i.e.*, the colloquial language of the northern part of Germany.

166

Plattenzustand. *See* **Zustand.**

Prachtex. Prachtexemplar.

Prachtexemplar. (bo.) splendid copy.

Pränumeration *or* **Abonnement.** subscription.

Predigt. sermon.

Preisschrift. prize essay.

Privatdruck. private publication.

Probebogen *or* **Korrekturbogen.** proof sheets.

Protokoll. minutes of a meeting.

Punkt. period.

Punktiermanier. stipple engraving.

punktierte Linie. dotted line.

R

Radierg. Radierung.

Radiergrund. (e.) etching ground.

Radierung. (e.) etching.

Rähmchen. (pr.) frisket.

ramponiert. damaged.

Randbemerkungen *or* **Marginalien,** *or* **Randglossen** *or* **Randnoten.** marginal notes.

Randglossen. *See* **Randbemerkungen.**

Randleiste. (b.) margin border.

Randnoten. *See* **Randbemerkungen.**

Randzeuge. (b.) witness, *i.e.*, leaf left uncut by the binder to show that the margin is not cut too much.

Rdnot. Randnoten.

Reglette *or* **Durchschuss. (pr.)** lead, reglet.

Reihe *or* **Folge.** series.

Remittenden. *See* **Auflagereste.**

rest. restauriert.

restauriert. repaired.

Revision, erste *or* **Autorkorrektur.** author's proof.

rh. W. rheinische Währung.

rheinische Währung. Rhenish currency.

Rm. (R.M.) Reichsmark.

rohes Exemplar. *See* **Exemplar, rohes.**

römische Schrift. *See* **Antiqua.**

Rotschnitt. red edged.

Rthr. Reichsthaler.

Rücken, fester. (**bb.**) tight back.

Rücken, loser. (**bb.**) loose back.

Rückenbildung. (**bb.**) backing.

Rückenschild. (**bb.**) label, lettering piece.

Rückentitel. (**b.**) binder's title.

Rücks. Rückseite.

Rückseite. Verso.

Runenschrift. runic characters.

S

S. V. Selbst-Verlag.

S. W. Süddeutsche Währung.

Satz *or* **Typenform.** (**pr.**) composition.

Satz, durchschossener. (**pr.**) leaded matter.

Satz, gesperrter. (**pr.**) spaced matter.

Satz, kompresser. (**pr.**) close matter, solid matter.

Satz, splendider. (**pr.**) widely spaced matter.

Schabmanier *or* **schwarze Kunst.** (**e.**) mezzotint.

Schafleder. sheepskin.

Schafleder, braunes. basil.

scharf beschnitten *or* **stark beschnitten.** cropped.

Schauspiel. drama.

Schiff. *See* **Setzschiff.**

schimmelig. mouldy.

Schliesse. *See* **Schloss.**

Schloss *or* **Schliesse.** clasp.

Schlussbl. Schlussblatt.

Schlussblatt. last leaf.

Schlusslinie *or* **Grundlinie.** (b.) bottom line.

Schluss-Vignette. (b.) tail-piece.

Schmähschrift *or* **Famosschrift** *or* **Pasquill.** libel.

schmalrandig. with narrow margins.

Schmitz *or* **dublierter Druck.** (pr.) set off, *i.e.,* a smut transferred from a freshly printed surface to another sheet.

Schmutzfleck. stain.

Schnauze *or* **Vorderschnitt.** (b.) fore-edge.

Schnitt, gepunzter. *See* **Schnitt, ziselierter.**

Schnitt, gesprenkelter. (bb.) sprinkled edges.

Schnitt (oberer) vergoldet. (bb.) gilt top.

Schnitt, unterer *or* **Schwanz.** (bb.) tail, lower edge.

Schnitt, ziselierter *or* **gepunzter Schnitt.** (bb.) tooled edges.

Schöndruck. (pr.) first form.

Schönschreibekunst. calligraphy.

Schrift, fette. (pr.) black faced type, bold faced type.

Schrift, geschwänzte. (pr.) tail type, descending letters.

Schrift, magere. (pr.) lightfaced type, lean-faced type.

Schriftkasten. (pr.) type-case.

Schriftkastenfach. (pr.) box in a type-case.

Schriftkegel *or* **Kegel. (pr.)** shank, body of a letter.

Schriftsetzer. *See* **Setzer.**

Schriftsteller *or* **Verfasser.** author.

Schrotblatt. (e.) dotted print.

Schuster. (pr.) new paragraph at the end of a page.

schw. u. r. gedr. schwarz und rot gedruckt.

Schwanz *or* **unterer Schnitt eines Buches. (bb.)** tail, lower-edge.

schwarz und rot gedruckt. printed in black and red.

schwarze Kunst *or* **Schabmanier.** mezzotint.

Schweinsleder. pig skin.

Schwnsl. Schweinsleder.

Segeltuch. (bb.) canvas, duck.

Seite, leere. blank page.

Seitenüberschrift. running title.

Semikolon *or* **Strichpunkt.** semicolon.

Separatabdruck. *See* **Sonderdruck.**

Setzbrett. (pr.) letter-board, composing board.

setzen. (pr.) compose.

Setzer *or* **Schriftsetzer. (pr.)** compositor.

Setzlinie. (pr.) composing rule, setting rule.

Setzmaschine. (pr.) type-setting machine.

Setzschiff *or* **Schiff. (pr.)** galley.

Sgr. Silbergroschen.

Signatur, falsche. (**b.**) signature with an asterisk.

Silbe. syllable.

Silbergroschen. old Prussian coin worth about 2½ cents.

Sitzungsberichte. proceedings.

soeben erschienen. (**bo.**) now published.

sog. sogenannt.

sogenannt. so-called.

Sonderdruck *or* **Separatabdruck.** reprint.

Sondertitel *or* **Untertitel.** subtitle.

Spalte. *See* **Kolumne.**

Spaltenlinie. (**pr.**) column rule.

spationieren. (**pr.**) to space.

Spatium *or* **Ausschlussstück.** (**pr.**) slug.

Spielkarten. playing cards.

Spiess. (**pr.**) blacks, *i.e.*, a space, quadrat or piece of furniture that rises and is imprinted on a sheet.

Spitzenornament. (**b.**) dentelle border.

Sprungrücken. (**bb.**) spring back.

Stabreim. alliteration.

Stege. *pl.* (**pr.**) furniture.

Steifband *or* **Pappband.** binding in boards.

steifbroschiert. (**bb.**) in boards.

Steif-Leinwand. (**bb.**) buckram.

stellenweise. here and there.

Stempel, feine. (**bb.**) petits fers, small tools.

Stern *or* **Notensternchen.** (**b.**) asterisk.

Stich. cut, plate, engraving.

Stich, gefalteter. folded plate.

stumpf anfangen. (**pr.**) commence even, flush.

Stundengebete. book of hours.

Subskribent. subscriber.

süddeutsche Währung. South German currency.

Superrevision *or* **Pressrevision.** press proof.

T

täglich. daily.

teilw. *or* **theilw.** teilweise.

teilweise. partly.

Thr. Thaler.

Tinte. ink.

Titelblatt fehlt. title-page lacking.

Trauerrand. mourning border.

Typendruck. (pr.) letter-press.

Typenform *or* **Satz. (pr.)** composition.

Typus. (pr.) type.

U

Überschlag *or* **Vorschlag. (b.)** head margin.

Überschrift *or* **Rubrik.** heading.

Übersicht *or* **Synopse.** synopsis.

übert. übertragen.

übertragen. translated.

umbrechen. (pr.) to make up.

Umdruckblatt. *See* **Auswechselblatt.**

Umklopfen. (bb.) rounding.

Umschlag. cover.

Umschreibung. transliteration.

unaufg. unaufgeschnitten.

unaufgeschnitten. not cut open.

ungeb. ungebunden.

ungebunden. unbound.

172

Unterkasten, Typen aus dem. **(pr.)** lower case.

Unterschlag. the blank space at the end of a page.

Unterstreichung *or* **Unterstreichen.** underscoring, underlining.

Untertit. Untertitel.

Untertitel *or* **Sondertitel.** subtitle.

V

V. Verlag.

V. A. Verlagsanstalt.

V. B. Verlagsbuchhandlung.

verd. verdeutscht.

verdeutscht. translated into German.

verg. vergoldet, vergriffen.

vergoldet. gilt.

vergriffen. suppressed.

Verlagsanstalt *or* **Verlagsbuchhandlung.** publishing house.

Verlagsort *or* **Erscheinungsort.** place of publication.

Verleger. publisher.

verletzt. damaged.

Versalbuchstabe *or* **Kapitalbuchstabe** *or* **Majuskel.** **(pr.)** capital letters.

verstaubt. stained with dust.

Versteigerung. *See* **Bücherversteigerung.**

Verweisungsbuchstaben. *pl.* **(pr.)** superiors.

Verweisungszeichen. **(pr.)** reference sign.

vierteljährlich. quarterly.

vollem Rand, mit. margin uncut.

Vorderdeckel. front cover.

Vorderschnitt *or* **Schnauze. (b.)** fore-edge.

Vorderseite *or* **ungerade Kolumne. (b.)** odd page, recto.

vorh. vorhanden.

vorhanden. in stock.

vorm. vormals.

vormals. formerly.

Vorrede *or* **Vorwort.** preface.

Vorsatztitel *or* **Schmutztitel. (b.)** half-title.

Vorschlag *or* **Überschlag. (b.)** head margin.

Vorsilbe. prefix.

Vorwort. *See* **Vorrede.**

W

W. Wappen.

w. weiss.

Währung. currency.

Wappen. coat of arms.

Wasserlinien. (pr.) waterlines.

weiss. white.

Weltkarte. map of the world.

Werke, ausgewählte. selected works.

Werke, sämmtliche. collected works.

Werksatz. (pr.) bookwork.

Werksetzer. (pr.) book compositor.

Widerdruck. (pr.) second form.

Widm. Widmung.

Widmung *or* **Zueignung** *or* **Dedikation.** dedication.

Wiedergabe. reproduction.

Winkelhaken. (pr.) composing stick.

wöchentlich. weekly.

wohlf. wohlfeil.

wohlfeil. cheap.

Z

Zeichenbändchen *or* **Lesezeichen.** bookmark.

Zeichnung. design, drawing.

zerknittert. mussed, crumpled.

Zeugkasten. (pr.) hell, *i.e.*, receptacle for broken and battered type.

Ziegenhaut. goatskin.

Zierbuchstabe. fancy letter.

ziselierter Schnitt. *See* **Schnitt, ziselierter.**

Zueignung. *See* **Widmung.**

zur Ansicht. (bo.) on approval.

Zusammenhang. context.

Zustand *or* **Plattenzustand.** (e.) state.

zweispaltig. in two columns.

Zwiebelfisch *or* **Eierkuchen.** (pr.) pie, *i.e.*, mixed type.

ITALIAN

A

a spese dell' autore. at the author's expense.

abbicci. alphabet.

abbonato. subscriber.

abbozzo *or* **schizzo.** sketch, rough draft.

accademie, pubblicazioni delle. publications of learned societies.

acciugajo. (b.) a book in very poor condition. Literal translation: a book only fit for wrapping up anchovies.

acqua forte *or* **incisione coll' acqua forte.** etching.

adèspota. (b.) author unknown.

album di ritagli *or* **estratti tagliati.** scrapbook.

allacciare. (bb.) to tie in.

amatore di libri *or* **collettore di libri.** bookcollector.

anche sotto il titolo. also under the title.

anepigrafo *or* **senza titolo.** anepigraphous, without title.

angolo *or* **punta** *or* **cantone di un libro.** corner of a book.

annata *or* **anno. (b.)** year.

annotazione. annotation.

annunzio. advertisement.

ant. (antip.) **antiporta.**

176

antiporta *or* **occhietto** *or* **falso frontispizio.** half-title.

antiporta figurata *or* **antiporta ornata.** frontispiece.

apòcrifo. not authentic.

approvazione *or* **licenza.** official sanction of a book.

articolo. (bo.) item.

articolo di fondo. editorial.

asse *or* **piatto in legno. (bb.)** wooden board.

assembramento di fogli. (bb.) gathering.

asta libraria *or* **vendita di libri all' asta. (bo.)** book auction.

asterisco. asterisk.

atlante d'imagini. large picture book.

atti. transactions.

atto. (b.) act.

avanti lettera *or* **prova avanti lettera. (e.)** proof before letter.

avviso. poster, placard.

B

balla. (pa.) ten reams.

bancone. (pr.) composing board.

barbone. (bo.) book, or lot of books, difficult to sell.

bassa cassa. (pr.) lower case.

bianca *or* **stampa in bianca. (pr.)** first form.

Bibbia. Bible.

biffato. (e.) canceled, *i.e.*, crossed out.

bimestrale. bimonthly.

blocco, in, *or* **in combutta** *or* **senza scelta. (bo.)** by the lot.

bollare. to stamp.

bollatura. stamping.

borchia *or* **fermaglio.** clasp.

bottello *or* **cartello** *or* **cartellino** *or* **etichetta.**
label, lettering piece.

bozza *or* **prova.** (pr.) proof-sheet.

bozza, ultima. (pr.) press-proof.

bozza di autore. (pr.) author's proof.

bozza in colonnini. (pr.) galley-proof.

bozza col rullo. brush-proof.

brache. (pr.) waste-sheets.

brachetta. (bb.) guard.

bustrofedone. boustrophedon.

C

c. con.

c. (*pl.* **cc.**) carta, carte, carattere.

c. t. con tavole.

calce. bottom of a page.

canale d'un libro *or* **davanti d'un libro** *or*
gola. (bb.) fore-edge.

cantone. *See* **angolo.**

capitello *or* **tranciafila.** (bb.) head-band.

capitolo. chapter.

capopagina *or* **testata illustrata.** (b.) head-
piece.

capoverso *or* **alinea.** paragraph, alinea.

car. carattere.

carattere *or* **lettera.** letter, type.

cart. (bb.) cartone.

carta. paper, card, leaf.

carta d'ammissione. card of admission.

carta bambagina. cotton paper.

ITALIAN

carta bollata. stamped paper.

carta geografica. map.

carta a mano. hand-made paper.

carta marmorea. marbled paper.

carta sugante *or* **carta asciugante.** blotting paper.

cartata *or* **faccia** *or* **pagina.** page.

cartatura *or* **cartolatura.** numbering of pages.

carte da giuoco. *pl.* playing cards.

carteggiare. to collate.

carteggio. collating.

cartellinato. labeled.

cartellino. *See* **cartello.**

cartello *or* **cartellino** *or* **etichetta** *or* **bottello.** (bb.) lettering piece, label.

cartolare. to number the pages.

cassa da caratteri. (pr.) type-case.

cassettino. (pr.) section of a type-case.

catalogo coi prezzi. priced catalogue.

cattivo stato, in. in bad condition.

cimèlio. very rare old book.

cod. codice.

codice. codex.

col. colonna.

collana *or* **raccolta.** collection.

collettore di libri *or* **amatore di libri.** book-collector.

colonna. column.

com. commento.

combutta, in, *or* **in blocco** *or* **senza scelta.** (bo.) by the lot.

cominciare in riga *or* **cominciare senza capoverso.** (pr.) commence even.

commento. commentary.

commercio librario. book-trade.

compiuto *or* **perfetto.** complete.

comporre. (pr.) to compose.

compositoio. (pr.) composing stick.

compositore. (pr.) compositor.

composizione. (pr.) form, composition.

composizione agevole *or* **roba buona. (pr.)** fat, *i.e.,* pieces of composition, for instance, running titles that are kept for future use and are not taken apart till the whole work is finished.

composizione interlineata. (pr.) leaded matter.

composizione serrata. (pr.) close matter.

composizione spazieggiata. (pr.) spaced composition.

comprare all' incanto. (bo.) to buy at auction.

con. with.

con note esplicative. with explanatory notes.

condizione, sotto. (bo.) on approval.

conferenza. lecture.

conferenziere. lecturer.

contenuto. contents.

contesto. context.

contornato. (pr.) boxed in.

contraffazione. unauthorized *or* illegal reprint.

copertina originale. publisher's cover.

copie invendute *or* **il fondo. (bo.)** remainders.

corpo *or* **opere complete. (b.)** collected works.

corpo d'un carattere. (pr.) shank.

correggiuóle. *pl.* **(bb.)** raised bands. .

correggiuóle, distanza fra le. (bb.) panel.

correttore. proofreader.

costola *or* **dorso d'un libro** *or* **schiena.** back of a book.

critica. criticism.

critico. critic.

crocétta. (pr.) dagger.

cuoio *or* **pelle.** leather.

cuoio di Russia. Russia leather.

curiosità. a book of which a few copies only are printed.

D

data di stampa. imprint year.

davanti d'un libro *or* **gola** *or* **canale d'un libro. (bb.)** fore-edge.

ded. dedica.

dedica. dedication.

dentelle. *See* **pizzo.**

deposito legale *or* **esemplari d'obbligo. (b.)** deposit copies.

deposito dei rappezzi. (pr.) hell; *i.e.*, a box into which a printer throws his broken type.

descriz. descrizione.

descrizione. description.

detto. called.

diario. diary.

didascalia. title, chapter headings.

difettoso *or* **imperfetto.** defective, imperfect.

disegnatore. designer.

disegno. design, drawing.

disopra dorato *or* **dorato in testa** *or* **taglio superiore dorato.** gilt top.

disopra del libro. (bb.) top, head of a book.

disotto del libro. (bb.) tail, lower edge.

dispensa *or* **fascicolo** *or* **puntata.** fascicle, number, part.

divisione *or* **sezione.** division, section.

dizionario. dictionary.

d'ogni settimana *or* **ebdomadario.** weekly.

doppio *or* **doppione** *or* **duplicato. (b.)** duplicate.

dorato sui fogli *or* **taglio dorato.** gilt edged.

dorato in testa. *See* **disopra dorato.**

dorso d'un libro *or* **costola** *or* **schiena.** back of a book.

dorso rigido. (bb.) tight back.

dorso a scatto. (bb.) spring back.

due punti. colon.

duerno. folio sheet.

duplicato. *See* **doppio.**

duplicatura. (pr.) double; *i.e.*, matter set up a second time by mistake.

E

ebdomadario *or* **d'ogni settimana.** weekly.

ecc. etcetera.

edizione dell' ancora. Aldine edition.

edizione di circostanza. work published for a special occasion, as a wedding, etc.

edizione contraffatta. *See* **contraffazione.**

edizione corretta. revised edition.

edizione economica. cheap edition.

edizione limitata *or* **edizione di pochi esemplari.** limited edition.

edizione non venale *or* **edizione fuori di commercio. (bo.)** edition not for sale.

edizione portatile. pocket edition.

edizione principe. first edition.

edizione purgata. expurgated edition.

elenco degl' indirizzi. directory.

ep. epistola.

epistola. letter.

errore di stampa. misprint.

esemplare di omaggio *or* **invio dell' autore** *or* **omaggio dell' autore.** presentation copy.

esemplare d'obbligo *or* **deposito legale.** deposit copy.

espurgato *or* **purgato.** expurgated.

estr°. estratto.

estratti tagliati *or* **album di ritagli.** scrap-book.

estratto. extract.

etichetta *or* **cartello** *or* **bottello.** label, lettering piece.

F

f. foglio, figurato, figura.

faccia *or* **cartata** *or* **pagina.** page.

facciata *or* **frontispizio.** title-page.

falso volume *or* **finto volume** *or* **libro bianco.** blank-book.

ferm. fermaglio.

fermaglio *or* **borchia.** clasp.

ferratura sulla legatura. (bb.) bosses.

ferri, piccoli. (bb.) small tools.

fiera di libri. book-fair.

figura. illustration.

fila. file.

filettato. (bb.) filleted.

filettato in oro *or* **filettatura d'oro. (bb.)** gold tooling.

filetto. (bb.) fillet.

filetto. (pr.) composing rule.

filoni della carta. (pa.) waterlines.

fin qui *or* **non si é pubblicato altro. (bo.)** no more published.

finale *or* **fregio. (pr.)** tail-piece.

finestra. the opening in a leaf caused by the cutting out of an illustration, with the margins left intact.

fogli impaginati. (bo.) advance sheets.

fogliaccio. waste-paper.

foglio. leaf.

foglio bianco *or* **guardia.** fly-leaf.

foglio bianco inserito. interleaf.

foglio vergine. blank page.

foglio volante. fly-sheet.

fol. foglio.

fondo, il *or* **copie invendute. (bo.)** remainders.

forma *or* **formato** *or* **sesto.** dimensions of a book according to the folding of the leaves.

formato. *See* **forma.**

frammento. fragment.

fraschetta. (pr.) frisket.

frate. (pr.) friar, *i.e.*, any part of a page which has not received the ink.

frontespizio. *See* frontispizio.

frontispizio *or* facciata. title-page.

frontispizio falso *or* frontispizio morto *or* titolo falso *or* occhietto. half-title.

funicella *or* spago. (bb.) page-cord.

fuori vendita *or* fuori commercio. (bo.) not for sale.

G

geroglifici. hieroglyphics.

ghiottornia. a very rare book of which only few copies were printed.

giornale. newspaper.

giornalista. journalist.

giustezza dei caratteri. (pr.) justification.

gola *or* davanti d'un libro *or* canale d'un libro. (bb.) fore-edge.

gora. water-stain.

got. gotico.

gotico. Gothic.

gr. grande.

grande. large.

guardia *or* foglio bianco. fly-leaf.

I

imbrachettare *or* imbragare *or* imbracare. (bb.) to supply a book with guards.

imbragare. *See* imbrachettare.

imbrattatura. (pr.) set off, *i.e.*, a smut transferred from a freshly printed surface to another sheet.

imp. impressione, impressioni.

impaginare *or* rifare. (pr.) to make up.

imporrato. mouldy.

impressione *or* **edizione.** impression, edition.

in blocco *or* **in combutta** *or* **senza scelta. (bo.)** by the lot.

in combutta. *See* **in blocco.**

incantare su di un libro. (bo.) bid on a book.

incartonato. in boards.

inchiostro. ink.

inchiostro da stampa. printer's ink.

incisione *or* **intaglio.** engraving.

incisione in acciaio. steel engraving.

incisione all' acqua forte. etching.

incisione di bulino. line engraving.

incisione a punteggiamenti. stipple engraving.

incorniciare *or* **inquadrare. (pr.)** to box in.

incunaboli. *pl.* incunabula.

indice dei nomi proprii. index of names.

indossare. (bb.) to back.

indossatura. (bb.) backing.

infanzia, libri per l'. juvenile literature.

iniz. iniziale.

iniziale. *See* **lettera iniziale.**

inquadrare. *See* **incorniciare.**

insegna *or* **marca tipografica.** printer's mark.

intagliatore. engraver.

intaglio. *See* **incisione.**

intercalazione. insertion, interpolation.

interfogliato. (bb.) interleaved.

interlineato. (pr.) leaded.

intestazione *or* **testata.** heading.

intestazione di lettera. letterhead.

intitolato. entitled.

invio dell' autore *or* **esemplare di omaggio** *or* **omaggio dell' autore.** presentation copy.

istoriato. with historical ornaments or illustrations.

L

lasciato *or* **lasciatura** *or* **pesce** *or* **svarione.** (**pr.**) out, *i.e.*, omission of a word or phrase by the compositor.

lavato. (**b.**) washed.

lavori avventizî *or* **lavori di fantasia.** (**pr.**) job printing.

legat. legatura.

legato in rustico. stitched.

legatore. binder.

legatoría. bindery.

legatura in cartone. (**bb.**) bound in boards.

legatura flessibile. (**bb.**) loose back.

legatura intera. (**bb.**) full binding.

legatura logora. worn binding.

legatura del tempo. (**bb.**) old original binding.

lesina. (**pr.**) bodkin.

lett. lettera.

lettera *or* **carattere.** (**pr.**) letter, type.

lettera capovolta. (**pr.**) turned letter.

lettera discendente *or* **lettera con asta discendente.** (**pr.**) tailtype.

lettera di fantasia. (**pr.**) fancy letter.

lettera guasta *or* **lettera logora.** (**pr.**) battered letter.

lettera iniziale *or* **iniziale. (pr.)** initial.

lettera logora. *See* **lettera guasta.**

lettera maiuscola. (pr.) capital letter.

lettera minuscola. (pr.) small letter, lower case letter.

lettera onciale. (pr.) uncial letter.

lettere piene. *pl.* **(pr.)** bold-faced type.

letterine di chiamata. (pr.) superiors.

lettore. reader.

libello. libel.

libraio d'assortimento. general bookseller.

libraio-editore. publisher.

libri per l'infanzia. juvenile literature.

libro con le barbe. book with rough edges.

libro a chiave. (b.) a book in which the names of persons or localities are disguised by the author.

libro in fogli. book in sheets.

libro con fogli chiusi. book as good as new, with leaves uncut.

libro alla macchia. a book printed secretly.

libro d'occasione. secondhand book.

libro di preghiere. prayer book.

libro xilografico. blockbook.

licenz. licenza.

licenza *or* **approvazione.** official sanction of a book.

lin. linea.

linea *or* **riga.** line.

linea di fondo. bottom-line.

linea punteggiata. dotted line.

luogo di stampa. place of imprint.

M

m. mezzo.

macchia. stain.

macchina da comporre. (pr.) composing machine.

maiuscoletti. *pl.* (pr.) small capitals.

manca il frontispizio. title-page lacking.

mappamondo. map of the world.

marca tipografica *or* **insegna.** printer's mark.

marezzato sui fogli. marble edges.

marg. margine.

marginatura di legno o di piombo. (pr.) furniture.

margine allargato. wide margin.

margine di lutto. mourning border.

marrochino. (bb.) morocco.

mbr. membr. membrana.

membrana *or* **pergamena.** parchment.

mensile *or* **mensuale** *or* **d'ogni mese.** monthly.

merletto. *See* pizzo.

messale. missal.

mezzo. half.

millesimo. (b.) date.

miniato. illuminated.

misc. miscelláneo.

miscelláneo. miscellaneous.

montato. mounted.

morto. (b.) discontinued.

mut. mutilato.

mutilato. mutilated.

N

nome composto. compound name.

non si é pubblicato altro *or* **fin qui. (bo.)** no more published.

nota in calce. foot-note.

nota della stampa *or* **nota tipografica.** imprint.

nota tipografica. *See* **nota della stampa.**

novella. tale, short story.

novità dell' anno. the new books of the year.

num. numer. numerato.

numerato. numbered.

O

occhietto *or* **falso frontispizio** *or* **antiporta.** half-title.

omaggio dell' autore. *See* **invio dell' autore.**

opera. work.

opera coronata *or* **opera a corona.** prize essay.

opera periodica. periodical.

opere complete. *pl. or* **corpo.** collected works.

opere póstume. *pl.* posthumous works.

opere riunite sotto una sola coperta *or* **volume miscellaneo.** pamphlet volume.

opere scelte. *pl.* selected works.

opuscolo. pamphlet.

orario. time-table.

orecchio *or* **canto ripiegato d'una pagina. (b.)** dog's ear.

orig. originale.

ornamenti a secco. (bb.) blind tooling.

ospedale. (b.) A book of which one or several leaves are missing.

P

pagina prima *or* **retto.** odd page, recto.

pagina rifatta. handwritten or photographed copy of a missing page.

pagina vergine. blank page.

paginatura continua. continuous pagination.

palinsesto. palimpsest.

parentesi quadre. brackets.

parentesi tonde. parenthesis.

pasticcio di caratteri. (pr.) pie, *i.e.*, printer's type mixed or unsorted.

pei tipi di. . . printed by. . . .

pelle di capra. goat skin.

pelle di porco. pig-skin.

pelle ruvida *or* **zigrino.** shagreen.

pelle di volpe. fox-skin.

perg. pergam. pergamena.

pergamena. parchment, vellum.

pesce *or* **lasciato** *or* **lasciatura** *or* **svarione. (pr.)** out, *i.e.*, omission of a word or phrase by the compositor.

piano. *See* **piatto.**

piatto *or* **piano** *or* **specchio. (bb.)** board.

piatto in legno *or* **asse.** wooden board.

piccoli ferri. (bb.) small tools.

piegatura. folding.

pizzo *or* **merletto** *or* **dentelle. (bb.)** dentelle border.

plagio. plagiarism.

portafogli. portfolio.

postilla. note.

pr. (princ.) principi, principiamento.

prefazione. preface.

prefisso. prefix.

premiato *or* **coronato.** awarded a prize.

prezzo lordo. (bo.) list price, published price.

prima facciata d'un folio stampato. (pr.) first form.

principi del libro. (b.) preliminary leaves.

principiamento. commencement.

proprietà letteraria. copyright.

prova *or* **bozza.** proof-sheet.

prova avanti lettera. (e.) proof before letters.

prova avanti qualunque lettera. (e.) plain prints, *i.e.*, proof without title or name of the engraver.

pubblicazione, data di, *or* **data di stampa.** imprint date.

pubblicazione, luogo di. place of publication.

punta *or* **angolo** *or* **cantone di un libro.** corner of a book.

punta secca. (e.) dry point.

puntata *or* **dispensa** *or* **fascicolo.** fascicle, part.

punteggiatura. punctuation.

punto. period.

punto esclamativo. exclamation point.

punto interrogativo. interrogation point.

punto e virgola. semicolon.

purgato. *See* **espurgato.**

Q

quad. quaderno.

quaderno di fogli. (pa.) quire.

quadretto. (pr.) quadrat.

quartino. *See* **rincarto.**

quindicinale. semi-monthly.

quotidiano. daily.

R

r. rame.

r. recto, retto. often printed as a superior character, *e.g.*, 14^r.

raffilato. (bb.) cut down.

rame. copper.

rattoppato. (bb.) reinforced.

redatto. edited.

refuso. (pr.) wrong font.

reg. registro.

registro. register.

relazione *or* **rendiconto** *or* **resoconto.** report.

rendiconto. *See* **relazione.**

resoconti. *pl.* proceedings.

resoconto. *See* **relazione.**

retto *or* **recto** *or* **prima pagina.** odd page, recto.

riassunto. summary.

rich. richiamo.

richiamo. (b.) catchword.

ricop. ricoperto.

ricoperto. (bb.) recovered.

rifare *or* **impaginare. (pr.)** to make up.

riga *or* **linea.** line.

riga di colonna. (pr.) column rule.

riga di testa. headline.

rileg. rilegato.

rilegato. rebound.

rincarto *or* **quartino. (b.)** inset.

ripiegato. folded.

riproduzione vietata. reproduction forbidden.

riscritto. re-written.

riservati tutti i diritti. all rights reserved.

rit. (ritr.) ritratto.

ritagli, album di *or* **estratti tagliati.** scrap-book.

ritratto. portrait.

rivista. review, magazine.

roba buona *or* **composizione agevole. (pr.)** fat, *i.e.*, pieces of composition, for instance, running titles that are kept for future use, and are not taken apart till after the whole work is finished.

romanzo. novel, romance.

S

satinatura. (pa.) calendering.

sbarbato *or* **tondato** *or* **tagliato. (bb.)** cut down, trimmed.

scelta. selection.

schiena *or* **costola** *or* **dorso. (bb.)** back of a book.

schizzo *or* **abbozzo.** sketch, rough draft.

sciup. sciupato.

sciupato. torn, injured.

scomporre. (pr.) to distribute the type.

scritto *or* **opera. (b.)** work.

194

scrittura. writing.

scrittura magra *or* **caratteri magri. (pr.)** light-faced type.

sec. secolo.

secolo. century.

sedicente. calling himself.

segn. segnat. segnatura.

segnatura con asterisco. (b.) signature with asterisk.

segno. bookmark.

segno di correzione. mark of correction (in proofreading).

senza millesimo. no date.

sequestrato. suppressed.

sesto *or* **forma** *or* **formato. (b.)** size.

settimanale *or* **d'ogni settimana** *or* **ebdomadario.** weekly.

sezione. section.

si stampi *or* **visto si stampi.** for press.

sillaba. syllable.

slegato. binding lost.

smacchiare. to remove spots.

smarginato. (bb.) cropped.

sotto condizione. (bo.) on approval.

sotto il torchio. in the press.

sottolineato. underlined.

sottoscrittore *or* **abbonato.** subscriber.

sottoscrizione. colophon.

sottotitolo. subtitle.

spago *or* **funicella. (bb.)** page cord.

spalla. (pr.) shoulder of a type.

spazî *pl.* **(pr.)** blacks, *i.e.*, a space, quadrat, or piece of furniture that rises and is imprinted on the sheets.

specchio *or* **piatto** *or* **piano.** board.

spese dell' autore, a. at the author's expense, privately printed.

spezzato. incomplete.

spezzatura. an odd volume of a set of books.

spolverare. to dust.

spurgo *or* **tincone.** a book of little value, difficult to sell.

stampa a colori. colored prints.

stampa in rilievo. anastatic printing.

stampa in volta *or* **volta. (pr.)** second form.

stampatore in lavori di fantasia. job printer.

stato. (e.) state.

stazzonato. crumpled.

stemma. coat of arms.

stoffa. (bb). cloth.

strato da incidere. (e.) etching ground.

stretto. oblong.

svarione. *See* **lasciato.**

T

tagliacarte. paper knife.

tagliato *or* **tondato** *or* **sbarbato. (bb.)** cut down, trimmed.

tagliato di un giornale. newspaper clipping.

taglio cesellato. (bb.) tooled edges.

taglio marmorizzato al pettine. (bb.) combed edges.

taglio spruzzato. (bb.) sprinkled edges.

taglio superiore dorato *or* **disopra dorato. (bb.)** gilt top.

tarlo *or* **tignuola** *or* **tarma.** bookworm.

tarma. *See* **tarlo.**

tarmato. worm-eaten.

tav. tavola, tavole.

tavola. table, plate.

tavola degli errori *or* **errata.** list of errata.

tavola delle materie *or* **indice** *or* **elenco.** table of contents.

tavola ripiegata. folded plate.

tavoletta de' legatori di libri. (bb.) sewing board.

tela grossa *or* **traliccio.** (bb.) buckram.

telaio di stamperia. (pr.) chase.

tesi. dissertation, thesis.

testata *or* **intestazione.** heading.

testata illustrata *or* **capopagina.** headpiece.

testimonio. witness, *i.e.*, leaf left uncut by the binder to show that the margin is not cut too much.

testo. text.

tignuola. *See* tarlo.

tincone. *See* **spurgo.**

tipi comuni. (pr.) body type.

tiratura. (pr.) impression.

tiratura a parte. reprint.

tiratura di pochi esemplari *or* **edizione limitata.** limited edition.

titolo collettivo. collective title.

titolo corrente. running title.

titolo falso. half-title.

titolo del legatore. binder's title.

tomo. volume.

tondato. *See* **tagliato.**

torchio. press.

torchio a cilindro. revolving press.

torchio a mano. hand-press.

torchio, sotto il. in the press.

trad. traduttore, traduzione.

tradurre. to translate.

traduttore *or* **traslatore.** translator.

traliccio *or* **grossa tela. (bb.)** buckram.

tranciafila *or* **capitello. (bb.)** headband.

tras. traslatore.

traslatore. *See* **traduttore.**

trasliterazione. transliteration.

tratto di penna. dash.

tratto d'unione. hyphen.

V

v. verso. often printed as superior character after the page number, *e.g.*, 18^v.

v. o. vedi oltre.

vaglia. money order.

vantaggio. (pr.) galley.

vedi. see.

vedi oltre. see below. *Literally*, see forward.

vendere all' incanto. (bo.) to sell at auction.

vendita di libri all' asta *or* **asta libraria.** book auction.

venditore di libri vecchi. secondhand bookseller.

verbale di un' adunanza. minutes of a meeting.

vergature *pl.* **(pa.)** wiremarks.

vignetta con dicitura. (e.) engraving with text.

virgola. comma.

virgolette. quotation marks.

visto si stampi *or* **si stampi.** for press.

vitellino. calf leather.

volta *or* **stampa di volta. (pr.)** second form.

volume, falso *or* **finto volume** *or* **libro bianco.** blank-book.

volume miscellaneo *or* **opere riunite sotto una sola coperta.** pamphlet volume.

volumetto. small volume.

Z

zigrino *or* **pelle ruvida.** shagreen.

LATIN

SOME LATIN ABBREVIATIONS AND TERMS OCCASIONALLY USED IN BOOK CATALOGS AND BIBLIOGRAPHIES

By FRANK KELLER WALTER

This list supplements the brief one in *Abbreviations and Technical Terms Used in Book Catalogs and in Bibliographies* (Boston Book Co., 1912). Like its predecessor, it is confined to abbreviations and terms used in the descriptions of books and again like its predecessor, it includes such expressions as actually are used, irrespective of their consistency or philological propriety. The number of Latin terms which the beginner will find in the ordinary trade and national bibliographies and in current catalogs of modern books is relatively small. The cataloger, order clerk, or reference assistant whose work lies even occasionally with books, prints or manuscripts of the 18th century or earlier, will find a different state of affairs. Since Latin was the universal language of the educated man, the earlier general bibliographies and catalogs of libraries were usually written in Latin and a profusion of Latin terms was used in the catalogs of booksellers. Even as late as 1838, Hain felt it advisable to use Latin throughout in his *Repertorium Bibliographicum*. Unfortunately, there was little or no agreement as to exact connotation of terms or as to form of abbreviation, and in many cases the context offers little or no help. The same is true even today of many continental booksellers, some of whom take their entries directly or at second-hand from bibliographers like Hain or Bauer, while some strike out boldly into systems of abbreviations of their own. Both in the old and in modern bibliographies the meanings as well as the spellings are post-classical and, in many cases, not to be found in any of the standard Latin dictionaries. The desire to avoid monotony by the use of synonyms of doubtful accuracy and expressions of only slightly different meanings adds to the confusion.

There is no attempt at completeness in this rough list and many terms have been included which may

seem unnecessary to the connoisseur while others
have been excluded which may now and then con-
front one in unexpected places. This has been un-
avoidable since there could be no completeness short
of a formal technical dictionary and the selection has
been made to depend on actual difficulties likely to be
met. Hain, as the source of many later works and of
thousands of fugitive entries and references, has received rather more attention than many of the others
and it is hoped that a fairly full list of terms frequently
used by that indefatigable, though sometimes incon-
sistent, bibliographer has been included. Many terms
and abbreviations in books used in the former list like
Cim, Kleemeier, Power, Rouveyre, though previously
excluded as of little use in a beginner's list have been
inserted here.

Three cautions are necessary in the use of any list
like this (1) There is no consistent principle followed
in many bibliographies and though *p.* may be the
usual abbreviation for *pagina*, one is quite as likely
to find *pag.* used in the same work. (2) The plural
is usually formed by doubling the final letter of
the abbreviation, *e.g.*,

p. Page; **pp.** Pages.
lit. litera. Letter; **litt.** literæ, Letters.
(3) The same abbreviation is often used indis-
criminately for both singular and plural, *e.g.*, **s.** for
both *signatura* and *signaturæ* as in Hain.

It is impracticable to list here all the books consulted. Among those from which considerable material was obtained are: Beck, C., *Jahrbuch der Bücherpreise*, v. 1—7, 1906–13 (Lpzg., 1907–14); Bauer,
J. J., *Bibliotheca Librorum Rariorum Universalis*,
6 v. (Nürnberg, 1770–74); *Caspar, C. N.* Book trade
bibliography and vocabulary of technical terms.
(Milwaukee, 1892); Cim, Albert, *Le Livre*, 5 v. (Par.,
1908); Copinger, W. A., *Supplement to Hain's
Repertorium Bibliographicum*, 2 v. (Lond., 1895–
1902); *Catalogue de la Bibliothèque de feu M. J.
Decaisne* (Paris, 1883); Dobbs, A. E. *Abbreviations,
British and foreign*, (Lond. 1911); Faulmann, Carl,
Das Buch der Schrift (Vienna, 1880); Hain, Ludovic,
Repertorium Bibliographicum, 2 v. (Stuttgart, 1826–38);
Pellechet, M., *Catalogue Général des Incunables des
Bibliothèques Publiques de France*, v. 1–2 (Paris, 1897);
Rouveyre, Edouard, *Connaissances Nécessaires à un
Bibliophile*. 10 v. 5th ed. (Paris, 1899). Valuable aid
both in the way of material and definition has been
received from many of the more general treatises

like Ames' *Typographical Antiquities;* Birt, T., *Das antike Buchwesen;* Blades' *Pentateuch of Printing* and his *Biography and Typography of William Caxton;* Brown's *Venetian Printing Presses;* Davenport's, *The Book, its History and Development;* Duff's *Early Printed Books;* Peignot, *Dictionnaire Raisonné de Bibliologie,* Reed's *Old English Letter Foundries,* Singer and Strang's *Etching, engraving and other methods of printing pictures* (Lond. 1907), and the excellent article by Hessels on *Typography* in the 11th edition of the *Encyclopædia Britannica.*

A

a. f. ad finem.

a. f. anni futuri. Of the following year.

a. h. v. ad hunc vocem.

a. i. (init.) ad initium.

a. p. (a. pr.). anni praesentis. Of the present year.

a. v. ad verbum.

absque. Without; — **registro.** Without register (of signatures, etc.)

acced. accedit. "There follows."

accuratus. Carefully prepared, accurate.

acta. Acts, proceedings.

ad. at, for; — **extremum.** At the end; — **finem.** At the end; — **initium.** At the beginning; — **litteram.** Literally (literatim); — **marginem.** At (or in) the margin; — **verbum (vocem).** At the word — (used in textual references).

addit.(t). additio (—ones). Addition(s).

adhaeret. (*perf. part.* **adhaesus**). (It) is joined with, fastened to or bound with; added at the end, appended. (*Hain.*)

adjunctus. Added to, bound with.

admodum. Very, quite, completely. *e.g.,* **Liber admodum rarus.** A very rare book.

adornatus. Embellished, decorated.

adp. *See* words beginning with **app.**

adversaria. Miscellany, commonplace books.

aen. aeneus. Copper. *e.g.,* **cum tabb. aen.** tabulis aeneis. With copperplates.

aet. aetat. Aged.

affinit. (**adfinit.**) Affinitas (adfinitas). *See* **arbor.**

agendum (or plu. **agenda**). Calendar, ritual, code, book of rules, schedule.

al. alia. Other (plu.). *e.g.* **al. exempla.** Other copies. (*Hain.*)

al.l. alia lectio (alii legunt). Other reading(s).

album amicorum. Autograph album.

albus. Blank (literally "white"). *e.g.* **c. duob. ff. albis.** With two leaves blank.

an. annus.

anglice. In English (English version or translation).

anni futuri. Of the following year.

anni praesentis. Of the present year.

annus. year.

antiquaria. (a) Relics, second-hand books. (b) stock of old books or relics.

apparatus. Prepared, edited, supplied.

approbatus. Approved. Used to indicate approval by official censor.

arbor. Tree. Used in phrases like **arbor affinitatis** (Chart or "tree" of relationships by marriage) and **arbor consan-**

.guinitatis (*or* consanguineus). (Chart or tree of blood relationships).

art. (artt.) articulus(-i). Part(s), division(s), article(s).

auct. (t). auctor(-es). Author(s).

augenda. Additions.

aux. auxilio. With the assistance [of].

B

biblioth. bibliotheca. Library (often in sense of "series").

bibliothecarius. Librarian.

breviarium. Breviary, abstract, abridgment, summary.

C

c. cum, custos, codex.

c. cum. (c.c. cum custodibus) c. m. tab. aeri incisis, cum multis tabulis aeri incisis; c.n. cum numero; c.pp.n. cum paginis numeratis; c. s. cum signaturis.

c. l. citato loco. (usually written l. c., loco citato). In the place or passage cited.

caetera desiderantur (caetera desunt). The rest lacking or missing.

calx (*Abl.* calce). End, bottom (of page). *e.g.* in calce, a calce (ad calcem). At the end, from (at) the bottom (of the page).

cap. caput, capitulum.

capitulum. Chapter, section or division.

capp. Capita. Plural of caput (chapter).

caret (*perf.* caruit). It is lacking. *e.g.*, f. 4 caret, "4th folio lacking."

carta. *See* **charta.**

centesimo et vigesimo-octavo. 128 mo. A book composed of sections folded into 128 leaves each. *See* **duodecimo.**

ch. (charact.) character(es). **ch. goth.** characteres gothici; — **maj.** characteres majores; — **majusc.** characteres majusculi; — **min.** characteres minores; **minim.** characteres minimi; — **minusc.** characteres minusculi; — **minut.** characteres minuti; — **nitid.** characteres nitidi; — **quadr.** characteres quadrati; — **rabb.** characteres rabbinici; — **rudiusc.** ch. rudiusculi; — **semig. (semigoth).** characteres semigothici.

chalcographus. Printer.

chalcotypus. Printer.

character(es). Character(s), letter(s). — **crassi.** Bold-faced characters; — **gothici.** Gothic (black letter or "text") characters; — **majores (majusculi).** large characters, capitals; — **minimi (minuti).** Very small characters; — **minores (minusculi).** Small (lower case) characters;— **missali** "Missal" characters; — **nitidi.** Beautiful, well-shaped, clear characters; — **quadrati.** Square, rectangular characters; — **rabbinici.** Rabbinical (Hebrew) characters;— **rudes.** "Rustic" characters (*Bradley*); "barbarous type" (*Ames*); crude, clumsy letters; — **rudiores. (rudiusculi.)** —type or characters with "rustic" characteristics;—**semigothici,** "Semigothic" characters, *i.e.,* with Gothic characteristics.

charta. (1) Paper, (more rarely, parchment). (2) Charter, letter or other writing.

circa. (**circiter, circum.**) About, nearly.

circumd., circumdat. circumdatus. Surrounded. *e.g.,* **circumd. ornamento xyl.** "Surrounded by wood-cut border."

circumscr. circumscriptio. Encircling inscription.

clavis. Key, explanatory appendix.

clericus. Sometimes applied to the rubricator of books and mss.

cod. codex. Manuscript with leaves folded in book form;—**quadratus.** Folio manuscript.

cohaeret. (*perf. part.* **cohaesus.**) Belongs with, bound with. *e.g.,* **cohaeret cum libello.** Bound with [another] pamphlet. **cohaeret proprie c. num. 2294.** Belongs properly with no 2294.

collatus. Collected, compiled. *e.g.* **collatis passim articulis.** Here and there in the collected articles.

collectio. Collection; — **scriptorum.** Collected writings.

collectus. Collected, compiled.

comm., comment. commentatio, commentator.

commentatio. Treatise, dissertation, commentary.

commentator. Commentator.

commentum. Note, comment. *e.g.* **c. commento ms.** With manuscript note.

206

complectitur. [It includes, comprises. *e.g.*, **complectitur libb. X-XII.** It comprises Bks. X-XII.

concl. conclu., conclusio. Conclusion.

conf. confer. (Rare. Usually **cf.**)

consang. consanguinitas. *See* **arbor.**

constat. Consists of, is composed of. *e.g.*, **Opus constat 54 capp.** "The work consists of 54 chapters."

contentorum, index —. Table of contents.

corpus scriptorum. Complete writings.

correct. correctio, correctus.

correctio(-ones). Correction(s).

correctus. Corrected.

corrigendum (-a). Correction(s).

crassus. Heavy, coarse. (*Cf.* **character.**)

cum. With; — **custodibus.** With catchwords; — **gratia et privilegio.** With favor and privilege (Official phrase cf authorization); — **multis tabulis aeri [ligno] incisis.** With many engravings in copperplate [or wood]; — **numero (-is).** With number(s) or numeral(s); — **paginis numeratis.** With numbered pages [or leaves]; — **privilegiis.** With privileges, or rights (of copyright, etc.); — **signaturis.** With signature numbers or symbols; — **tabulis.** With tables or plates.

cus. (cust.) custos (-todes). Catchword(s).

D

d. delinea(vi)t, dedica(vi)t, dona(vi)t.

d. a. dicti anni. of the year cited.

d.d. (dd). dono (*or* donum) dat (*or* dedit).

d. q. s. de quo supra. Concerning the article or citation above.

dedic. dedicatio. Dedication.

dedicat. Dedicates.

dedicatus. Dedicated.

deest (*plu.* **desunt**). Is (are) lacking. *e.g.*, **haec ult. verba desunt.** "These last words are lacking."

del., delin. delineavit. "In old engravings . . . often indicated the man (not necessarily the original artist) who copied the design on the plate for the engraver."

delenda. Things which should be cancelled. Frrata.

desid. desiderata. Books or other articles desired. Desirable books or other articles.

differt (*plu.* **differunt**). It differs.

dir. direxit. Sometimes used in sense of **excudit.** *q. v.*

donatus. The, "Ars grammatica" of Ælius Donatus was much used in the Middle Ages as a beginner's book in Latin. From this, the term *donatus* came to be applied to any introductory Latin grammar, and, by further license, to any introductory treatise.

donec corrigatur. "Temporary or partial prohibition of a book not absolutely condemned. . . . Books so marked might be bought, sold and used, provided that in the existing edition the corrupt passages were either blotted out or corrected by pen, and in all subsequent editions omitted or modified." —*Brown. Venetian Printing Presses*, p. 12.

dono dedit. Given, donated.

duodecimo. 12mo. (12°) A book between 6⅞ and 7⅞ in. (17.5–20 cm.) high. The older terminology, still in use in Europe, named books from the number of leaves into which a sheet was folded. Thus a duodecimo was composed of sheets folded into 12 leaves (24 p.) each; a quarto, one of sheets folded into 4 leaves each, etc. In such cases, the size of the unfolded sheet is usually also indicated by its trade name, *e.g.*, Crown 8vo, an octavo printed on sheets of Crown paper (15 x 20 in.) In older books, fold only is generally indicated.

E

e. c. exempli causa. For example. More frequently **e.g.,** exempli gratia.

ed. (*plu.* **edd.**). edidit (*plu.* **ediderunt**). He has edited, published, issued; or **editus.** Edited, published, issued.

ed. Editio; — **opt.** editio optima; — **ster.** editio stereotypa; — **ult.** editio ultima.

editio. Edition; — **aucta.** Enlarged edition; — **emendata.** Corrected edition; — **optima.** Best edition; — **originalis.** Original edition; — **perrara.** Very rare edition; – **rara.** Rare edition. — **stereotypa.** stereotyped edition;—- **ultima.** last edition.

eff. effigies. Portrait, illustration.

ej., ejusd. ejusdem. Of the same.

elenchus. Table of contents.

emendatio (-ones) Correction(s), change (s).

emendatus. Corrected, emended.

empt. emptus. Bought.

eod., eodem. In the same, at the same.

ep.(p). Epistula(e).

epilogus. Epilogue.

epistula(e) (epistola(e)). Letter(s), epis-
tle (s).

errator. collectio. erratorum collectio. List of
errata.

erratum(a). Error(s). Also used for list
of indicated or corrected errors.

ex. From. **ex-dono.** Gift of —; **ex
meis.** From my library; **ex museo
(musaeo).** From the library of —.

exarata. writings, works. The better and
earlier form is **exaratio (ones).**

exc. excipe. except.

ex., exc. excudit (excudebat). "In old engravings . . . often indicated prints exe-
cuted by workmen under the supervision
of the master engraver whose name is
attached." (*Singer & Strang*)

excitatus. Cited. (*Hain.*)

excl. excludens, exclusus. Excluding, excluded.

excus. excusus. Composed, written.

exempl. exemplum (-a). Copy (copies).

exemplar (-ia). Copy (copies).

exiguus. Small, thin.

expensa. Expense. **ad expensas —**, At the expense of —. Published (printed) for.

expict. expictus. Illuminated, colored.

expl., explic. explicit. The end. ("It is ended.")

expr. expressus. Printed, portrayed.

exsculptor librorum. Printer. (*Uncommon.*)

extr. extremo. At the end.

F

f. fecit. (**q. v.**)

f. folium (*pl.* **folia**); — **maj.** folium maius (majus) — **max.** folium maximum; —**min.** folium minus. More commonly found in Italian form **folio.**

f. l. **falsa lectio.** Incorrect reading.

fasc. fasciculus. Part, number, section of serial publication.

fec., fecit. He did it. Attached to name of engraver to indicate his work. Often has added **aq. fort.** (aqua forte), "done in acid," *i.e.*, etched.

ff. folia.

fin. finis.

flor. (florent.) florens (-entes), floruit.

florens (florentes). With floral or other decorative designs. *e.g.*, **c. litt. initial. flor.** "With decorated (ornamented) initial letters, "Blooming letters."

florilegium. Anthology. (*cf.* Eng. "Speaker's Garland.")

floruit. He flourished, or was prominent.

fo. folio. **fo. ro.** folio recto; **fo. vo.** folio verso.

folium (usually in Italian form **folio**). Book 30 cm. or more (11⅞ in. high), (b) book composed of sheets folded into two leaves or four pages each. *See* also **duodecimo.** (c) the running numbers indicating the pages of a book.

folium (folia). Leaf. Folio (book size or fold); — **majus.** Large folio; — **maximum.** Great folio; — **minus.** Small folio.

foll. folia. Leaves. (Rare form used by Hain. Usual form, **ff.**)

forellus. Parchment, forel.

forte. Probably. *e.g.*, **forte Romae.** "Probably [printed] at Rome."

fronte, in —. In the front; On the fly-leaf.

G

g. gothici; **g. ch.** gothici characteres.

gallice. In French; French version.

germanice. In German; German version.

glossa (-ae). Manuscript note(s); **glossae interlin. (interlineares).** Interlinear notes; **glossae marginales.** marginal notes.

graece. In Greek; Greek version.

H

h. a. hoc anno. In this year.

h. l. hoc loco. In this place.

h. m. huius mensis. Of this month.

hebr. hebraice. In Hebrew; Hebrew version.

hispanice. In Spanish; Spanish version.

I

i. e. id est. That is.

ic., icon. Figure, engraving. **c. ic.** cum iconibus. With engravings.

impressor (librorum). Printer.

impressus. Printed.

impressum (*noun*). Imprint.

in albis. blank.

in extenso. Completely, fully, entirely.

in limine. At the beginning.

in manu. on hand, in stock, available.

incipit. [It] begins. Here begins.

inc., incis. incisus. Engraved.

incl. inclus. inclusus. Included.

ind. index;—**libror. prohib.** index librorum prohibitorum;—**ind. nom.** index nominum.

index. Index, list; — **contentorum.** Subject index or table of contents; — **expurgatorum (expurgatorius).** List of books condemned by the censor. (Usually applied to the list of books prohibited by the Roman Catholic church; also termed **index librorum prohibitorum.**) — **materiarum.** Subject index or table of contents; — **nominum.** Index of names, name list.

indicatio errorum. List of errata.

infrequens. Scarce.

init., initial., initialis. Initial.

inscr. inscriptio, inscriptus.

inscriptio (-ones). Inscription(s), title(s).

inscriptus. Inscribed, entitled.

insertus. Inserted.

insign. insigne. Mark, sign, device. *e.g.* **insign. typogr.,** insigne typographi. "Printer's mark."

integer. Entire, complete, perfect.

interpr. interpres. Translator.

interscriptus. Written between. Interlined.

introduct. introductio. Introduction.

inv., invt. invenit. He designed it.

inventu difficilis. Hard to find, scarce.

it. item. Also, the same.

L

l. l. loco laudato.

la. litera. *q. v.*

latus. Wide. *e.g.,* **lato margine.** With wide margin.

lect.(t). lector(es). Reader(s).

leg. legit (legunt). He reads, they read.

libellus. Small book, pamphlet.

lib. (libr.). liber. Book.

librarius. Bookseller, keeper of a circulating library; hence, librarian. Scribe, or copyist of manuscripts.

lignus. Wood. *e.g.* **ligno incisus** (*or* **sculptus**). Engraved on wood.

lin. linea (linia). Line.

lit.(t.) litera (littera). Letter. For styles *see also under* **character.** Hain generally uses the form **litera** with abbreviations lit. and litt. for singular and plural respectively. Others use the preferred classical form littera with litt. for abbreviation for singular or sometimes for both singular and plural.

litera(e). (littera(e)). Letter(s). literae florentes. Decorated or ornamented letters; — literae initiales. Initial letters; — literae reclamantes. Catchwords.

ll. libri. Books; lineae. Lines.

loco laudato. In the place indicated.

M

m. m. pr. manu mea propria.

m. pp. m. pr. manu propria.

m. pr. mensis praeteriti.

majus. Larger. folium — ; Large folio.

majusc. majusculus(-i). Large or capital letter(s).

male. Badly, improperly, erroneously. *e.g.*, male numeratus. Incorrectly numbered.

manu. By hand, *e.g.*, manu adscriptus. Added by hand, manuscript addition. — propria. with his own hand, *i.e.*, autograph.

mea propria. with my own hand.

marginal. marginalia. Notes or other matter in the margin.

max. maximus. Very large, largest. *e.g.*, 4 max. Great quarto, very large quarto.

med., in — in medio. In the middle.

membrana. Parchment.

menda (-ae). Fault (s), error (s). *e.g.,* **ab infinitis mendis purgatus.** Freed from many errors.

merus. Only, nothing but, *e.g.,* **meri textus 14 l. meri comment. 28 l.** 14 lines, text only; 28 lines, notes only.

minimus. Smallest, very small. In the form **minimo.** sometimes used to indicate books below 3 inches in height; *i.e.,* from 64mo. to 128mo.

minor. Small. (*lit.* smaller), rather small. *e.g.,* **f. minus.** Small folio. The term **minores** is sometimes applied to small books (*i.e.* below 12mo) generally. *See also* **minimus.**

minusc. minusculus (-i). Small, or lower-case letter (s).

missal. missalis. Relating to a missal. *e.g.,* **litt. missal.** Large letters like those used in missals. "Canon" (48 pt.) type, so-called because this sized letter was used in early missals

mp., mpp. manu propria. *q.v.*

mut. mut. mutatis mutandis. After making necessary changes.

mutato nomine. With changed name. **mutato titulo.** With changed title.

mutilus. Mutilated.

N

n. nomen. Name. *e.g.,* **n. typ.** nomen typographi. Name of the printer.

n. (*plu.* **nn.**). numeratus (-i). Numbered.

n. (nn.) numerus(i). Number(s).

n. n. nomen nescio.

ni. numeri. Numbers.

nigro. In black.

nihil obstat. "Nothing to prevent." Approved. Formula of official approval by Catholic censor.

nitidus. Beautiful, clear, neat. *e.g.*, **editio nitida.** Handsome edition.

nom. nomen. Name.—**nescio.** Author unknown, anonymous.

nonagesimo sexto. 96mo. A book made of sheets folded into 96 leaves each. *See also* **duodecimo.**

nota (ae). Note (s), mark, sign.

notatio (-ones). Mark, cipher or sign.

notitia (ae). Mark, or sign of identity. *e.g.*, **notitia typographi.** Printer's mark (*Hain*).

numquam antea impressus. Never before printed.

O

obvius. Met with, obtainable. *e.g.*, **non facile obvius.** Not easily obtainable.

occurrens. Met with, appearing, offering or presenting itself. *e.g.*, **non frequenter occurrens.** Infrequently offered.

oct. octavo. A book between 20 and 25 cm (7⅛–9⅛ in.) high. A book composed of sheets folded into 8 leaves each. *See also* **duodecimo.**

octo–decimo. 18mo. *See* **duodecimo.**

omissus. Omitted.

omnia quae supersunt (extant). All that remain. Used of "literary remains" and of complete extant works of an author.

op. posth. opus posthumum. Posthumous work.

opella. Small book, pamphlet. **(libellus.)**

opus regale. Sumptuous, magnificent work, (literally "royal work").

opusculum. Small work or volume, part of a printed work.

ord. ordo (ordines). Series, order, arrangement. *e.g.,* **ordo quarternorum.** Arrangement in quaternions ("fours").

ordine. In series.

P

p., pp., pag.(pagg.). pagina(ae). Page (s), leaf (leaves). Copinger uses **pp.** in the latter sense. Most use **ff.** (folia) in sense of "leaves" and **pp.** (paginae) for "pages."

p. a. per annum. By the year.

p. t. praetermisso titulo.

pars (partes). Part (s), section (s).

pegit. He made, or composed it. **I. D. pegit.** "Iohn Day pegit." "John Day made it."

plagula (ae). Sheet (s) [of paper].

plano, in —. in sheets. Sometimes used of unfolded prints, maps, broadsides, etc.

pleno titulo. *See* **titulo.**

plur. plurimus. Many. *e.g.,* **cum tabb. plu.** With many tables.

post. After, subsequent to. *e.g.,* **post 1470.** Later than 1470.

post. posterior. Later. *e.g.,* **ed. post.** Second, or later, edition.

ppt. praeparatus. Prepared, provided.

pr. primus, principium.

praeced. praecedens. Preceding. *e.g.,* **praeced. index.** Index preceding. **praeced. pr. p. tab.** Table (or plate) preceding first page.

praef. (praefat). praefatio. Preface, prologue.

praemissus. Put before, preliminary. *e.g.,* **praemissa sunt 4ff in quorum pr. hic tit.** "There are 4 preliminary leaves on the first of which is this title."

praestans. Remarkable, excellent, superior.

praetermisso titulo. omitting the title.

pret. pretium. Price.

pretiosus. Costly.

primus. First. *e.g.,* **42 ff. cum primo albo.** 42 folios, the first blank.

principium. Beginning. **in principio.** In the beginning, at the top.

prohemium. *See* **prooemium.**

prolog. prologium (prologus). Prologue, preface, introduction.

prooem. prooemium.

prooemium (prohemium). Introduction, preface, proem.

punctus. Wormeaten.

purgatus. Freed from errors, corrected.

Q

q. s. quid (quae) supra. The thing (s) noted above.

qm. quondam. Formerly. (Used after changed title, name of author or firm name.)

quad. (quadrat). quadratus. Square, rectangular.

quadragesimo-octavo. 48mo. *See also* **duodecimo.**

quae supersunt. *See* **omnia quae supersunt.**

quarto. A book between $9\frac{7}{8}$ and $11\frac{7}{8}$ in. (26–30 cm.) high. *See also* **duodecimo.**

quatern. quaternio.

quaternio (-ones). (*a*) Section of four sheets each folded once (*i.e.*, 4 sheets, 8 leaves, or 16 pp.). A book made up of these sections is "in quaternions" or "in 4's." (**4ns**). (*b*) Webster defines **quaternion** as "A sheet of paper folded twice; also, a quire of 4 sheets thus folded." (*a*) is the customary bibliographic meaning.

quintern. quinternio (-ones). Section of five sheets each folded once. (*i.e.*, 5 sheets, 10 leaves, or 20 pp.). "In quinternions" or "in 5's." (**5ns**). *Cf.* **quaternio.**

R

r. regalis. *e.g.*, **f. r.** folium regale.

r. ch. romani characteres.

r. r. reservatis reservandis. With due allowances.

rabb. ch. rabbinici characteres.

rabbinicus. rabbinical (Hebrew). **litterae rabbinicae.** Rabbinical letters.

rar. rarus.

rarescit. It is rare.

rarior. Rather rare.

rarissime. Very rarely.

rarissimus. Very rare.

raritas. Rarity. *e.g.,* **immensae raritatis.** Of great. rarity.

rarus. Rare.

recognitus. Reviewed, revised. **Cura recognitus.** Revised with care.

red. redditus. Translated, repeated, delivered.

registr. registrum (-a). Alphabetical table of contents, etc. Register.

rel., reliq. reliqua. The remainder, the rest. "Literary remains."

repert. repertorium. Catalogue, systematically arranged list or summary.

retro. On the back, backward, "above" (**vide retro,** "See above").

rr. rarissime, rarissimus.

rub. ruber. Red.

rubro. In red. (From **ruber,** "Red") *e.g.,* **Insign. typogr. rubr.** Red device of printer. **rubro et nigro impressus.** Printed in black and red.

rubrum. Colophon (*Uncommon*).

rud. rudis. Crude, clumsy. *See* **character.**

rudior. Rather crude or clumsy.

S

s. sequens, signatura.

s. sine. **s. c.** sine custodibus; **s. pp. n.** sine paginis numeratis; **s. s.** sine signaturis.

s. e. e. o. Salvo errore et omissione. Errors and omissions excepted. Used also in plural form.

s. s. n. Signato suo nomine. Signed with his own name.

saec. saeculum (a). Century (-ies).

scriptor (-es). Author (s), writer (s).

sculpt. sculptus. Engraved.

scutum impressoris. Printer's armorial device.

sedecimo (sexto decimo.) 16mo. A book between $5\frac{7}{8}$ and $6\frac{7}{8}$ in. (15–17½ cm.) high or composed of sections of 16 leaves each. *See* **duodecimo.**

semig. semigothicus (-i). Semi-Gothic. Applied to a type with modified Gothic characteristics.

septuagesimo-secundo. 72mo. Book of sections of 72 leaves each. *See also* **duodecimo.**

seq., sq., sequ. Sequitur. It follows.

seq., sequ., sequen. Sequens, sequentia. Following.

sextern. sexternio (-nes). Section of six sheets each folded once. *Cf.* **quaternio.**

222

sexagesimo-quarto. 64mo. *See also* **duo-decimo.**

sic. "Thus." Indicates exact spelling, etc., of original, particularly when original is erroneous.

siglae. Abbreviations or contractions of words or syllables, particularly in manuscripts and incunabula. *e.g.,* **Nr** for **noster; Dns,** for **Dominus,** etc.

sine. Without; — **custodibus.** Without catchwords; — **menda** (*plu.* **mendis**). Without a fault (or faults), perfect; — **nota** (or **notis** (*plu.*)). Without place date, or name of printer; — **paginis numeratis.** Without page numbers.

situ, in —. In its proper place or position.

ss. scriptores. Writers, authors.

ss. Semis. Half.

subjunct. subjunctus. Appended, added to.

subscr. (**subscript.**). subscriptio (-ones). Signature (s), superscription (s).

subseq. subsequens. Following, subsequent.

sup. superior. Upper. *e.g.,* **sup. marg.** Upper margin.

superlibros (**superexlibris**). "Owner's coats of arms impressed in gold upon the book's sides." Mark of ownership on cover of book, usually stamped or gilt device.

T

t. titulus. Title.

t. (**tom.**). tomus. Volume.

t. p. titulo pleno.

t.t. titulo toto.

tab. tabula. Table; — **alphabetica.** Alphabetical table; — **quaestionum.** List of questions.

term. terminat. Ends. *e.g.*, **term. lib. septimus.** "End of book 7."

tern. ternio (-ones). Section of three sheets each folded once. *Cf.* **quaternio.**

testamur. Testimonial [usually unofficial] to the value of a work.

titulus in extenso. Full title.

titulo pleno. With full title. *i.e.*, with all the titles of honor of the author, subject of a biography, etc. Sometimes less correctly used in place of **titulo toto.**

titulo toto. With full title. *i.e.*, Complete title of book given.

tli. tituli *pl.* of titulus.

tract. Tractatus. Treatise, tract.

translatus. Translated.

trib. tribus. (Abl. of **tres.** "three"). *e.g.*, **in trib. lin.** In three lines.

trigesimo-secundo. 32mo. A book between 4 and 5 in. (10–12½ cm.) high or composed of sections of 32 leaves each. *See also* **duodecimo.**

trigesimo-sexto. 36mo. A book composed of sections of 36 leaves each. *See also* **duodecimo.**

typ., typogr. typographus. Printer.

typus (-i). Type (s), letter (s), character(s). **typi tornatissimi.** Ornamental or decorated letters (**literae florentes**).

U

u. i. (inf.) ut (ubi) infra: As below. In the book or passage cited below.

ubi supra. Above. In the work or passage cited above.

ult. ultimus. The last. At the end.

unicus. Unique, sole.

V

v. verte.

v. e. vide etiam. See also.

v. l. varia lectio. A different reading.

vacat. Is blank. *e.g.*, **f. 80 vacat.** Folio 80 blank.

vacuus. Blank.

vademecum. Small handbook.

vba. verba. Words.

vera effigies. True likeness, fac-simile.

vero. Truly, certainly. *e.g.*, **vero omissae sunt.** They have certainly been omitted.

versio (-ones). Version (s).

verte. Turn over.

vetustus. Old, ancient. *e.g.*, **g. ch. vetusti.** Ancient Gothic characters.

vic. (viz.) videlicet. Namely.

vid. videtur. It seems, probably. *e.g.*, **Venetiis ut vid.** Probably [printed] at Venice.

vigesimo-quarto. 24mo. A book between 5 and 5⅞ in. (12½–15cm.) high or composed of sections of 24 leaves each. *See also* **duodecimo.**

vivum, ad —. From life. *e.g.*, **ad vivum del.** Drawn from life.

vulgo. Commonly, generally. *e.g.*, **Schwarzerd, vulgo Melancthon.** Schwarzerd, commonly called Melancthon.

X

xyl. xylographicus, xylographum (-a).

xylographum.(a). Early wood-cut(s), block-book (s), xylograph (s).

xylographicus. Pertaining to wood-engraving. *e.g.*, **c. figg. xyl.** With wood-cuts.

SPANISH

A

á plana y renglón *or* **á plana renglón.** copied word for word.

á la rústica *or* **en rústica** *or* **cosido. (bb.)** stitched.

abrir las hojas. to cut the pages.

acaba de publicarse. (bo.) now published.

academias, trabajos de. society publications.

actas. proceedings.

adorno tipografico. typographical ornament.

agregado *or* **añadido. (pr.)** new matter.

agua fuerte *or* **grabado al agua fuerte.** (e.) etching.

aguatinta. (e.) aquatint.

album de recortes. scrapbook.

alzado. (bb.) gathering.

añadido. *See* **agregado.**

anales. annals.

anaquel para tipos. (pr.) letter board.

año de imprenta. imprint date.

anteport. anteportada.

anteportada. page with half title.

aparte. separately.

apostill. apostillado.

apostillado. with marginal notes.

aprob. aprobación.

aprobación. approbation.
aviso. advertisement.

B

bala de papel. ten reams.
balada. ballad.
baraja. a pack of playing cards.
barniz blando. (e.) soft etching ground.
barniz de grabadores. (e.) etching ground.
bastardillas. *See* **letras bastardillas.**
bien conservado *or* **en buen estado. (bo.)** in good condition.
bigote. (pr.) short rule, dash rule.
bimestral. bi-monthly.
blanco (pr.). first form.
bocarán. (bb.) buckram.
borrado. canceled.
bramante *or* **cuerda. (pr.)** page-cord.
broche para cerrar un libro. (bb.) clasp.
bruñidor. (bb.) burnisher.

C

cabezada de libro. (bb.) headband.
caja. (bb.) case.
caja alta. (pr.) upper case.
caja baja. (pr.) lower case.
caja de letras. (pr.) type case.
cajetín. (pr.) section of a type case.
cajista. (pr.) compositor.
cajista de libros. (pr.) book compositor.
canto inferior de un libro. (bb.) tail, lower edge.
cantonera. (bb.) corner of a book.

228

cantos cincelados. (bb.)   tooled edges.

cantos encarnados *or* **cantos rojos. (bb.)**
red edges.

cantos jaspeados. (bb.)   marble edges.

cantos sin cortar. (bb.)   rough edges.

capítulo.   chapter.

carácter *or* **letra. (pr.)**   character, letter.

carátula *or* **portada.**   title-page.

carnero. (pr.)   hell, *i.e.*, a receptacle for
broken types.

carta.   letter.

cartel.   poster, placard.

cartel de comedia.   play bill.

cartera.   portfolio.

cartibana *or* **escartibana** *or* **uña. (bb.)**   guard.

cartón fuerte.   pasteboard.

centón.   cento.

cob.   cobre.

cobre.   *See* **grabado en cobre.**

colaborador.   joint author.

colación.   collation.

colacionar *or* **comparar.**   to collate.

colector de libros.   book-collector.

coma.   comma.

comenzar igual. (pr.)   to commence even.

comercio de libros.   booktrade.

comido por el comején.   wormholed.

comisión, en *or* **condicionalmente. (bo.)**   on
approval.

comparar.   *See* **colacionar.**

compartimiento. (bb.)   panel.

compilador.   compiler.

componedor. (pr.)   composing stick.

composición *or* **forma. (pr.)** composition, form.

composición espaciada. (pr.) spaced composition.

composición regleteada. (pr.) interlined composition, leaded matter.

composición sólida. (pr.) close matter.

compuesto *or* **hecho.** edited, prepared.

con notas explicativas. with explanatory notes.

condicionalmente. *See* **comisión, en.**

contenido. contents.

continuará. continued.

cordeles de lomo de un libro *or* **nervios. (bb.)** bands.

corondel *or* **raya de columna. (pr.)** column rule.

corondeles. *pl.* **(pa.)** wiremarks.

corrección de pruebas. proof reading.

corrector de pruebas. proof reader.

corregido. revised.

corta-papeles. paper-knife.

cosido. (bb.) stitched.

cosido entero. (bb.) stitched uncut.

cotidiano *or* **diario.** daily.

cruz. (pr.) dagger.

cuad. cuaderno.

cuaderno. composition book.

cuadrado. (pr.) quadrat.

cubierta deteriorada. worn binding.

cubierta original. publisher's cover.

cuenta del autor, por. (bo.) at the author's expense, privately published.

cuento. tale.

cuerda *or* **bramante.** (pr.) page-cord.

cuero *or* **piel.** leather.

cuero de Moscovia *or* **cuero de Rusia.** Russia leather.

cuerpo del tipo. (pr.) shank, body of a type.

D

derechos de autor *or* **propiedad literaria.** copyright.

desencuadernado. binding lost.

devocionario. prayerbook.

diario *or* **periódico.** newspaper.

diccionario. dictionary.

directorio *or* **anuario.** directory.

disertación. dissertation.

div. fol. diversa foliación.

diversa foliación. various pagings.

división *or* **guión.** hyphen.

dorso *or* **lomo.** (bb.) back.

dos puntos. colon.

duplicado. (pr.) double, *i.e.*, matter set up a second time by mistake.

E

e. del. i. escudete del impresor.

edición apócrifa *or* **edición fraudulenta.** an edition in every way unchanged except for the title-page.

edición barata. cheap edition.

ejemplar regalado. presentation copy.

en buen estado. (bo.) in good condition.

en prensa. in the press.

en publicación. current.

en rústica. *See* **á la rústica.**

encabezamiento. heading.

encabezamiento de carta. letter head.

encordelar. (bb.) to tie in.

encuadernación, taller de. bookbindery.

encuadernación entera *or* **pasta entera. (bb.)** full binding.

encuadernación de lujo *or* **encuadernación á la real. (bb.)** sumptuous binding.

encuadernador. bookbinder.

encuadrar con reglas. (pr.) to box in.

enhilar. to file.

enlomado. (bb.) backing.

ensuciar. to soil.

entrada, papeleta de. card of admission.

entrega *or* **fascículo.** part, fascicle.

err. errata.

errata tipográfica *or* **falta tipográfica.** misprint.

esbozo. *See* **esquicio.**

escartibana *or* **cartibana** *or* **uña. (bb.)** guard.

escritor *or* **autor.** author.

escritura. writing.

escudete del impresor. printer's scutcheon.

espacio. (pr.) space.

esquicio *or* **esbozo.** sketch, rough draught.

estampa en colores. color-print.

estampa de humo *or* **media tinta. (e.)** mezzotint.

estampa en madera. (e.) woodcut.

estampadura en seco *or* **fileteado en seco. (bb.)** blind tooling.

estampador *or* **impresor.** printer.

etiqueta. (bb.) lettering piece, label.

expurgado. expurgated.

F

f. foja.

falsa portada. *See* **frontis, falso.**

falso frontis. *See* **frontis, falso.**

falta la portada *or* **falta de portada.** title-page lacking.

falta tipográfica. *See* **errata tipográfica.**

fe de erratas. list of errata.

feria de libros. (bo.) book-fair.

fileteado. filleted.

fileteado en oro. (bb.) gold tooling.

fileteado en seco *or* **estampadura en seco.** **(bb.)** blind tooling.

firma *or* **signatura. (b.)** signature.

firma con asterisco. (b.) signature with an asterisk.

florón. (b.) vignette.

foja *or* **hoja.** leaf.

forma *or* **composición. (pr.)** form, composition.

fornitura. (pr.) furniture.

fraile. (pr.) friar, *i.e.*, any part of a page which has not received the ink.

frasqueta. (pr.) frisket.

fróntis, falso *or* **falsa portada.** half title.

G

galera. (pr.) galley.

galerada. (pr.) galley proof.

grabado al agna fuerte. (e.)   etching.

grabado al buril. (e.)   line engraving.

grabado en cobre. (e.)   copper plate engraving.

grabado crible. (e.)   dotted print.

grabado á puntos. (e.)   stipple engraving.

grabado á tres colores.   three-color print.

grabador.   engraver.

guarda.   fly-leaf, end-paper.

guía de ferrocarriles *or* **itinerario.**   time-table.

guión *or* **división.**   hyphen.

H

h. en. b.   hoja en blanco.

ha dejado de publicarse.   discontinued.

hebdomadario *or* **semanal.**   weekly.

hecho *or* **compuesto.**   edited, prepared.

hierros pequeños. (bb.)   small tools.

hilera.   row, file.

hoja en blanco.   blank leaf.

hoja doblada.   dog's ear.

hoja intercalada. (b.)   interleaf.

hoja volante. (bb.)   fly-sheet.

hojas de autor. *pl.* **(bo.)**   advance sheets.

hojas preliminares. *pl.* **(b.)**   preliminary leaves.

hojas sin cortar.   uncut leaves.

hojear un libro.   turn over the leaves of a book.

hombro. (pr.)   shoulder of a type.

imp.   impreso.

imponer. (pr.)   to make up.

impr. imprenta.
imprenta á claroscuro. (e.) chiaroscuro.
impresión de relieve. anastatic print.
impreso por un lado. printed on one side.
impreso en rojo. rubricated.
impresor *or* **estampador.** printer.
impresor de trabajos menudos. job-printer.
intercal. intercalado.
intercalado. inserted, interpolated.
interlínea *or* **regleta. (pr.)** lead.
interlineado. (pr.) leaded.
itinerario *or* **guía de ferrocarriles.** time-table.

J

jeroglíficos. hieroglyphics.
justificación. (pr.) justification.
juventud, literatura para la. juvenile literature.

L

l. letra.
l.g. letra gótica.
lector. reader.
letra *or* **carácter. (pr.)** letter, character, type.
letra de adorno *or* **letra de capricho** *or* **letra florida. (pr.)** fancy letter.
letra de capricho. *See* **letra de adorno.**
letra descendente. (pr.) tail-type.
letra florida. *See* **letra de adorno.**
letra inicial. (pr.) initial.
letra machucada. (pr.) battered letter.
letra mayúscula. (pr.) capital letter.
letra minúscula. (pr.) small letter.

letra montante. (pr.) kerned letter.

letra revuelta *or* **letra empastelada.** (pr.) turned letter.

letra de tortis. (pr.) black letter, gothic letter.

letra usual. (pr.) body type.

letras bastardillas *or* **letras cursivas** *or* **letras italianas** *or* **letras venecianas.** (pr.) italics.

letras cursivas. *See* **letras bastardillas.**

letras italianas. *See* **letras bastardillas.**

letras monacales. (pr.) monk's letters.

letras negras. (pr.) bold faced types.

letras venecianas. *See* **letras bastardillas.**

letras voladas *or* **letras superiores.** (pr.) superiors.

libelo. libel.

librero-editor. publisher.

libro auxiliar *or* **libro de referencia.** reference book.

libro en blanco. blank book.

libro de horas. book of hours.

libro de láminas. picture book.

libro de lance. *See* **libro de segunda mano.**

libro á llave. a book in which the proper names of persons or localities are disguised by the author.

libro en papel. unbound book.

libro en rama. book in sheets, book in quires.

libro de referencia. *See* **libro auxiliar.**

libro de segunda mano *or* **libro usado** *or* **libro de lance.** (bo.) secondhand book.

libro xilográfico. blockbook.

lic. licencia.

licencia. permission, license.

línea del pie de la página. bottom line.

línea de puntos. dotted rule.

línea de reclamo. direction line.

lingote. (pr.) slug.

listo para ponerle en prensa *or* **puede imprimirse. (pr.)** for press.

llamadas. *pl.* **(pr.)** reference marks.

llamado. called.

lomo hueco. (bb.) loose back.

lomo de resorte. (bb.) spring back.

lomo rígido. (bb.) tight back.

lugar, sin. no place.

lugar de edición. place of publication.

lugar de imprenta. place of printing.

M

maculatura. (pr.) waste sheet.

mad. madera.

madera. wood.

mano de papel. (pa.) quire.

mapa geográfico *or* **carta geográfica.** map.

mapamundi. map of the world.

máquina de alimentación. (pr.) feeding machine.

máquina para componer las letras. (pr.) composing machine.

máquina de copiar. copying machine.

marca de agua. (pa.) water-mark.

marca del impresor. printer's mark.

marcador. book-mark.

margen ancha. wide margin.
materia muerta. (pr.) dead matter.
media caña. (bb.) fore-edge.
media tinta *or* **mezzo tinto** *or* **estampa de humo. (e.)** mezzotint.
memoria. report.
memorias. *pl.* memoirs.
mensual. monthly.
merc. de libr. mercader de libros.
mercader de libros. bookseller.
mezzo tinto. *See* **media tinta.**
minutas de un cuerpo deliberante. minutes of a meeting.
misal. missal.
mohoso. mouldy.
muestras, primeras. (pr.) first proof.

N

nervios *or* **cordeles de lomo de un libro. (bb.)** bands.
nervios falsos. (bb.) false bands.
no cortado. (b.) uncut.
no se ha puesto á la venta *or* **no se vende. (bo.)** not for sale.
no se vende. *See* **no se ha puesto á la venta.**
nombre compuesto. compound name.
nota al pie. foot-note.
novela. novel.

O

obra coronada *or* **obra premiada.** prize-essay.
obra premiada. *See* **obra coronada.**

obras completas. collected works.

obras escogidas. selected works.

obras póstumas. posthumous works.

olvido. (pr.) out, *i.e.*, omission of a word or phrase by the compositor.

orl. orlado.

orlado. (pr.) framed, boxed in.

orlar *or* **encuadrar con reglas. (pr.)** box in.

P

p. ej. por ejemplo.

p. en b. página en blanco.

página impar. (b.) odd page, recto.

página par. (b.) even page, verso.

paginación continua. (b.) continuous pagination.

pal. palabra.

palabra. word.

pap. papel.

papel de algodón. cotton paper.

papel de calcar. tracing paper.

papel pautado *or* **papel reglado** *or* **papel rayado.** ruled paper.

papel secante. blotting paper.

papel de seda *or* **papel de culebrilla.** tissue paper.

papel sellado. stamped paper.

papel trabajado á mano. hand made paper.

papeleta de entrada. card of admission.

paréntesis angulares. (b.) *pl.* brackets.

párrafo nuevo. paragraph.

pasta entera *or* **encuadernación entera.** full binding.

pastel. (pr.)   pie, *i.e.*, mixed type.

pautado *or* **reglado** *or* **rayado.**   ruled.

pegado.   mounted.

percalina.   book muslin.

perdido.   missing.

pergamino.   parchment.

periódico *or* **diario.**   newspaper.

peso fuerte.   dollar.

pf.   peso fuerte.

pie de imprenta.   imprint.

pie de mosca. (pr.)   reference sign.

pie de una página.   bottom of a page.

piel de cabra.   goatskin.

piel de carnero.   sheepskin.

piel de cerdo.   pigskin.

piel de zapa *or* **chagrèn. (bb.)**   shagreen.

piel de zorra. (bb.)   fox-skin.

plancha de componedor. (pr.)   composing board.

plana *or* **página.**   page.

plana y renglón, á.   copied word for word.

pno.   pergamino.

polilla.   bookworm.

por cuenta del autor.   at the author's expense.

por ejemplo.   for instance.

portada, falsa.   *See* **frontis, falso.**

prec.   precioso.

precio de catálogo.   published prize, list price.

precioso.   precious.

premiado *or* **coronado.**   awarded a prize.

prensa.   press.

prensa, en.   in the press.

prensa de cilindro. (pr.) revolving press.

prensa de dorar. (bb.) gilding press.

prensa de mano. (pr.) hand-press.

pro. proemio.

proemio. introduction.

prol. prólogo.

prueba antes de la letra *or* **prueba de artista.**
(e.) proof before letters.

prueba sacada con escobilla. brush proof.

pruebas. *pl.* proof sheets.

publicado. published.

puede imprimirse. (pr.) *See* **listo para ponerle en prensa.**

punta seca. (e.) dry point.

puntizones. (pa.) waterlines.

punto de admiración. exclamation point.

punto y coma. semicolon.

punto de interrogación. interrogation point.

punzón. (pr.) bodkin.

Q

que se llama. calling himself.

quincenal *or* **bimensual.** semi-monthly.

R

r. y n. rojo y negro.

rama. (pr.) chase.

rasgo de pluma. dash.

raya de columna *or* **corondel. (pr.)** column rule.

raya de luto. (pr.) mourning border.

reclamo. (b.) catchword.

recogido por orden del gobierno ó tribunal para impedir la circulación ó publicación. suppressed.

recop. recopilación.

recopilación. compendium, summary.

recorte de periódico. newspaper clipping.

recortes, album de. scrapbook.

red. redondo, redonda.

redondo. round.

reencuadernar. rebind.

regleta. (pr.) composing rule, setting rule.

reimp. reimpresión, reimpreso.

reimpresión. reprint.

reimpreso. reprinted.

remate de libros. book auction.

remendado. (bb.) repaired.

remiendo, trabajos de. job printing.

renglón *or* **línea.** line.

repintar. (pr.) to set off, to double.

resma. (pa.) ream.

retiración. (pr.) second form.

revista. review, magazine.

revista *or* **segunda prueba. (pr.)** second proof.

rojo y negro. printed in red and black.

rotulado. (bb.) labeled.

rústica, á la *or* **cosido.** stitched.

S

s. siglo.

sangrar. (pr.) to indent.

sangría. (pr.) indentation.

satinación. (pa.) calendering.

semanal *or* **hebdomadario.** weekly.

seudónimo. pseudonym.

signo de corrección. (pr.) mark of correction.

sílaba. syllable.

sin contar. (bo.) by the lot.

sin rayar. unruled.

sototítulo. (b.) subtitle.

subrayado. *n.* underscoring, underlining.

subrayado. *adj.* underscored, underlined.

sumario. summary.

suscripción. subscription.

suscriptor. subscriber.

T

tabla de nombres. index of names.

taller de encuadernación. bindery.

también con el título. also under the title.

tapas de madera. (bb.) wooden boards.

tejuelo *or* **tejuelito. (bb.)** lettering piece.

tela para velas. (bb.) duck.

telar. (bb.) sewing board.

timbramiento *or* **timbrado.** stamping.

tinta. ink.

tinta de imprenta. printer's ink.

tipo. type.

tipos delgados *or* **tipos de poco cuerpo.** (pr.) lightfaced types.

tir. .tirado.

tirado. printed.

tít. título.

titulado. entitled.

título. title.

título del encuadernador. binder's title.

título general. collective title.

título de página *or* **línea de cabeza** *or* **título con palabras.** headline, live heading, running title.

todo publicado. no more published.

tomo de varias *or* **colección ficticia.** pamphlet volume.

trabajos. transactions.

traductor. translator.

trimestral. quarterly.

V.

v. (v°.) verso.

v. en b. verso en blanco.

vendedor de libros usados. secondhand bookseller.

versal *or* **letra mayúscula.** (**pr.**) capital letter.

versalitas. *pl.* (**pr.**) small capitals.

versión *or* **traducción.** translation.

verso en blanco. (**b.**) verso blank.

viñeta *or* **florón.** vignette, headpiece.

virgulillas *or* **comillas.** quotation marks.

vitela. (bb.) calf.

Z

zarzuela. musical comedy.

SWEDISH

A

adresskalender. directory.

afd. afdelning.

afdelning. section.

afdrag, första. (e.) plain print.

afdrag af förrådssättning. (pr.) galley proof.

afdrag med text. (e.) proof with letters.

afdrag utan text. (e.) proof before letters.

afh. afhandling.

afhandling. dissertation, paper, treatise.

afskuren. (bb.) cut down.

afskuren, kort. (bb.) cropped.

äfven under titel *or* **också under titel. (b.)** also under the title.

ål. (pr.) bodkin.

allt utgifvet. (b.) no more published.

anfangsvignet. (b.) headpiece.

anföringstecken *or* **citationstecken.** quotation marks.

anmärkare *or* **utläggare** *or* **kommentator.** annotator, commentator.

anslag *or* **plakat.** poster, placard.

år. year.

arbeten, samlade. collected works.

årgång, löpande. (b.) current publication.

ark, rentryckt *or* **profark. (bo.)** advance sheet.

arkföljd *or* **läggens ordning. (bb.)** gathering.

årlig. annual, yearly.

årsböcker. *pl.* annals.

årsredogörelse *or* **årsberättelse.** annual report.

årstryck *or* **pliktexemplar.** (b.) deposit copies, *i.e.*, copies which the printers are by law obliged to send to certain libraries.

B

bal af papper. ten reams.

begynnelsebokstaf. (pr.) initial.

belagdt med kvarstad *or* **beslagtagen.** suppressed.

berättelse *or* **redogörelse.** report.

beslagtagen. See **belagdt med kvarstad.**

bilderbok. picture-book for children..

bind, höga *or* **upphöjda bind.** (bb.) raised bands.

binda in. to bind.

bindestreck. hyphen.

bjuda på en bok. (bo.) bid on a book.

bläck. ink.

blindsida. (b.) blind sheet.

blindstämplar. *pl. See* **blindtryck.**

blindtryck, *or* **med blindstämplar.** (bb.) blind tooling.

bok, ohäftad. *See* **bok i exemplar.**

bok i exemplar *or* **ohäftad bok.** (bo.) book in sheets, book in quires.

bok papper. (pa.) quire.

bokägarmärke. (b.) bookplate, ex libris.

bokanmälan. (bo.) booksellers' announcement of new books.

bokauktion. book-auction.

bokbindare. bookbinder.

bokhandelspris *or* **boklådspris. (bo.)** published price, list price.

boklådspris. *See* **bokhandelspris.**

boklista *or* **katalog.** catalogue.

bokmal. bookworm.

bokmarknad. (bo.) book-market.

bokrygg. back of a book.

bokryggs förfärdigande. (bb.) backing.

boksnitt. *See* snitt.

bokspänne *or* **knäppe.** book-clasp.

bokstaf. (pr.) character, letter.

bokstaf, skadad *or* **trasig bokstaf. (pr.)** battered letter.

bokstaf, stor *or* **versal** *or* **majuskel. (pr.)** capital letter.

bokstaf, upp- och nedvänd. (pr.) turned letter.

bokstaf, utsirad. (pr.) fancy letter.

bokstafsföljd. alphabetical order.

bokstafstil *or* **stil** *or* **typ. (pr.)** type.

boktryck. (pr.) bookwork.

boktryckare. printer.

boktryckargosse. (pr.) printer's devil.

boktryckarkonst. art of printing.

bönbok. prayer-book.

börja utan indrag. (pr.) commence even.

bred. wide.

bref. letter.

brefhufvud. letter-head.

brefvexling. correspondence.
broschyr. pamphlet.
buringravyr. line engraving.
bryta om. (pr.) to make up.
byte. exchange.

C

ciseleradt snitt. (bb.) tooled edges.
citationstecken *or* **anföringstecken.** quotation marks.

D

daglig. daily.
död kolumntitel. (pr.) page number, dead heading.
dubblett *or* **duplikat.** duplicate.
duplikat. *See* dubblett.

E

efterlemnade skrifter. posthumous works.
efterskrift *or* **post scriptum.** postscript.
eftertryck. (b.) unauthorized reprint.
ej afskuren. uncut.
etsgrund. (e.) etching ground.
ettbladstryck. (b.) broadside.

F

fals. (bb.) guard.
falsa. (bb.) to fold.
falsben. (bb.) folding stick.
fårskinn. (bb.) sheepskin.
fårskinn, brunt *or* **basan. (bb.)** basil.
felfritt exemplar. (bo.) perfect copy.

fet stil. (pr.) blackfaced type, boldfaced type.

fickformat. pocket edition.

fileter i guldtryck. gilt fillets.

fjäderrygg. (bb.) spring back.

flygblad *or* **ströskrift (b.)** fly-sheet.

flygskrift *or* **broschyr. (b.)** pamphlet.

fodr. fodral.

fodral. case.

förbättr. förbättrad.

förbättrad. improved.

föreg. föregående.

föregående. preceding, earlier.

företal. (b.) preface.

förgyld. (bb.) gilt.

förhandlingar. proceedings.

förlag, på eget. (bo.) privately published.

förläggare *or* **förlagsbokhandlare. (bo.)** publisher.

förlagsrätt. copyright.

formram.(pr.) chase.

förrådssättning, afdrag af. (pr.) galley proof.

försättsblad *or* **försättspapper. (b.)** fly-leaf.

förstafvelse. prefix.

förstärkt. (bb.) reinforced.

fortel. (pr.) fat, *i.e.*, pieces of composition, for instance, running titles that are kept for future use and are not taken apart till the whole work is finished.

fortlöpande paginering. continuous pagination.

fortsättning. continuation.

fortsättning följer. to be continued.

frågetecken. interrogation point.
framsnitt. (bb.) fore-edge.
friexemplar. *See* **gåfvoexemplar.**

G

gåffrerad. (bb.) goffered.
gåfvoexemplar *or* **friexemplar.** presentation copy.
gemensam titel *or* **hufvudtitel.** collective title.
genombläddra. turn over the leaves of a book.
genoms. genomsedd.
genomsedd. revised.
getskinn. (bb.) goatskin.
godtköpsupplaga. cheap edition.
götisk stil. (pr.) black letter.
grafstickel. (e.) burin, graver.
gravering med grafstickel *or* **buringravyr. (e.)** line engraving.
gravyr. (e.) engraving.
gravyr i punktmanér *or* **gravyr i punktermanér. (e.)** stipple engraving.
guldpressning. (bb.) gold tooling.

H

h. häftad.
häfta ark. (bb.) to tie in.
häftad. stitched, sewed.
häftlåda. (bb.) sewing-board.
häftning i pappband. (bb.) binding in boards.
halfband. (bb.) half-binding.

250

halfklot. (bb.) half cloth.

handlingar. transactions.

höga bind *or* **upphöjda bind. (bb.)** raised bands.

höger sida. (b.) odd page, recto.

hopviken plansch *or* **inviken plansch. (b.)** folded plate.

horarium. book of hours.

hörn af en bok. corner of a book.

hufvudlinje *or* **rubrikrad. (b.)** headline.

hufvudtitel *or* **gemensam titel. (b.)** collective title.

hundöra. dog's ear.

hvar annan månad. bi-monthly.

I

inbinda ånyo. rebind.

inbindning. binding.

inbindning, sliten. worn binding.

indrag. (pr.) indentation.

indraga. (pr.) to indent.

inledande onumrerade blad. (b.) preliminary leaves.

innehållsförteckning. (b.) table of contents, index.

inrama med linjer. (pr.) to box in.

inskjutning. (b.) insertion, interpolation.

inviken *or* **hopviken.** folded.

inviken plansch *or* **hopviken plansch.** folded plate.

J

jämn sida *or* **vänster sida. (b.)** verso, even page.

juftläder *or* **ryssläder. (bb.)** Russia leather.

K

kägel. (pr.) shank, body of a letter.

kallnål radering *or* **torrnål radering. (e.)** dry point.

kapitäler. (pr.) small caps.

kapitaling. (bb.) head-band.

kart. kartonerad.

kartonerad *or* **styfhäftad.** in boards.

kartong. (b.) a cancel.

kast. (pr.) type-case.

kastfack. (pr.) box in a type-case.

kilskrift. cuneiform letters.

klb. (bb.) klotband.

klot, styft. (bb.) buckram.

klotband. cloth binding.

klotryggsband. (bb.) binding with cloth back.

klrb. (bb.) klotryggsband.

knäppe. (b.) clasp.

kolumnsnöre. (pr.) page cord.

kolumntitel, död. (pr.) dead heading, page number.

kolumntitel, lefvande. (pr.) live heading, running title.

kopparstick. (e.) copperplate-engraving.

korrekturläsare. proof-reader.

korrekturtecken. mark of correction in proof-reading.

kors. (pr.) dagger.

kort afskuren. cropped.

kritteckning. crayon.

kursivstil. (pr.) italics.

kustod. (b.) catchword.

kvartalsvis, utkommande. (b.) quarterly.

L

lägga af. (pr.)   distribute the types.

läggens ordning *or* **arkföljd. (bb.)**   gathering.

lärdt sällskap.   learned society.

lärftsband.   heavy cloth binding.

läskpapper.   blotting paper.

ledare *or* **redaktionsartikel.**   editorial.

lefvande kolumntitel. (pr.)   running title, live heading.

lik.   out, *i.e.*, omission of a word or phrase by the compositor.

linjerad.   ruled.

löpande årgång.   current publication.

lrftbd.   lärftsband.

lustspel.   comedy.

lyxupplaga.   edition de luxe.

M

mager stil. (pr.)   lightfaced types, leanfaced types.

makulaturark.   waste sheets.

makulerad.   canceled.

månadsskrift.   monthly publication.

månatlig.   monthly.

marginal, bred.   wide margin.

marmoreradt snitt. (bb.)   marble edges.

marokäng. (bb.)   morocco.

maskäten *or* **maskstungen.**   wormholed.

maskhål.   wormhole.

maskstungen. *See* **maskäten,**

mässbok.   missal.

mellanslagen. (pr.)   leaded.

mjukt skinnband. limp leather.

mögelfläck *or* **vattenfläck.** mildew, water stain.

möglad. mouldy.

munk. (pr.) friar, *i.e.*, any part of the page which has not received the ink.

munkstil. (pr.) monk's letters.

N

namndikt. acrostic.

nedfläckad. stained.

neds. nedsatt.

nedsatt pris. reduced price.

notsiffra. (pr.) superiors.

nr. nummer.

nummer. number.

ny rad. (b.) paragraph.

nyss utkommen. (bo.) now published.

O

obunden. unbound.

också under titel *or* **äfven under titel.** also under the title.

öfversatt. translated.

öfversättare. translator.

öfversättning. translation.

öfversigt. synopsis.

öfverskrift *or* **rubrik.** heading.

oillustr. oillustrerat.

oillustrerat. without illustrations.

ombrytare. (pr.) impositor.

omskrifning. transliteration.

omtr. omtryck.

SWEDISH

omtryck. reprint.

ordbok *or* **lexikon.** dictionary.

ort, utan. no place.

P

på eget förlag. privately published.

paginering, fortlöpande. (b.) continuous pagination.

papp. pasteboard.

papp-pärmar. *pl.* boards.

papper, marmoreradt. marble paper.

papper, reffladt. ribbed paper.

papper, tjockt. heavy paper.

papper, tunnt. thin paper.

pappersknif. paper-cutter.

pappersomslag. paper jacket.

pärm. cover.

påseende, till *or* **till benäget påseende. (bo.)** on approval.

per stycke. (bo.) apiece.

pergamentband. parchment binding.

pgb. pergamentband.

planschverk. book chiefly consisting of plates.

pliktexemplar. *See* **årstryck.**

portf. portfölj.

portfölj. portfolio.

ppr. papper.

predikan. sermon.

prenumeration *or* **abonnement.** subscription.

pressad rygg. (bb.) decorated back.

pressförgyllning. (bb.) gold tooling.

3333

55

55

presskorrektur *or* **reviderkorrektur.** **(pr.)**
last proof.

primaform. (pr.) first form.

prisbelönt. awarded a prize.

profark *or* **korrekturark.** advance sheet,
proof-sheet.

protokoll. minutes of a meeting.

punktermanér. *See* **punktmanér.**

punktmanér, gravyr i. (e.) stipple engraving.

R

rabatt, utan. no discount.

rad. (b.) line.

rad, ny. (b.) paragraph.

radutslutning. (pr.) justification.

räfskinn. (bb.) fox-skin.

ram. border, frame.

randen, inre. (b.) inside border.

randning i papper. (pa.) wiremarks.

randornamentering. decorated border.

rar *or* **sällsynt.** rare.

rätt. rättelser.

rättelser. corrections, errata.

rättelser saknas. list of errata missing.

red., redig. redigerat.

redigerat. edited.

redaktionsartikel *or* **ledare.** editorial.

redogörelse *or* **berättelse.** report.

remmika. (pr.) frisket.

ren sida. blank page.

renskrifvet exemplar (pr.) fair copy.

rentryckt ark. (pr.) advance sheet.

restupplaga. (bo.) remainders.

reviderkorrektur *or* **presskorrektur.** (**pr.**)
last proof.

revy. review.

rödt snitt. (**bb.**) red edges.

rödtryck, med. rubricated.

rubrikrad *or* **hufvudlinie.** headline.

rygg, fast. (**bb.**) tight back.

rygg, lös. (**bb.**) loose back.

rygg, pressad. (**bb.**) decorated back.

ryggfält. (**bb.**) panel.

ryggtitel. binder's title.

ryssläder *or* **juftläder.** (**bb.**) Russia leather.

S

saga. tale.

saknas. missing.

sakregister. (**b.**) index.

sällskap, lärdt. learned society.

sällskapsskrifter. society publications.

sällsynt *or* **rar.** scarce, rare.

samlingsband. pamphlet volume.

sammanbundet med. (**b.**) bound with.

sammandrag. abstract.

sammanhang. context.

sats, mellanslagen. (**pr.**) leaded matter.

sats, spärrad. (**pr.**) spaced composition.

sätta. (**pr.**) to compose.

sättare. (**pr.**) compositor.

sättbräde. (**pr.**) letter-board, composing
board.

sättlinje. (**pr.**) composing rule.

sättskepp. (**pr.**) galley.

se ofvan. see above.

segelduk. (bb.)   duck.

sekundaform. (pr.)   second form.

sida, höger. (b.)   odd page, recto.

sida, jämn *or* **vänster sida.** (b.)   verso, even page.

sida, ren. (b.)   blank page.

silkespapper.   tissue paper.

skadad bokstaf *or* **trasig bokstaf.**   (pr.) battered letter.

skadadt.   mutilated.

skådespel.   drama.

skära i stil. (bb.)   to bleed.

skb.   skinnband.

skinn.   leather.

skinnband. (bb.)   leather binding.

skinnryggsband. (bb.)   binding with leather back.

skiss.   sketch, rough draft.

skjuta ut en form. (pr.)   impose.

skönlitteratur.   literature, *i.e.*, fiction and poetry.

skrb. (bb.)   skinnryggsband.

skrifbok.   blank book.

skrifter, efterlemnade.   posthumous works.

skrifter, utvalda.   selected works.

skriftställare *or* **författare.**   author.

slaktad.   binding lost.

sliten inbindning.   worn binding.

slutrad. (b.)   bottom-line.

slut-underskrift. (b.)   colophon.

slutvignet. (b.)   tailpiece.

smädeskrift.   libel.

smutsfläck.   stain.

smutstitel. (b.) half-title, bastard-title, fly-title. ·

snitt. (bb.) edges.

snitt, ciseleradt. (bb.) tooled edges.

snitt, kammarmoreradt. (bb.) combed edges.

snitt, marmoreradt. (bb.) marble edges.

snitt, öfre. (bb.) head, top.

snitt, rödt. (bb.) red edges.

snitt, sprängdt. (bb.) sprinkled edges.

sorgespel. tragedy.

sorgkant. mourning border.

spaltlinje. (pr.) column rule.

spänne. *See* **bokspänne.**

spärra. (pr.) to space.

spärrad sats. (pr.) spaced composition.

spelkort. playing cards.

spetsbordyr. (bb.) dentelle border.

spis. (pr.) blacks, *i.e.*, a space, quadrat or piece of furniture that rises and is imprinted on the sheets.

sprängdt snitt. (bb.) sprinkled edges.

st. stycke.

stadium. (e.) state.

stafrim. alliteration.

stafvelse. syllable.

stålstick. (e.) steel-engraving.

stämpelpapper. stamped paper.

stämpla. to stamp.

stämplar, små. (bb.) petits fers, *i.e.*, small tools.

stånd, i godt. in good condition.

steg. (pr.) furniture.

stentryck. lithography.

stereot. (pr.) stereotyperad. ·

stereotyperad. stereotyped.

stil *or* **bokstafstil** *or* **typ. (pr.)** types.

stil, fet. (pr.) boldfaced types.

stil, götisk. (pr.) black letter.

stil, mager. (pr.) lightfaced types, lean-
faced types.

stilkast. (pr.) type-case.

stjärna. asterisk.

ströskrift *or* **flygblad.** fly-sheet.

struket. expurgated.

stycke. (bo.) piece.

styfhäftad *or* **kartonnerad. (bb.)** in boards.

subskribentsamlande. (bo.) canvassing ·
booktrade.

svårläst manuskript. (pr.) bad copy.

svartkonstmanér. (e.) mezzotint.

svibelfisk. (pr.) pi, *i.e.*, types mixed.

svinskinn. (bb.) pig skin.

T

tankstreck. dash.

tidning. newspaper.

tidningsurklipp. newspaper clipping.

tidtabell. time-table.

till benäget påseende. (bo.) on approval.

tillegnande. (b.) dedication.

tills. tillsammans.

tillsammans. (bo.) in all.

titel, gemensam *or* **hufvudtitel. (b.)** collective title.

titel, utan. anepigraphous, without title.

260

titelbl. titelblad.

titelblad saknas. title-page lacking.

titelfält. (bb.) lettering piece.

titelplansch. (b.) frontispiece.

titelupplaga. (b.) a so-called new edition in every way unchanged, except for the title-page.

tjockt papper. heavy paper.

topp, förgyld. gilt top.

torrnål radering *or* **kallnål radering.** (e.) dry point.

träpärmar *pl.* wooden boards.

träsn. träsnitt.

träsnitt. woodcut.

trefärgstryck. three color print.

trespaltig. in three columns.

tryck med upphöjda linjer. (pr.) anastatic printing.

trycka. (pr.) to print.

tryckår *or* **utgifningsår. (b.)** imprint date, year of publication.

tryckeri. (pr.) printing office.

tryckfärdig. (pr.) for press.

tryckfel. misprint.

tryckfelsförteckning. table of errata.

tryckning *or* **upplaga.** impression, edition.

trycksvärta. (pr.) printer's ink.

tunnt papper. thin paper.

två gångar i månaden. semi-monthly.

U

under tryckning. (pr.) in the press.

underslag. (b.) bottom of a page.

understruken. underscored.

understrykning. underscoring.

undertecknadt. signed.

undertitel. (b.) sub-title.

ungdomsskrifter. juvenile literature.

upphöjda bind *or* **höga bind. (bb.)** raised bands.

upphört att utkomma. (b.) discontinued.

uppklistrad. (b.) mounted.

upplaga i fickformat. pocket edition.

upplaga, godtköps. cheap edition.

upplaga, liten. limited edition.

uppskuren. cut open.

uppslagsbok *or* **handbok.** reference book.

urval. selection.

utan rabatt. no discount.

utgången ur bokhandeln. (bo.) out of print.

utgifningsår *or* **tryckår.** imprint date, date of publication.

utgifningsort. place of publication.

utklippsalbum. scrapbook.

utläggare *or* **anmärkare.** annotator.

utropstecken. exclamation point.

utsirad bokstaf. (pr.) fancy letter.

utstruket. (e.) canceled.

utvalda skrifter. selected works.

V

vänster sida *or* **jämn sida.** verso, even page.

vapensköld. coat of arms.

vattenfläck *or* **mögelfläck.** waterstain, mildew.

vattenlinjer *pl.* **(pa.)** waterlines.

vattenstämpel. (pa.) watermark.

veckoblad. weekly newspaper.

veckligen. weekly.

verldskarta. map of the world.

vinkelhake. (pr.) composing stick.

vinkelparentes. brackets.

Lightning Source UK Ltd.
Milton Keynes UK
UKHW022012090119
335262UK00010B/851/P